WRITTEN IN THE SNOWS

WRITTEN IN THE SNOWS

Across Time on Skis in the Pacific Northwest

LOWELL SKOOG

MOUNTAINEERS
BOOKS

MOUNTAINEERS BOOKS is dedicated to the exploration, preservation, and enjoyment of outdoor and wilderness areas.

1001 SW Klickitat Way, Suite 201, Seattle, WA 98134
800-553-4453, www.mountaineersbooks.org

Printed in Canada
Distributed in the United Kingdom by Cordee, www.cordee.co.uk
24 23 22 21   1 2 3 4 5

Copyeditor: Kris Fulsaas
Design and layout: Jen Grable
Cartographer: Martha Bostwick
All photographs by the author unless credited otherwise
Back cover of paperback edition photos, left to right: *Spectators for the 1931 Cle Elum Ski Club tournament* (Central Washington University Archives and Special Collections, Cle Elum Ski Club Collection); *Dean Collins and Rene Crawshaw just outside the Mount Baker ski area* (Carl Skoog); *Skiing above Paradise in 1948* (Spring Trust for Trails)
Cover and interior illustrations: Jen Grable
Frontispiece: *Stephanie Subak skis Primus Peak in North Cascades National Park.*

Library of Congress Cataloging-in-Publication data is on file at https://lccn.loc .gov/2021014553. The ebook record available at https://lccn.loc.gov/2021014554.

Mountaineers Books titles may be purchased for corporate, educational, or other promotional sales, and our authors are available for a wide range of events. For information on special discounts or booking an author, contact our customer service at 800-553-4453 or mbooks@ mountaineersbooks.org.

 Printed on recycled and FSC-certified materials

MIX
Paper from responsible sources
FSC® C016245
FSC
www.fsc.org

ISBN (paperback): 978-1-68051-290-8
ISBN (hardcover): 978-1-68051-580-0
ISBN (ebook): 978-1-68051-291-5

An independent nonprofit publisher since 1960

TO TOM AND NANCY

IN MEMORY OF STEPH AND CARL

IDAHO

BRITISH COLUMBIA

WASHINGTON

OREGON

PACIFIC OCEAN

Spokane

Colville

Republic

Winthrop

Loup Loup

Okanogan

Columbia River

Chelan

Lake Chelan–Sawtooth Wilderness

Lake Chelan

Wenatchee

Mission Ridge

Ephrata

Pasco

Dayton

Walla Walla

Leavenworth

Cle Elum

Ellensburg

Yakima

Toppenish

Goldendale

Satus Pass

Mount Stuart

Snoqualmie Pass

Naches Pass

Stampede Pass

Crystal Mountain

Cayuse/Chinook Passes

Mount Rainier NP

White Pass

Goat Rocks Wilderness

Mount Adams

Mount Adams Wilderness

Columbia River

Hood River

Mount Hood

Government Camp

Portland

Kalama

Mount St Helens National Volcanic Monument

Olympia

Tacoma

Shelton

Seattle

Everett

Bellingham

Mount Baker Wilderness

Mount Baker

Mount Shuksan

North Cascades National Park

Three Fingers

Stevens Pass

Alpine Lakes Wilderness

Glacier Peak

Glacier Peak Wilderness

Lyman Lake

Cascade Pass

Stehekin

Harts Pass

Barron

Pasayten Wilderness

Ross Lake

Port Angeles

Deer Park

Hurricane Ridge

Mount Olympus

Olympic National Park

Flapjack Lakes

Puget Sound

Vancouver Island

Columbia River

Winthrop

CONTENTS

PROLOGUE

FAINT TRACKS

The slopes are quiet as I arrive in early morning at the Summit West ski area at Washington's Snoqualmie Pass. Groomers have tilled the runs, but the lifts won't begin running for another hour or so. I unload my skis from the car and apply nylon climbing skins to ascend the hill without riding the chairlift. With no other skiers on the mountain, I head up the middle of the slope and take the shortest route toward the Cascade crest. I'll be out of the ski area before the public arrives.

Within a half hour, I reach the top of the groomed ski run and enter a gentle vale leading toward Beaver Lake. No snow has fallen recently, and the ungroomed snow surface is crusty and rough. A strong wind blows, a sign that a weather system is approaching from the coast. I'll want to finish my tour before the next storm arrives. Beyond Beaver Lake, thin snow makes it easy to locate the Pacific Crest Trail, a narrow, snowy corridor wending through ancient trees. I remove my climbing skins and glide along the trail, avoiding creeks and other obstacles as I traverse the old growth above Lodge Lake. In contrast to the cleared and manicured ski resort, this forest has been growing undisturbed for the past century. I imagine myself transported back in time.

Over the next couple hours, I travel along the snow-covered trail, cross a powerline corridor, follow an old logging road, and encounter freshly groomed cross-country ski tracks. Eventually the Pacific Crest Trail crosses a big clearing to reenter ancient forest. I've ventured

Opposite: *Skiing at Paradise in the 1930s* (Giese Archives)

The author scouting The Mountaineers Patrol Race route during the winter of 2001

about five miles from my starting point at Snoqualmie Pass and now I'm in terrain seldom visited in winter. Hard old snow masks the trail in the woods, and I lose track of it. Not having hiked in this area before, I can only guess at the trail's location based on my altimeter and topo map. As the slope grows steeper, I struggle to maintain solid footing on my skis. They slip on an ice crust and I fall headfirst, bending one of my ski poles.

Since I packed light and neglected to bring a repair kit, I scold myself. *This is serious, Lowell. You need to take it more seriously.* I stow my skis, put on crampons, and continue climbing on foot. A few hundred feet higher, I locate the trail again and switch back to skis. Then I see them: "orange-colored tin shingles high on trees and placed so that one was always in sight ahead," a description in journals published long before I was born. This is what I've come for.

It's often said that knowing the history of a place makes traveling there more interesting. This could not be demonstrated more vividly than during my solo outing south of Snoqualmie Pass. The orange markers seem like relics from a lost time. They are old, older than the Pacific Crest Trail, older than the Snoqualmie Pass ski area, older even than any rope tow or chairlift in America. Placed in the early 1930s by members of The Mountaineers, a local outdoor club, these tin shingles mark the route of an annual ski race held in the years before World War II. Reading about the venerable Patrol Race inspired my trip. In 1933 a party of nine Mountaineers placed five hundred markers along a route spanning almost

20 forested miles between Snoqualmie Pass and Stampede Pass. Most of the markers are gone now, victims of forest fire or a logger's axe. But a few remain. I wonder whether anyone spotting them in recent years knows of their origin. I wonder whether any of the skiers who placed the markers are still living.

A week after my first scouting trip, I spend another day exploring the Patrol Race route on skis from the opposite end, near Stampede Pass. Two weeks after that, I traverse the entire route from north to south by myself. I have not yet been able to find anyone interested in joining me. The trip marks the beginning of my fascination with a forgotten chapter in Washington ski history and the first of many such journeys.

———————

It's fair to say that skiing runs in my family. My mother didn't ski much by the time I was a teenager (I am the fifth of six children), but I knew her family had been skiers, based on old stories and family photographs. Mom's parents were born in Sweden, and a treasured

My grandmother Elsa Olsson (second from left) with her siblings Anna, Karl, and Hildur in Sweden, circa 1910

My father, Dick Skoog, during a ski vacation in Yosemite in December 1945

family picture shows Elsa, my *mormor*, or mother's mother, with three of her siblings on skis when they still lived in Scandinavia. My parents grew up in Minnesota. It seemed to me that my dad had always been a skier, and I regret never asking him how he got started. Dad died relatively young of heart failure when I was in college. For at least a decade before that, it was a settled matter in our home that while Mom preferred church on Sundays, Dad would rather go skiing. We kids usually went with him.

Dad and his older brother, Jim, were ski jumpers as well as downhill skiers. In the 1950s and 1960s, Nordic ski jumping was a vital sport in the Northwest. It had diminished from its heyday in the 1930s and 1940s, but it was still an active club sport with regular events. Dad and Jim were members of the Kongsberger Ski Club, organized by a group of Norwegian jumpers and populated by an enthusiastic bunch of local-born skiers. In the 1950s the Kongsbergers built a tiny eight-foot-by-eight-foot cabin and practice jump a few miles east of Snoqualmie Pass. I remember accompanying Dad and my brother Gordy to the Kongsberger site to watch them practice their jumps. After a morning of sledding and watching the jumpers, I'd squeeze into the cabin to warm up, surrounded by the smell of leather boots and wet wool, entranced by the jumpers' stories, often told in Norwegian- or Swedish-accented English.

I understood intuitively that skiing was older and richer than what a kid from Seattle experienced riding the rope tows. That feeling has stuck with me ever since. Years later, after my father had passed away and I realized that his peers were disappearing too, I felt an urgency to learn more about their stories and, by extension, more of Dad's own story. Those stories have been written in the snows—destined to fade with the passing of seasons and of generations.

I never took up ski jumping, at least not in the Norwegian style. My father retired from jumping by the late 1960s, and my brother Gordy moved on as well. My siblings became alpine skiers, ski instructors, and ski patrollers. We weren't full-time professionals by any means. Instructing or patrolling was something we did one day a weekend to earn a free lift ticket to ski the other day. My brothers and I came of age during the emergence of freestyle skiing in the 1970s. One friend joked that we should start a Million Moguls Ski Club, because we had probably skied that many bumps over the years, cycling the chairlifts at Snoqualmie Pass, Crystal Mountain, and other Northwest ski areas.

While some of my college friends got seriously into freestyle skiing, I drifted in another direction, toward mountaineering. Alpine climbing opened my eyes to the wilderness mountains of the Pacific Northwest, country hinted at in views from Northwest ski areas but only truly experienced after leaving the roads and chairlifts behind. After I graduated from the University of Washington in 1978, I landed an engineering job and dove into local mountaineering with a passion sharpened by having to squeeze my adventures into weekends and short vacations from work. I bought a pair of Ramer ski-touring bindings and mounted them on a used pair of K2 skis from Gordy. My friend Gary Brill gave me some old strap-on climbing skins. After modifying the Ramers to fit my climbing boots, I had a serviceable setup for ski mountaineering. Each spring, before the alpine climbing season was under way, I explored the Cascade and Olympic Mountains on skis, retracing classic routes and pioneering a few new ones as well.

Mountaineering has a long tradition of written history and vivid storytelling. Yet in ski mountaineering, I found few records to indicate where Northwest skiers had been and what they had done. In the fall of 2000, I began to seek out records and talk to old-time skiers to learn more about the story of human-powered skiing in the Northwest. I was interested in how ski resorts had come to be, since in several cases ski mountaineers had located the sites that were later developed. In 2012, as several Northwest ski areas approached fiftieth or seventy-fifth anniversaries, local writers compiled fine histories of those areas.

I had faith that the story of human-powered skiing in the Northwest would include tales worth telling, characters worth meeting, scenes to inspire, and surprises to be uncovered. After two decades of effort, frustration, delight, and even heartbreak, I feel that ultimately that faith has been justified.

Opposite: *An unidentified man skis at Paradise on Mount Rainier, circa 1907.* (University of Washington Libraries, Special Collections, Albert H. Barnes Collection)

CHAPTER 1

A FAR WHITE COUNTRY

"As a boy in Minnesota, I had my own skis," remembered Howard Hanson in a newspaper story almost sixty years later. "When we moved to Seattle in 1889, my father induced me to give away the skis. He said the climate here was too mild for skiing and the mountains were inaccessible, for lack of roads." Hanson, who served as a Washington state legislator and Seattle attorney in the early 1900s, never forgot his boyhood love of skiing. "Naturally, I longed for my skis," he recalled wistfully.

Hanson was not alone. In the 1880s, nearly two hundred thousand Norwegians immigrated to the United States. Many were young people fleeing poverty who left

Mount Rainier from Tacoma City Hall, December 1894; the railroad line can be seen crossing the tide flats. (University of Washington Libraries, Special Collections, Alvin H. Waite Collection)

family farms that were too small to divide any further. The Midwest was a popular destination for families like Hanson's. Some continued to the Pacific Northwest, where mining, forestry, and fishing offered opportunities to start a new life. Those who settled in western Washington and Oregon realized that they must set aside a cherished part of their old life—skiing.

From his new home in Seattle, Hanson could see mountains in nearly every direction. To the west rose the mysterious Olympics; to the north, the cone of Mount Baker; to the south, massive 14,410-foot Mount Rainier. On a clear winter day, hundreds of miles of snowy peaks beckoned along the eastern skyline between Mount Baker and Mount Rainier. But the mountains were no more accessible than distant clouds. To travel crude wagon roads for 50 miles or more to find skiing was out of the question. The low country where Hanson lived was mild and rainy—a place for umbrellas and overshoes, not skis.

In the early days, Seattle was isolated not only from its nearby mountains but from all of America. For Seattle founder Arthur Denny, coming to the Northwest had been an exhausting journey. During the summer of 1851, the Denny party traveled west by wagon from Illinois to Portland, Oregon. Three months later, they sailed from Portland to Puget

Sound, landing at Alki Point on a gray November day. Though the Duwamish people had inhabited Seattle comfortably for many generations, the newcomers would require some time to feel at home. "I can't never forget when the folks landed at Alki Point," recalled the captain's wife. "It rained awful hard and the starch got took out of our bonnets and the wind blew, and when the women got into the rowboat to go ashore they were crying every one of 'em."

From the beginning, Denny felt that the future of Seattle lay in connecting to the east: "I came to the coast with the belief that a railroad would be built across the continent to some point on the northern coast within the next fifteen or twenty years, and [I] located on the Sound with that expectation." Denny would have to wait longer than he'd hoped. In 1853, when the Washington Territory was established, Congress authorized the reconnaissance of potential rail routes from the Mississippi to the Pacific. Isaac Stevens, Washington's first territorial governor, was put in charge of the Northern Pacific survey. This survey proposed a route from the east with two branches, one down the Columbia River to Fort Vancouver and the other over the Cascade Mountains to Puget Sound. After the Northern Pacific Railroad bill was approved by Congress in 1864, more detailed surveys were launched.

From 1867 to 1872, scouts for the railroad explored Cascade passes north of the Columbia River. On the North Cascades crest between Stevens Pass and the Skagit River, Daniel C. Linsley investigated potential routes both north and south of Glacier Peak in 1870. With his Native guides, he crossed Kaiwhat Pass above the headwaters of Lake Chelan, which was buried under a deep June snowpack. Though he was no skier, Linsley was perhaps the first white person to emulate the way his Native guides traversed their snowy environment: "In coming down [from the pass] I practiced the plan pursued by the Indians, to-wit, sitting down upon the snow and allowing the force of gravity to take me down, using a stout stick as a brake to regulate the speed. It may have not been, and indeed I am convinced it is not the most dignified pose of traveling known, but it was an eminently successful one in my case."

While Linsley and others searched for the best crossing of the Cascade Range, construction of the Northern Pacific Railroad was beginning in Minnesota. Development focused on the Columbia River as the main rail line, with the trans-Cascade route as a secondary branch. The railroad reached Puget Sound in 1883 via the Oregon side of the Columbia River gorge, a ferry across the river to Kalama, Washington, and a line that ran north from there to Tacoma.

In 1853, two years after the Denny party had landed in Seattle, there arrived another pioneer whose life would help set the scene for the introduction of skiing in the Cascade Mountains. That September, James Longmire led the first wagon train over Naches Pass, a 4,900-foot gap in the Cascades north of Mount Rainier. Longmire settled with his family near Washington's future state capital, Olympia. In 1870 he guided to Mount Rainier the first two parties to climb to its summit. After Longmire's own climb of the mountain in 1883, he discovered mineral springs near the foot of Rainier and struck the idea of developing the springs as a resort. He filed a mineral claim, cleared a trail to the site, and built a cabin. In 1890 he opened the Longmire Springs Hotel, two stories with a downstairs lobby and five guest rooms. With a crew of Native laborers, Longmire extended the road from Ashford to the hotel a few years later. The resort's success helped accelerate the movement for a national park, which was established at Mount Rainier in 1899. Within a decade, the resort would serve as the base camp for the first skiers on the mountain.

With the arrival of thousands of Scandinavians to America in the 1880s, and the gradual development of roads into Northwest mountains a decade later, the stage was set for skis to make their appearance. As the railroad neared completion in 1882–83, the Northern Pacific's immigration agencies lured thousands of British, German, and Scandinavian settlers onto its land grant. Some settled along the Columbia River near Hood River, Oregon, along the route of the old Oregon Trail. This area just east of the Cascade Range experiences colder winters than settlements near the coast. During the 1880s, residents of the Hood River valley built a tourist road from the Columbia River to the northeastern flank of Mount Hood. A tent camp was initially established, and in 1889 the Cloud Cap Inn was constructed on the mountain at an elevation of nearly 5,900 feet. The inn was built from native stone and beams of silver fir hauled by horse teams two miles up the mountain slope. Next to the construction of the railroad through the Columbia River gorge, the inn was considered the most important development project in the valley at the time.

The winter of 1889–90 brought deep snow and severe storms. Many feared that the new inn would be blown away or crushed by heavy snows. To see how the inn had fared, Will and Doug Langille set out on homemade skis in February. They reached Elk Beds cabin on the first day and the inn a day later. The day was sunny and warm, and meltwater dripped from the eaves. The inn was unharmed. This was the first recorded ski trip to the north side of Mount Hood and the earliest reference to skiing I've found in the Cascades between Mount Hood and the Canadian border. According to Portland newspaperman and skier Fred McNeil, the Langille trip dispelled the myth among local residents that winter weather at timberline could not be endured. A month later, the Langilles, along with photographer A. B. McAlpin, carried an 18-inch-by-22-inch plate camera to the inn to photograph winter scenes. The success of these trips helped popularize the idea of winter recreation on Mount Hood. Due to the proximity of the railroad, it was easier in the 1890s to get to the north side of Mount Hood than to Government Camp, which in later years became the gateway from Portland to skiing on the mountain's southern flank.

The Mazamas mountaineering club was founded in 1894 by a group of Oregon climbers during a July ascent of 11,240-foot Mount Hood. Several years later, in February 1903, a trio of Mazamas organized a ski expedition to the mountain's south side. They traveled by wagon to Tollgate (now a Mount Hood campground) above Rhododendron, then backpacked with their skis to Government Camp, where the men were guests of club member Oliver C. Yocum, manager of the Mountain View House. Colonel Lester L. Hawkins made their skis, about ten feet long and six inches wide with toe-strap bindings. Martin Gorman and T. Brooke White completed the party, each of whom carried a nine-foot pole for balance. None of the men had previous ski experience, but they returned from the trip with great enthusiasm. White predicted that "the time would come when more people would visit Mount Hood in the winter than in the summer." The trip received a lot of attention, though local forest ranger Dick Maupin had already been skiing around Summit Prairie for several years. By 1911 Yocum's wife, Ann, wrote, "We have had quite a lot of company several times this winter. It is quite the fad to come up here for the ski riding."

In Washington, stories of skiing first appeared in the north-central Cascades east of Everett. In the 1870s and 1880s, gold and silver had been discovered at Silver Creek, about 10 miles northeast of Index, and at Monte Cristo, on the other side of Poodle Dog Pass at the head of the Sauk River. In 1892 and 1893, a railroad was built from the port of Everett on Puget Sound to Monte Cristo. A year later, a steam-driven rotary snowplow arrived, enabling trains to run to the town site throughout the winter. It was a boom year, and Monte Cristo became the largest mining effort ever undertaken in western Washington.

Even before the railroad arrived, men wintered in the mountains surrounding Monte Cristo to seek their fortune. An article in the *Monte Cristo Mountaineer* noted that prospectors always observed New Year's Day to stake claims on ground where the previous owner hadn't done the required assessment work: "All day on Tuesday, Dec. 31st, men could be seen, well provided with snowshoes, ski, provision, flat bottles, alpenstocks and hatchets, taking their devious way up the hillsides south, north and east, nearly all of whom remained out overnight, in order to place their stakes on coveted ground exactly at midnight."

The winter of 1892–93 brought especially heavy snowfall. Henry Pennycock, in charge of a camp seven miles down from Monte Cristo, reported that more than 36 feet of snow fell during the winter. In late April, seven feet of snow remained on the ground at the camp and more than three feet at Silverton, a few miles down the valley. "They are hauling goods to Silverton on sleighs, and have been packing on ponies to the Hoodoo mine, three and a half miles above Silverton, all winter," Pennycock wrote. "Traveling is all done on snowshoes or on Norwegian ski."

The editor of the *Inter-Cascade Miner* at Galena, at the mouth of Silver Creek, described the view from his window in February 1893: "The office windows command an extensive view of the business and residence portions of the town, and the hours of labor are frequently enlivened by the gyrations and lofty tumbling that a man and a pair of able-bodied Norwegian snow-shoes [i.e., skis] can execute when a slight misunderstanding arises between them. The snow-shoes invariably come out on top while the man is buried, head down in the snow."

A WONDERLAND OF SNOW AT MOUNT RAINIER

In 1883, as its line to Tacoma neared completion, the Northern Pacific Railroad launched a promotional campaign to attract travelers to the Northwest. To draw attention to Mount Rainier, the railroad invited a distinguished group of Europeans to visit the mountain in the company of Northern Pacific geologist Bailey Willis. The party included Professor James Bryce, a writer and member of the British Parliament, and Professor Karl von Zittel, a geologist. Following their visit, they wrote of Rainier, "The peak itself is as noble a mountain as we have ever seen in its lines and structure. The combination of ice scenery with woodland scenery of the grandest type is to be found nowhere in the Old World, unless it be in the Himalayas, and, so far as we know, nowhere else on the American Continent."

Bryce and von Zittel published a report expressing the hope that Mount Rainier would be treated as a national park. Their 1883 proposal went nowhere, but ten years later Willis revived it. His proposal eventually attracted the support of scientists, mountaineers, and Northwest civic leaders. The Northern Pacific, whose land grant included the area of Mount Rainier, stayed discreetly in the background during this campaign. Mount Rainier National Park was established in 1899 in a deal that gave the Northern Pacific prime forestland in exchange for the ice and rock it had owned on Mount Rainier.

After the establishment of the national park, John Bagley became president of the Tacoma Eastern Railway and set out to extend the line from Tacoma to Ashford, just six miles west of the park boundary. The railroad was completed in 1904 and stage service was inaugurated over the remaining 12 miles to Longmire. The first day-trippers to the park arrived that summer. Visitors could now leave Tacoma at 9:00 a.m. and arrive at Ashford by noon. In 1906 the railway opened the second hotel in Mount Rainier National Park, the National Park Inn, with room for sixty guests located opposite the Longmire Springs Hotel. James McCullough of Ashford was the inn's winter caretaker, and by 1909 he and

Alfred B. Conrad of Eatonville had become the first two permanent rangers employed in the national park.

Rainier was the first national park to be patrolled exclusively by rangers, without resort to US Army troops. A ranger cabin was built at Paradise, but it was unused in winter. It's possible, perhaps even likely, that McCullough or Conrad used skis around Longmire in winter, but ski trips to Paradise would probably not have been a regular part of their duties. One of the earliest known skiers on Rainier was Thor Bisgaard, a Norwegian who moved to the Northwest in 1907. He took a job with the Northern Pacific in Tacoma and visited the mountain with skis. Snapshots in Bisgaard family albums and a photo by Albert H. Barnes at the University of Washington suggest that these trips may have started as early as 1907, but the precise date is unknown. However, by 1909 recreational skiing on Mount Rainier had definitely arrived.

The year 1909 was auspicious in the Pacific Northwest. Mount Rainier National Park was ten years old. The Klondike Gold Rush of 1897 had made Seattle a boomtown, and the city celebrated its prosperity by hosting its first world's fair, the Alaska-Yukon-Pacific Exposition (AYP). Between June and October 1909, nearly four million people attended the AYP. The automobile was just beginning to transform America. The previous fall, Henry Ford had started production of his Model T, known as the "Tin Lizzie." To launch the exposition, the first auto race across North America was started in New York City at the exact moment that President Taft opened the AYP in Seattle. Twenty-three days later, four cars rumbled into Seattle, with the climax of the transcontinental race being the rugged crossing of Snoqualmie Pass.

Young, energetic, and well traveled throughout the Northwest, thirty-two-year-old Milnor Roberts, dean of the University of Washington's College of Mines, was one of the AYP organizers. He proposed that the exposition be held on the UW campus, where he planned sports events for the AYP. (His father, William Milnor Roberts, had been chief engineer for the Northern Pacific during most of the years of its construction.) During spring break in 1909, Milnor Roberts planned an unusual holiday in the Cascades. In March he and a small group of friends arrived at the National Park Inn at Longmire. The party included Roberts and his sister, Milnora; their friend Frank Dabney; and Dabney's wife, Mary, and daughter Edith, among others. By special arrangement, inn watchman James McCullough allowed the group entry, and they spent the next week enjoying day trips skiing on the slopes of Eagle Peak, the Ramparts, and Paradise Valley.

The government road to Paradise was still under construction and would not be plowed in winter for another twenty to thirty years. The Paradise Inn did not yet exist, and the

Milnor Roberts skiing on the University of Washington campus, probably during the 1920s (University of Washington Libraries, Special Collections, Social Issues Collection)

only structure in the area was the small ranger cabin. The goal of the Roberts outing was to reach Paradise Valley on skis. The shortest route from Longmire to Paradise was the horse trail along the Paradise River, a six-mile trek. Since the trail was unbroken through deep snow, the party made several trips toward Paradise, each time pushing the route farther up the valley. Two groups eventually reached Paradise. The first, including Milnor Roberts, reached the ranger cabin and enjoyed views of Mount Rainier rising above the head of the valley. Roberts wrote, "The only toilsome part of the journey was at Narada Falls, where we were forced to navigate our skis sidewise, in crab fashion, up the steep slope."

On March 24, Edith Dabney and Milnora Roberts, accompanied by McCullough, skied to Sluiskin Falls, well beyond the point the first party had reached. They left Longmire at 8:00 a.m. and climbed to Paradise Valley, where they found the snow piled 20 to 30 feet deep. McCullough, who had been employed since 1892 and was familiar with ascents made over many years, said Dabney and Roberts were the first women to make a ski trip to Paradise Valley and that theirs was the first trip of any kind to reach the elevation of Sluiskin Falls so early in the year. Milnor Roberts later wrote, "As both the ladies had ascended Rainier in summer, they could enjoy to the utmost the wonderful view of the snow-clad range spread out before them." The party made their way back to Longmire in waning daylight, returning to the hotel in darkness at 9:00 p.m.

The Roberts outing to Mount Rainier was reported in the *Seattle Times*, the *Seattle Post-Intelligencer (P-I)*, and the *Tacoma Ledger*. In a letter to Mountaineers historian Eugene Faure a half century later, Milnor Roberts recalled, "As we traversed the open slopes, now smooth with a great depth of snow, our skis hidden deep in the powder snow slid quietly along to make the only marks of man's presence even for a day, or at least the only visible one. The possibilities of Paradise as a winter resort so impressed us that I wrote an article for the *National Geographic Magazine* [which] published it with some of our photos in the June 1909 issue with the title 'A Wonderland of Glaciers and Snow.'" In that article Roberts wrote, "So far as ski sport is concerned, it would be difficult to imagine more perfect riding than can be had on the many miles of varied slopes in Paradise Park."

EARLY OUTINGS WITH THE MOUNTAINEERS

After completing its line from Kalama to Tacoma, the Northern Pacific turned its attention to completing the trans-Cascade route between Ellensburg and western Washington. The Stampede Pass crossing (via switchbacks) opened in 1887. Seattle celebrated with "jollifications" that almost eclipsed those of 1883 when the railroad first reached Puget Sound. As rail historian Kurt Armbruster wrote, "A great bonfire blazed on Front Street, skyrockets whooshed into the night, revolvers were emptied with abandon, and a long Victorian conga line snaked uptown to the *Post-Intelligencer* office." The Stampede Pass tunnel opened in 1888, eliminating the need for switchbacks over the pass.

The second trans-Cascade route opened in 1893, when the Great Northern Railway under James J. Hill completed its line by an intricate series of switchbacks over 4,056-foot Stevens Pass. In 1897 construction began on the two-and-a-half-mile Cascade Tunnel under the pass. It opened to trains in December 1900, beginning the era of large-scale logging in western Washington and organized winter recreation by groups such as The Mountaineers.

Founded in 1906 by 151 charter members, more than half of them women, The Mountaineers was largely a Seattle-based organization, with members clustered in Everett and Tacoma as well. The club organized outings in both summer and winter, the latter initially

The Roberts ski party posed outside the National Park Inn at Longmire in 1909. From left to right: Milnora Roberts, Mrs. Worrall Wilson, Sally Nieman, Edith Dabney, Frank and Mary Dabney, Milnor Roberts, Carl F. Gould; Waldemar Nieman is not shown. (University of Washington Libraries, Special Collections, Social Issues Collection)

Left: Mountaineers skiers enjoy Paradise Valley during one of their early outings on Mount Rainier. (University of Washington Libraries, Special Collections, Mountaineers Collection) *Right: Catherine Winslow skiing during The Mountaineers' New Year's outing to Paradise in 1916–17* (Washington State Historical Society)

limited to the foothills of the Cascades. As Lulie Nettleton wrote in the 1913 *Sierra Club Bulletin*, "Since snow—fluffy, exhilarating, real snow—does not come to Seattle, Seattleites must seek the snow. Consequently, it has become the annual custom for the Mountaineers to go back to the hills and spend New Year's enjoying winter sports usually confined to colder lands." Several of the club's earliest winter trips were made to Index or Scenic Hot Springs along the Great Northern Railway. The Scenic Hot Springs Hotel was built three miles below the west portal of the original Cascade Tunnel after the railroad was completed. The Mountaineers started going there around 1910, after the hotel was rebuilt following a fire.

The Tacoma Mountaineers turned their attention to Mount Rainier as a winter destination. Over the New Year's holiday of 1912–13, the Tacoma branch organized its first winter outing, under the leadership of A. H. Denman. With Seattle and Everett members joining in, fifty people attended. "Since the average resident of this mild climate is not equipped for deep snow," Nettleton wrote, "the sudden demand for cold-weather articles had caused a rush upon Alaskan outfitters, and calls upon friends from colder regions." Equipped with Alaskan mukluks, Canadian and Alaskan snowshoes, and a few Norwegian skis, the party rode the Tacoma Eastern Railway to Ashford, then walked 12 miles to the National Park Inn at Longmire. Most of the party had never used snowshoes before, and one member wrote that at night the lobby resembled a repair shop.

Most of the party stayed close to Longmire during their snowshoe wanderings. Six, including Nettleton, pressed on to Paradise through a snowstorm. "[We] stood spellbound in an unreal world," she recalled. "Paradise Valley is charming as a home of mountain flowers and exquisite verdure, but as we saw it, robed in a mantle of snow a score of feet in depth, it attained a dignity and majesty that will make it stand alone in the gallery of mountain memories." Milnor Roberts and his sister Milnora attended this outing, but written records don't mention them using skis. The only skier named was Olive Rand, a young woman who apparently borrowed a pair in a misguided moment. Her skis were described as "two lanky slabs of wood, with turned-up ends and a pair of simple loops for harness which quite failed to keep the runners straight or, for that matter, to keep them on her feet at all."

In 1913–14 the party was smaller, but the trip highlight was an overnight visit to Paradise. The men slept in John Reese's private cabin, and the women slept in the nearby ranger cabin. J. Harry Weer wrote, "The scene was beyond description—a panorama in white, sparkling in the starlight, dotted here by trees, streaked there by wind-swept ridges; the graceful Tatoosh Range on one hand and the majestic monarch of the region on the other."

During the 1915–16 New Year's outing, Thor Bisgaard, a member of the Tacoma Mountaineers, offered ski instruction to any interested member. Important changes were coming to the mountain around this time. Stephen Mather, who would soon become the first director of the National Park Service, convinced Seattle business leaders in 1915 to form the Rainier National Park Company and build an inn at Paradise. Construction started in the summer of 1916, and the inn was prepared to open the following summer. Members of The Mountaineers persuaded Mather to erect a shelter hut at Camp Muir, designed by Mountaineers architect Carl F. Gould, who had been in Milnor Roberts's 1909 ski party.

For the New Year's outing of 1916–17, The Mountaineers arranged to stay at the new Paradise Inn, which would not formally open until summer, as its first informal guests. Food and other provisions were transported to the inn ahead of time, and sixty-eight Mountaineers tramped to Paradise after a night at Longmire. Over the next two days, Mountaineers parties ventured to Sluiskin Falls, Cowlitz Rocks, McClure Rock, and the new stone hut at Camp Muir—the first time the camp had been reached on snowshoes and one of the earliest visits in winter.

Writing in the *Mountaineer Bulletin* in 1917, Kathryne Wilson described Paradise as "a new Mecca for winter sports." Due to the difficult access, however, Paradise would not truly become a winter resort for at least a decade, and The Mountaineers would largely have the valley to themselves through the early 1920s. But the first tentative step had been made to establish Mount Rainier as the center of winter sports in the Pacific Northwest.

THE GENTLE ART OF SKIING

By 1905 rail traffic to the Pacific Northwest had grown so dramatically that the Northern Pacific and Great Northern Railways were glutted. The Chicago, Milwaukee, and St. Paul Railroad announced that it would build a line from Evarts, South Dakota, to Puget Sound over the Cascade Mountains. For its Cascade crossing, the Milwaukee Railroad chose Snoqualmie Pass, a historic wagon route in the 1870s and 1880s before the opening of the Northern Pacific Railroad over Stampede Pass ended the era of wagon transportation over the Cascades. The Milwaukee Railroad completed its line over Snoqualmie Pass in the spring of 1909, just in time for the Alaska-Yukon-Pacific Exposition. Around this time, the old wagon road was improved for the AYP's New York–to–Seattle auto race. Like the earlier lines over Stampede and Stevens Passes, the Milwaukee Railroad initially crossed Snoqualmie Pass on a surface track; the station at the summit was called Laconia. Except during severe conditions, the Milwaukee Railroad was kept open throughout the winter.

In February 1912, four Mountaineers stepped off the train at Laconia Station into 10 to 12 feet of snow. They donned snowshoes for the first time and spent three days camping and traveling to the head of the Snoqualmie River (the valley that would later hold the

Waiting at Rockdale Station (University of Washington Libraries, Special Collections, Mountaineers Collection)

The Mountaineers' Snoqualmie Lodge in 1914; designed by Carl F. Gould, the lodge was built near Lodge Lake, on the opposite side of the Cascade crest from today's ski areas. (The Mountaineers Archives)

Alpental ski area). Upon their return, one of the men wrote a short but enthusiastic trip report for the club's monthly *Bulletin*. This excursion began an association between The Mountaineers and Snoqualmie Pass that would last more than a century.

During a summer outing in the Olympics in 1913, The Mountaineers decided to build a lodge in the Cascades that club members could use throughout the year. They sought a location reachable by train within a few hours from the city that would provide trips of a day or several days' tramping and make enjoyment of winter sports possible. After scouting several possibilities, they chose a site just west of Snoqualmie Pass, on a knoll 500 feet above the Milwaukee Railroad tracks. Big Lake, a quarter mile from the lodge site, would later become known as Lodge Lake, after The Mountaineers' Snoqualmie Lodge.

Sunday mornings, during the summer of 1914, Mountaineers would take the train to a stop below the lodge hill, where together with lumber, shingles, bricks, and other building materials, they were unloaded. They carried the supplies up the trail and worked through the day at the lodge site until it was time to catch the evening train home. Arthur Nation Sr. became the hero of the year for carrying the cookstove from the railroad stop to the lodge on his back. Designed by Gould, the Mountaineers architect who had designed the stone hut at Camp Muir, the lodge was finished that summer and club members began using it immediately.

Meanwhile, the Milwaukee Railroad had been struggling to keep its surface line over Snoqualmie Pass open in winter. Following the hard winter of 1912–13, the railroad worked in earnest to complete a tunnel route. The tunnel would run beneath the Cascade crest for two miles, from Rockdale Creek west of the pass to Hyak, near the northern tip of

HAPPY LODGE DAYS

"Each year the ski gains in popularity," Mountaineers club member Crissie Cameron wrote in 1923. "The festive ski-runner now flits scornfully by the deliberate snowshoer. The sight-seeing columns of snowshoers retort that they enjoy more of the beauties of nature, and have even been heard to allude to our old friends the hare and the tortoise."

Elizabeth Kirkwood, writing in 1924, added, "People did not talk about snowshoes, it was all about skis. When the three-quarter-mile ski run became too safe and tame for the speedy ones, they took to the rock-pile course and annihilated distance." The following year, Florence McComb concluded, "Skiing is decidedly in the ascendancy for the long winter season at Snoqualmie Lodge and the snow-shoe is as much out of style as the 'covered wagon,' though it still has a few staunch supporters who like to plant their feet firmly and know that they will stay put."

Clayton Crawford expressed the feelings of many Mountaineers when he wrote in 1915, "Every trip to the Lodge and every contribution of time, labor, or money seems to make the members fonder of it." Describing the charms of winter, he wrote, "Big Lake freezes into a field for snowshoe races and other sports of winter outings, the landscapes are symphonies in white and dark green, moonlight turns the forest to fairy land, and the Lodge seems more inviting than at any other time of the year; the great fireplace, filled with logs that blaze defiance to the cold outside, warms the heart as well as the body, intensifies Mountaineer good fellowship, invites the singers to do their best, the storytellers to be most brilliant and all to dream of happy Lodge days past and happier still to come."

Snowshoe race winners on Lodge Lake in 1920 (Art and Grace Marzolf collection, The Mountaineers Archives)

Keechelus Lake, on the east side. The Snoqualmie Tunnel opened to trains early in the winter of 1914–15, just in time for the first winter season at the Mountaineers' new lodge. To reach the lodge in winter, they rode the Milwaukee Railroad to Rockdale Station at the west end of the Snoqualmie Tunnel. From there, they walked a mile of uncleared track (the old surface line) to Lodge Creek, then climbed the snow-covered trail to the lodge. Train schedules weren't very tight in those days, and the railroad allowed trains to stop to pick up passengers alongside the tracks. The drawback was that lodge users might have to wait for up to three hours in blowing snow or driving rain for the train to appear. That was the price to be paid for a weekend in the mountains.

Before The Mountaineers arrived, there were few trails in the area, so club members scouted and cut new ones. The Cascade Crest Trail, proposed by club member Joseph T. Hazard in 1926, follows paths in the Snoqualmie Pass area established by The Mountaineers in the years after they built their lodge. In 1916 club members blazed a trail from the lodge southward to Silver Peak. The trail was cleared for hiking soon thereafter.

In February 1915 the Seattle Mountaineers held the first of what would become their annual winter outing at the lodge. Washington's birthday was chosen as the date for their

Fairman B. Lee tries skis in 1919, when most Snoqualmie Lodge visitors were still using snowshoes. (University of Washington Libraries, Special Collections, Mountaineers Collection)

long-discussed winter carnival. Snowshoe races were held on Lodge Lake and skis soon appeared. During the 1918 outing, three pairs of skis at the lodge were in constant use. Members proposed a ski and toboggan course that was cleared during the following summer. "Over one hundred sizable trees" were felled to create a toboggan and ski course 50 feet wide by 300 feet long, ending at Lodge Lake.

Skiing slowly grew but remained less popular than snowshoeing throughout the 1910s. Mountaineer Celia Shelton wrote in 1918, "The masters of the gentle art of skiing take on a superior air, and let it be known that the lowly snowshoe has no caste at all in the world of winter sports. A trip to Snoqualmie Lodge is usually enough, however, to establish the snowshoe solidly in favor as a very present help in trouble, with skis holding first place in the popular opinion on Lodge Lake and the toboggan course."

Opposite: *A jumper takes flight during the 1922 ski tournament on Mount Rainier.* (Photo by Ingrid P. Wicken courtesy California Ski Library)

CHAPTER 2

THE BIG SNOW

With its maritime climate, Seattle rarely gets much snow in winter. Snow in town is a novelty that quickly becomes a nuisance because of the city's steep hills and limited ability to clear them. Scandinavians who grew up skiing and who settled in Seattle in the early 1900s were frustrated because snow never lasted long enough to encourage development of the sport here. But events in the winter of 1916 began to change this. That January was unusually cold. Lakes around the city froze over, and during the last weekend of the month, three thousand skaters flocked to Green Lake on a Sunday afternoon.

Over a period of three days, 29 inches of snow blanketed the city. The one-day record for snowfall in Seattle, 21½ inches, was established on February 1. At 10:00 a.m. that day, the grandstand at the University of Washington's Denny Field buckled under the weight of new snow. The following afternoon, the dome of St. James

During the Big Snow of February 1916, 29 inches of snow fell on Seattle in a single storm. Here, L. C. Twito skis along 6th Avenue near University Street. He and other Norwegians made their own skis and thus had no problems in getting around town. (The Nordic Heritage Museum Collection, Seattle, 1999.020.013)

Cathedral collapsed. Newspapers reported similar cave-ins all around western Washington. Streetcars were disabled and five-foot drifts clogged residential streets. The Smith Tower, the tallest building in the western United States at the time, hurled rooftop avalanches onto pedestrians below. The *Seattle Times* reported that the city was "in the Clutch of the Snow King." As Seattle slowly dug itself out during the days that followed, *Times* editorials exhorted citizens to "clean your sidewalks!" and "clean off that roof!" and "clean out the alleys."

By the end of the week, odd tales of citizens coping with the snow were widespread. The *Seattle P-I* ran a fanciful account of one Henry Steinkopf, who wrote, "For fifteen years I have enjoyed the reputation of being the model citizen of our neighborhood . . . perfectly lamblike except under great provocation." Steinkopf, who had never skied before, was persuaded by his Norwegian neighbor to borrow a pair of skis for a trip to the grocer. During the downhill run for home, he lost his groceries, his watch, his cash, and his temper after crashing into Rev. Mr. Lukenwater, the local pastor. "I repeat," he wrote to the *P-I* editor, "that I lost all that was dear to me save my family because of those deceitful skis." The story distilled through humor what non-Scandinavians imagined might happen if they tried skiing.

On Sunday, February 6, the *Times* printed an unusual announcement: "Ski jumping and speed skiing today will be introduced to the Seattle public. . . . The committee in charge of the event believes that this is the first display of ski jumping ever staged in Seattle." Three men worked late Saturday night to prepare a ski jump on Fourth Avenue North, one of the city's steepest streets, in the Queen Anne neighborhood near the Fremont Bridge. "The contest Sunday," explained organizer John Sagdahl, "is in the nature of an experiment. For many years, a number of ski jumpers from Norway who are now businessmen here have been attempting to create interest in the sport without success. We believe that skiing is one of the most thrilling sports in existence, both from the skier's and spectator's viewpoint."

Front page of the Seattle Times on February 7, 1916 featured ski jumpers (clockwise from upper left): A. Flakstad, Reidar Gjolme, and L. Orvald.

The event was an expression of the distinctly Norwegian ideal of *friluftsliv*, loosely translated as "open-air living." Growing up where snow and skiing were a way of life, the ski-jumpers-turned-businessmen pined for snow-covered hills and the sport of their youth. A once-in-a-lifetime dump of snow in the city was simply too wonderful to waste. The ski jumping exhibition was front-page news on Monday. Warming temperatures, light rain, and sticky snow failed to deter ten jumpers from competing. Reidar Gjolme, general agent of the Norwegian American (steamship) Line, won the event with a leap of 43 feet. L. Orvald was second with 38 feet, and three jumpers tied for third.

The snow didn't last long enough for a planned second exhibition. A rapid thaw flooded Northwest rivers, and the Great Northern Railway cancelled its trains through the mountains due to avalanche danger. Life in the city returned to a soggy routine. For the men who participated in the exhibition, however, the event stirred powerful memories of their skiing youth. In the months that followed, they discussed how they might revive ski jumping and put it on a firmer footing in the region. By the next winter, they had a tentative solution.

Seattle newspapers announced in February 1917 the "First Ski Tournament Ever Held in the Northwest" at Scenic Hot Springs, on the Great Northern line below Stevens Pass. In addition to mineral baths and "an invigorating atmosphere," Scenic offered skis and toboggans for guest use on a small slope carved out of the forest behind the hotel. Five silver cups were put up for the event, with contests for both men and women. The Great Northern Railway offered a special two-dollar-and-eighty-cent roundtrip rate for the tournament. About 150 people traveled from Seattle to watch the tournament.

Nineteen skiers entered the event, traveling from Seattle, Tacoma, and even Victoria and Vancouver, British Columbia. They included Thor Bisgaard of Tacoma and the winner of two previous winter's competition in Seattle, Reidar Gjolme, who had competed on the famous Holmenkollen jump in Norway in 1902. Jumps of 80 to 100 feet were expected, although the newspapers acknowledged that "some of the men who will compete have had many seasons pass their heads since they essayed the flight through the air on skis."

The tournament on February 4 was marred by rain and sticky snow. Gjolme won the meet with jumps of 70, 76, and 72 feet. Birger Normann of Tacoma was second. Due to the difficult conditions, Normann was the only jumper to stand up after his leaps. The highlight of the tournament was a young Norwegian woman, twenty-four-year-old Olga Bolstad, who arrived during the event and asked to borrow a pair of skis. "Although an unknown when she arrived," newspapers reported, "she speedily became the most talked-of person in the tourney, owing to her sensational jumping." Bolstad cleaned up the women's prizes and was awarded honorable mention in the men's events for her jumping.

Organizers realized that Scenic Hot Springs was not an ideal location for skiing. At an elevation of only 2,200 feet above sea level, Scenic receives as much rain in winter as snow. Fortunately, Bisgaard knew another option—Mount Rainier—as well as any skier. He had attended The Mountaineers' New Year's outing at Paradise just five weeks before the Scenic tournament and knew that the Paradise Inn would open to the public that summer. At an elevation of 5,400 feet, Paradise often holds snow into July.

After meeting with Thomas H. Martin, proprietor of the new inn, Bisgaard organized an event unprecedented in America: a midsummer ski tournament. The tournament was scheduled for July 29, 1917. Paradise Inn opened before the road was cleared of snow, and the first guests saw their baggage delivered on sleds. Publicity for the event announced that Olga Bolstad, "the most sensational lady ski-jumper in the Northwest," would be competing. The newspapers advised that "novices who wish to try their luck on the queer looking skis will be given an opportunity to do so, and some of the professionals will give instructions in their proper use."

Warm sunshine greeted the spectators, and Mount Rainier presided over the scene in a robe of brilliant snow. A feeling of celebration filled the air, and the tournament unfolded like a coming-out party, with the sport of skiing as the debutante. The ski jump was constructed on the east slope of Alta Vista, just a few hundred yards above the

Olga Bolstad won the first ski tournament held on Mount Rainier; she defeated all the male competitors. (Photo by Asahel Curtis courtesy Washington State Historical Society, WSHS.1943.42.40132)

inn. As the *Tacoma News Tribune* put it, "One of the most picturesque athletic events of the season was last Sunday's ski tournament on the slopes of Mount Tacoma. The beautiful Camp of the Clouds was the scene of the tourney, and the ideal weather made the day one long to be remembered. One side of the hill was deep with snow, while the other was green and decked with tulips, anemones and fragrant flowers. Summer and winter seemed to have met for the occasion."

Gjolme entered the meet but did not win this time. Bolstad defeated all the men to become the first ski champion crowned on Rainier. Newspapers reported that she had come to America four years earlier from Åmot, Østerdalen, Norway, where she learned to ski traveling to and from school. "Olga Bolstad, the pretty Seattle girl, was the greatest center of attraction among all the ski jumpers," wrote the *News Tribune*. "Her lightness

Competitors line up for the 1923 cross-country ski race on Mount Rainier; Hans Otto Giese, wearing number 15, is next to the pole with the Norwegian flag. (Giese Archives)

and grace made her a favorite with all, and she seemed to skim through the air like a bird. . . . The girl champion has been made an honorary, lifelong member of the Puget Sound Ski club [later the Northwest Ski Club]." The men accepted their defeat with grace. The Pacific Northwest had a new spectator sport, and Olga Bolstad was its first star.

A year later, the tournament on July 7, 1918, was billed as a "big sport classic." Nearly four hundred came to watch, helped by the opening of the auto road a day before the meet. Bolstad was the center of attention. "The little Seattle woman was easily the favorite of the spectators, who cheered her lustily when she made her appearance on the long slide," reported the *News Tribune*. "She made beautiful runs of exceptional length, with poise." Although she jumped well, Bolstad failed to repeat her victory. She placed fourth, after Sigurd Johnson of Tacoma and two other men. The result inspired an oddly matter-of-fact headline in the *News Tribune*: "Man Defeats Woman in Ski tournament." The men's acceptance of Bolstad on Mount Rainier is remarkable in light of sexist attitudes that prevailed in the sporting world for decades to come. Women's ski jumping would not be permitted in the Olympic Games until 2014, almost a century after Bolstad's victory on Rainier.

After the 1918 contest, the organizers made the tournament an annual classic. The 1919 postwar event was the first tournament in which jumps longer than 100 feet were recorded. Sigurd Johnson won in 1919 and 1921, while L. Larson of Aberdeen was champion in 1920. The tournament date was shifted to July 4 to attract more spectators.

According to the *News Tribune*, "Nowhere else on the American continent, outside of remote regions of the North, can be found conditions which would permit a ski meet while the sun is pouring down its heat and driving sweltering humanity to vacational scenes of rest and relaxation."

In 1922 and 1923 the organizers, now called the Northwest Ski Club, worked to expand the tournament beyond the local community. Professionals were invited from Colorado, the Midwest, and British Columbia. Gjolme, who had been involved since the first ski jumping exhibition in Seattle, was one of the club directors; he later became president of the Seattle Ski Club. Another director was Howard Hanson, who as a boy in Seattle had been induced to give away his skis.

The 1923 tournament attracted more than a thousand spectators, despite a one-mile hike in snow from Narada Falls to Paradise. One of the competitors was Hans Otto Giese, newly arrived from Germany and a veteran of the 1922 Olympic Games. He had been a member of "the pack" in the groundbreaking 1921 ski film *A Fox Hunt in the Engandine*, known in English simply as *The Chase*. The movie, by German filmmaker Arnold Fanck, featured Austrian ski-meister Hannes Schneider (as the fox) chased by eighteen German and Norwegian hotshots. Giese would become one of the fathers of alpine skiing and ski mountaineering in the Northwest in the decade that followed.

As skiing spread throughout the Northwest during the 1920s, the Fourth of July tournament on Mount Rainier fell by the wayside. Other events took its place, and what had been a curiosity on a Seattle street in 1916 became a sport enjoyed by many. By the early 1930s, Paradise would become the premier ski resort in the Northwest. The far white country that beckoned to settlers in the 1800s would become their grandchildren's winter playground.

SKIMMING THROUGH THE AIR: A CENTURY LATER

I learned of Olga Bolstad and her victory on Mount Rainier during some of my earliest research into Northwest skiing history. I dreamed of reenacting her tournament on old ski gear for its centennial in 2017. I felt somewhat daunted when I realized that I would be sixty years old in 2017 and maybe ski jumping at that age wouldn't be such a good idea. But as the years passed, reality proved kinder than my fears, so I decided to go ahead with the plan. I posted invitations on a couple of internet forums seeking skiers who might like to participate. I was reluctant to organize something extravagant, figuring that the Park Service would require a permit or block the event entirely if it got too big. Ultimately my best accomplices for the venture were family and a few close friends.

Homemade harness adapted to antique toe irons on a pair of 1930s-era skis

My brother Gordy had fond memories of ski jumping as a kid, when our dad was still active in the sport. Gordy had Dad's old leather boots and jumping skis, which he said Dad had bought from Olympic champion Toralf Engan in the 1960s, when Engan visited the Northwest for a tournament at Leavenworth. Gordy's best high school friend, Eric Lindahl, was a former freestyle skier and a fan of ski nostalgia, so he too was in. My son Tom and his friend Lee Swedin were also eager to go. Lauren Frohne, a videographer with the *Seattle Times*, became interested after attending a talk I gave earlier in the season, so she and writer Evan Bush and staff photographer Mike Siegel also came along. We met in the Paradise parking lot on a brilliant morning in late June. Just as in 1917, the day brought cloudless skies and bright sunshine. But unlike 1917, the Paradise Inn now stood next to a parking lot filled with hundreds of cars. By 9:00 a.m. the lot was nearly full. Visitors on snowshoes, skis, sneakers, and every sort of footwear in between set out from the parking lot on snowy trails leading up toward Alta Vista or around the mountain toward Edith Creek basin.

The most likely spot for the original ski tournament was on the southeastern flank of Alta Vista at around 5,800 feet elevation. Following a well-packed snowy trail from the Paradise Inn, we hiked up a few hundred feet to the site in about a half hour and discussed where to build our jump. I had borrowed a pair of 1930s-era wooden skis from the basement of The Mountaineers clubhouse in Seattle. The edgeless skis had toe irons but no harness, so I fashioned crude bindings using polyurethane ski straps and parts from my neighborhood hardware store. My boots were a pair of old but serviceable leather climbing boots. To be honest, I thought my boots probably offered better control than Dad's old jumping boots, which had very little ankle support. A few of us had rummaged old clothing to wear. I had a vintage shirt and vest from a neighborhood thrift store, a homemade tie, and a wool driving cap. In honor of Olga, I picked up some small Norwegian flags to plant in the snow as well as a larger American flag. While sunny, the day was breezy, and the flags fluttered wildly as we scouted and constructed our jump.

Gordy identified the problem with our hill: there was no out-run. Well-formed jumping hills have a steep landing area that transitions smoothly to a flat zone, which continues

The author on Mount Rainier, celebrating the centennial of Olga Bolstad's victory in 1917

rising to an uphill slope, making it easier for jumpers to stop. Our hill transitioned from an acceptably steep landing slope to a slope that was only a bit less steep, which continued for 500 vertical feet to the bottom of Paradise Valley. During Gordy's first jump, one of his skis came off, and it ran all the way to the river. It was undamaged, but he had to walk down and fetch it. Newspaper records indicate that jumps as long as 120 feet were recorded during tournaments at Paradise in the 1920s. We weren't sure where they had built a jump that would offer that much distance. With our sloppy boots and old skis, sticky snow was a problem. Just a little stickiness on the in-run could throw a skier off balance. I sprinkled ice cream salt over the in-run to prevent this from happening.

Without a proper out-run, we had to figure out how to stop after our jumps. My home-made bindings offered little control over my skis, so I decided to jump with a bamboo pole in one hand. Upon landing, I could brace by dragging the pole on one side while turning the skis in that direction to stop. This worked well, and I fell only once in several jumps. Gordy found it impossible to turn Dad's skis with his old boots, and he didn't have a pole, so each of his jumps ended with a crash.

On most of my jumps, I was happy just to ski away without falling. But on my fourth flight, I felt a touch of the magic that must have inspired the old jumpers. The in-run was fast, with no stickiness, and my skis ran true. When I sprang, there was a sensation of floating on air—balanced and, for a brief moment, suspended. I landed softly, leaned my pole into the snow, and gradually skidded to a stop. Had Olga been watching, I would have tipped my hat to her.

Eric, Tom, and Lee jumped on modern alpine ski gear, with plastic boots and sturdy bindings. To mimic the Nordic style, they schussed without ski poles. To measure the jumps, I placed markers on the snow using cherry Kool-Aid. Lee had the longest jump, more than 50 feet. In the end we each had a few good jumps, no one got hurt, and we cleaned up the site before we left. I brought medals, which we awarded to Lee and Tom, and gag gifts for everybody else. It was a beautiful day on the mountain, and we were inspired to think of the dawning of Mount Rainier skiing on a day very much like it one hundred years earlier.

FROM THE MINES TO THE SKY

The Olympic and western Cascade Mountains share Seattle's maritime climate. They get a mix of snow and rain throughout the winter, depending on elevation. At 3,000 feet Snoqualmie, the lowest of the Cascade passes, is just high enough to offer reliable skiing in most years. But until the 1930s, the road over Snoqualmie Pass was closed in winter, preventing

Young skiers in Cle Elum proudly display their skis. (Central Washington University Archives and Special Collections, Cle Elum Ski Club Collection)

the development of skiing there. Thirty miles east of Snoqualmie Pass is Cle Elum, founded in the 1880s after most of its Native American inhabitants had been relocated to the Yakima Valley. Shielded from warmer coastal air by the Cascades, Cle Elum is high enough at 2,000 feet to usually have snow on the ground in midwinter.

Cle Elum and its smaller neighbor, Roslyn, were born as coal mining towns. The towns came alive in 1884, when coal was discovered in the hills above Roslyn. Railroads ran on coal in those days, and the Northern Pacific was building its line toward the Cascade Mountains. The railroad reached Cle Elum in 1886 and opened to the coast through Stampede

Pass the following year. By the 1920s, however, mining at Cle Elum had begun a gradual downturn and would end completely by the 1960s.

In the early years of mining's decline, the community found a new diversion during the winter months through skiing. A note in the February 11, 1921 issue of the *Cle Elum Echo* recorded that a party of twelve skiers had enjoyed a day near Lake Cle Elum "sliding, gliding, rolling and tumbling down to Mr. Spratt's cabin." By 1924, the newspaper (by then

EARLY NORTHWEST SKI CLUBS

It is remarkable how isolated Northwest ski communities were from each other in the early 1900s, judging by accounts from the time. Addressing the Kiwanis Club in 1932, John Bresko spoke of how the Cle Elum Ski Club had introduced the sport of skiing to the Northwest with its annual tournament in 1924. Bresko overlooked, perhaps, the midsummer ski tournaments on Mount Rainier from 1917 through 1923, the year before Cle Elum's first winter carnival. At least one competitor at Cle Elum in 1924 had jumped at Mount Rainier the previous July.

Organized skiing on a smaller scale had been happening at several other locations, including outings to Mount Rainier by The Mountaineers in the mid-1910s and at their Snoqualmie Lodge in the early 1920s, where the club's first ski tournament was held in 1922. In 1919 Everett Mountaineers spent Washington's birthday at the Silverton hotel, a few miles down from Monte Cristo, which they reported was "plentifully supplied with snowshoes, toboggans, and skis." The following July 4, an informal ski tournament was held in Glacier Basin, 2,000 feet above Monte Cristo. "No prizes were handed out," wrote mining historian Philip Woodhouse. "The only trophy was the joy of competition."

Likely the earliest ski contest in the Northwest took place far from the Cascade Mountains. At Spokane, near the Washington-Idaho border, a ski running and jumping exhibition was held in the winter of 1913, organized by Olaus Jeldness. The January 20 *Spokesman-Review* reported on the event held at Browne farm on Moran Prairie. Ole Larsen and Engwald Engen made individual leaps of more than 100 feet and a tandem jump over 80 feet long. A mining engineer born in Norway, Jeldness is recognized today as the father of skiing in western Canada. In the 1890s he organized and won ski tournaments at Rossland, British Columbia, where he lived and worked at the time. Around 1907 Jeldness moved to Spokane, where he retired and became an important member of the local Scandinavian community until his death in 1935.

Coordination between Northwest ski clubs finally arrived in 1930 with the formation of the Pacific Northwest Ski Association, which began with six clubs: Seattle, Leavenworth, and Cle Elum in Washington and Cascade, Hood River, and Bend in Oregon. In the beginning, the association was devoted almost entirely to ski jumping, which intimidated beginners. But alpine skiing soon took hold of the sport because it appealed to every skier.

combined with the *Cascade Miner* as the *Miner-Echo*) reported, "There are now hundreds of ski riders in this district."

In 1921 John "Syke" Bresko and friends formed a skiing group associated with the Kiwanis Club, which created a course at South Cle Elum with a ski jump and toboggan run in the fall of 1923. Around the same time, Bresko, John Koester, and Russ Connell built the Summit Lodge, a three-walled shelter three miles north of Cle Elum on the ridge above the Teanaway Valley. Besides the lodge, the site included a ski takeoff and the Rocky Run, an obstacle course with five jumps.

Cle Elum organized its first ski carnival in 1924, held at the Kiwanis course at South Cle Elum with more than a thousand spectators. Four professional jumpers competed, all from towns west of the mountains. John Holen of Seattle made the longest jump of the day, 83 feet. According to the *Miner-Echo*, Holen last jumped at Mount Rainier on July 4, during the last summer tournament organized by the Northwest Ski Club. The Kiwanis carnival included an amateur contest won by Walt Anderson from the nearby community of Easton. Anderson, who would go on to key roles in the US Forest Service, later became one of the most important early skiing boosters in central Washington.

The Cle Elum ski tournament became an annual event. Carnivals at both the Kiwanis and Summit Lodge courses were held in 1925. The Kiwanis awards were presented between shows at Lane Theatre, which featured the pioneering ski film *The Chase*. In 1926 both the amateur and professional tournaments were moved to the Summit Lodge, which had the most reliable snow, since it was located 1,000 feet above town.

The contests were designed for local fun as much as serious competition. With names like Devils Dive, Camels Hump, and Goose Fashion Glide, courses were laid out for boys and girls under fifteen, for men and women, and for amateurs and professionals. The forerunner for the jumping event was introduced as "Mr. Swanson, Champion of the World, Out to Set New Records." Dressed in a farmer costume, this character laid down the first track over the jump and, according to the *Miner-Echo*, "nearly ruined the course landing." He was followed by Mrs. Swanson, "a typically dressed mate, who also did justice to the course busting introductory." After their runs, the Swansons were unmasked as tournament organizers Russ Connell and John Koester.

Tony Sandona, dubbed "the human tumbleweed," took second place on the Hell's Dive in the upset of the day: he "rolled over the landscape in front of the Summit kitchen like a playful kitten and when he cleared the Hell's Dive course in nice style all judged the successful glide to have been an accident." In the ladies gliding event, Connell entered the course dressed as Mysterious Miss Hanson of Alaska, "fully ten feet tall, wearing yellow

BACK VIEW OF THE 80 FOOT TOWER
WITH A 46 DEGREE SLOPE.
ON OUR $5.000 SKI HILL.

rolled stockings, bedaubed with cosmetics and well gifted in the pursuits of flapperism, but all to no avail so far as the judges were concerned." More than six hundred people witnessed the ten-event program.

For the 1928 event, a new cabin was constructed at the Summit site, and the crowd was estimated at more than four thousand. Spectators began hiking up from Cle Elum at 9:00 a.m. "For four hours a steady stream continued, wending its way up the mountain like the gold rush of the 'Forty-Niners.'" Visiting experts arrived from around the Northwest, including Giese of Seattle, who honored his German roots by competing on behalf of the Black Forest Ski Club.

The tournament reached a milestone in 1931, when the Snoqualmie Pass highway remained open throughout the winter for the first time. This produced the largest crowd ever, reported to be around five thousand. To handle the crowds, organizers arranged for visitors to be trucked from First Street in Cle Elum to the Number 7 mine tunnel, at which point they loaded onto an electric tramway (known as a mantrip) normally used by miners. The tram entered the tunnel and rolled its passengers up and into the mountain. Higher on Cle Elum Ridge, where the coal vein outcropped, the tram unloaded its human cargo after a ten-minute trip underground. From there, a half-hour hike on snow led to the Summit Lodge.

During a test run two weeks before the tournament, the underground railroad worked flawlessly. "The crowd behaved, nobody stood up and got their heads beamed against the 'low roof,' and the party arrived safe and sound on the upper end," reported the *Miner-Echo*. However, on tournament day a woman from west of the mountains stood up while passing through the tunnel and suffered a scalp wound. She was treated at the hospital and rode home by car over Snoqualmie Pass. During the jumping event, Portland's John Elvrum was the winner with a leap of 128 feet.

In the long run, the well-maintained highway meant doom for Cle Elum skiing. Two weeks after the 1931 Summit Lodge tournament, the Seattle Ski Club held its second annual tournament at Beaver Lake near Snoqualmie Pass. With a crowd estimated at ten thousand, the tournament doubled as the Pacific Northwest tryout for the 1932 Olympic Games at Lake Placid. Elvrum won again, with a jump of 180 feet. The Cle Elum Ski Club responded to the challenge of Beaver Lake by constructing a $5,000 ski jump tower and ramp, which plunged 117 feet at a maximum angle of 46 degrees. The jump was used during

Rear view of Cle Elum's $5,000 ski hill, built in 1932 (Central Washington University Archives and Special Collections, Cle Elum Ski Club Collection)

the 1932 tournament but remained unused the following year because of high winds. As attention shifted to Snoqualmie Pass and its Beaver Lake jump, the Cle Elum tournament was never held again. Skiing in Cle Elum flourished in the 1920s because of the reliable access that railroads provided, but it died in the 1930s because the railroad could not compete with the even greater freedom offered by the automobile.

Opposite: *Herbert Strandberg (left) and Fred Ball ski along the Patrol Race route in the 1930s.* (Meany Lodge Collection)

CHAPTER 3

SKIS TRIUMPHANT

During the 1920s, when the Snoqualmie Pass highway remained closed in winter, Cle Elum skiers looked for other slopes to extend their season. They found them near Stampede Pass. About 20 miles west of Cle Elum, the Northern Pacific Railroad cuts through the Cascades via the Stampede Pass tunnel. The tunnel is at 2,800 feet beneath the main Cascade divide, an area with a longer snow season than towns, such as Cle Elum, farther east. The east portal is called Martin, while the west is called Stampede. Both sites had railroad shacks in the 1920s and 1930s, and the railroad would let passengers off at either location on request.

In the early 1920s, Martin was the favorite spring destination for Cle Elum skiers. The *Cle Elum Miner-Echo* reported in March 1924 that thirty skiers had enjoyed "the finest ski grounds found in years." A year later about fifty Cle Elum skiers made the trip in early April, joined by skiers from Ellensburg, Tacoma, and Yakima. In

Taking it straight near Stampede Pass (Photo by Othello P. Dickert courtesy The Mountaineers Archives)

1926 the annual Martin ski party brought out more than seventy-five skiers, and the Northern Pacific Railroad provided a special coach for the event.

Skiers from The Mountaineers in Seattle had similar ideas, and in February 1928 they organized their own first weekend outing to Stampede Pass. Arriving from the west, the Seattle Mountaineers spent the night at Stampede rather than at Martin. On Saturday most of the party climbed from the railroad shacks with skis in hand to the ranger cabin near Stampede Pass, arriving in a snow and sleet storm. After a long break at the cabin to warm themselves and eat lunch, they returned by skiing down "glorious long slopes and ideal snow conditions."

The next morning, they were joined by six men who had spent all of Saturday skiing to Stampede Pass from The Mountaineers' lodge near Snoqualmie Pass, a distance of about 18 miles. This country had never been traveled on skis before, and the party—Rudy Amsler, Andrew "Andy" Anderson, Alex Fox, Lars Lovseth, Bill Marzolf, and William J. "Bill" Maxwell—had trouble finding their way. "When they reached the neighborhood of Dandy Pass," wrote Fred Ball in an unpublished account, "it was late in the afternoon and there was a lot of discussion and disagreement as to which way they should go. With the uncertainty and approaching night they decided to spend the night where they were, and to this end they enlarged a hole around a dead snag, lining the bottom with boughs and making a bench around the outside so they could sit or lay. They then set fire to the snag with such success that they were alternately driven out of the hole by the heat and back in by the cold, so all in all it was not a restful night. At first light of morning they continued down toward Stampede and arrived at the railroad buildings to join the outing at breakfast time."

This trip from Snoqualmie to Stampede Pass demonstrated how much the club's skiers had improved since their early years at Snoqualmie Lodge. "In the old days we did not learn to ski," Mountaineers member Paul Shorrock recalled, "we just put on skis and started out." Most Mountaineers in those days could hardly be called skiers. They were more like sledders on a pair of boards. This began to change as a few experienced skiers shared their knowledge with club members. One of those was Rudy Amsler, a Swiss who immigrated to the Northwest after World War I. Amsler attended the club's New Year's outing at Mount Rainier in 1924–25 and agreed to visit Snoqualmie Lodge to offer pointers in skiing. The club's monthly *Bulletin* noted, "Mr. Amsler has been good enough to show some of our members more about skiing and about the difficult skiing turns than they would ever be able to read out of books." Club member Laurence Byington recalled, "Until Rudy Amsler started the group on the path to learning the fine art of Telemarks and Christianias, we 'herring-boned' up and 'ran it straight.'"

Rudy Amsler was a Swiss guard on the Italian frontier during World War I. After immigrating to the United States, he taught Mountaineers how to ski "under ski control." (Rudolf Amsler collection, The Mountaineers Archives)

At Snoqualmie Lodge, snowshoes were now as rare as skis had been a few years earlier. As enthusiasm for skiing grew, The Mountaineers discussed building a second base to handle the overflow from the lodge. Some members envisioned a series of huts located a day's trek from one another, like in Europe or the Appalachians. In June 1928, after the successful outing to Stampede Pass, Bill Maxwell proposed building a ski hut in that vicinity to accommodate fifty people. The proposal was approved, and club president Edmund S. Meany purchased fifty-four acres of Northern Pacific land near Martin for $125 and donated the land to the club. Construction began in September, and the cabin (dubbed the Meany Ski Hut) was dedicated on Armistice Day in November.

The enthusiasm for skiing generated by the Meany hut was reflected in the 1929 *Mountaineer Annual*, which was designated as a "Special Ski Number" and filled with long articles about the sport. Six new ski trophies were established that year: cross-country skiing trophies for men and women; trophies for ski jumping, slalom, and downhill racing; and the Patrol Race trophy, donated by Andy Anderson and Norval Grigg. Patrol races had been part of the 1924 and 1928 Winter Olympic Games, though unlike The Mountaineers' race, the Olympic event also included target shooting. The stated purpose of The Mountaineers' Patrol Race was to develop and promote cross-country skiers and skiing and to make better known the area along the Cascade crest between Snoqualmie and Stampede Passes. The Patrol Race trophy would be awarded to the fastest three-person team to race over the 18-mile route from Snoqualmie Lodge to Meany Ski Hut.

Bill Maxwell, described by a friend as "one of the most enthusiastic ski-fiends I ever knew," captured the spirit of the time in a fictional tale written for the 1929 *Mountaineer Annual*. Called "Skis Triumphant: A Story That Could Be True," the tale follows Jim Connor, a young outdoorsman who tries skiing for the first time at Snoqualmie Lodge and resolves to master the sport. Two years later, with a few club friends, he sets out from the lodge toward Meany. Near Tinkham Peak, they witness a US Mail plane making a crash landing. Springing into action, Connor rushes to help, giving "an exhibition of his marvelous dexterity on skis." After describing a winter bivouac, a successful rescue, and the timely delivery of the mail, Maxwell concludes, "Skiing skill had triumphed!"

The Mountaineers touted Meany Ski Hut as the most accessible ski area in the Northwest, and it really was. The train ride from Tacoma or Seattle to Martin took a leisurely

Meany Ski Hut in the 1930s (Meany Lodge Collection)

three hours. From the station at Martin, the hut was just a five-minute walk. On the downside, the hut lacked indoor plumbing until the late 1930s.

THE PATROL RACE

The winter of 1929–30 was the first in which all of The Mountaineers' eight ski trophies were contested. The most unusual of these was the Patrol Race. "Patterned after the popular military patrol races in Europe," wrote participant Andy Anderson, "it is the only event of its kind in this country so far as we have been able to ascertain." The course followed a high route between the two club lodges via the Silver Peak Trail, Olallie Meadows, the

EARLY SKIING TECHNIQUES

Since the early 1900s, ski techniques have been grouped into two categories, Nordic and alpine, based mainly on the equipment and how it is used.

Nordic skiing emphasizes mobility over varied terrain and relies on boots and bindings that allow the skier's heels to lift at all times. Nordic skiing has three traditional disciplines: cross-country, downhill (based on the telemark turn), and jumping.

Alpine skiing is focused on skiing downhill, using bindings that clamp the heels down during the descent. Although the Norwegians invented all of the techniques described below, the christie was popularized in the 1920s by Hannes Schneider from the Arlberg region of the Austrian Alps, thus the terms "alpine skiing" and "Arlberg technique" for this style of skiing.

Christiania or **christie:** Named for the Norwegian capital of Christiania (now Oslo), this skidded or carved turn is performed with the feet more or less side by side, best done with the heels firmly clamped down. Advanced christies are done with the skis parallel throughout the turn (little or no stem—see below). In an open christie, the ski tips are splayed apart and the ski on the inside of the turn is the driver.

Telemark: Named for the Telemark region of Norway, this turn is performed with the outside leg driven forward and the inside leg bent as in a curtsy. Telemark turns, unlike christies, work best with bindings that allow the skier's heels to lift.

Stem: This movement consists of putting the skis into a snowplow position to facilitate the start of a turn. The stem can be performed by sweeping or lifting either ski. Stemming can be used with either a telemark or a christiania but is usually associated with the latter.

Gelandesprung: In this jump associated with alpine skiing, the skier pulls up the knees after springing into the air. The skier may boost the takeoff by thrusting the poles in the snow during the jump. In contrast, Nordic ski jumping is performed without ski poles and the skier's body is straight, leaning forward over the skis during flight.

Mirror Lake Trail, Yakima Pass, Meadow Creek, Dandy Creek, and Baldy Pass. Each individual and team was required to carry certain equipment, and each racer's pack had to weigh at least twelve pounds. Teams drew for starting order, starting five to ten minutes apart, and all three members of a team had to finish within a two-minute period. Climbing skins or sleeves were prohibited, and racers were allowed to use only ski wax for climbing.

The route became quite popular during the 1930s. "Any novel or whimsical idea could easily set in motion a trip across," Fred Ball wrote in the 1963 club annual. "It was quite a satisfaction suddenly to appear on the lane at Martin complete with pack and to answer the question 'Where did you come from?' by saying, 'Oh, we've just come from the Lodge.'"

It may have been just such a trip that took place in the winter of 1930, when a young man named Morris Jenkins was living in a cabin near the shore of Mirror Lake. Unable to find winter work during the Depression, he and a friend heard about the Mirror Lake cabin and decided to try their luck at fur trapping. By January they had run traplines on snowshoes for miles between the cabin and Keechelus Lake but had caught only two marten and two ermine. Discouraged, the friend left to look for other work, leaving Jenkins alone in the wilderness.

The hardest thing to bear was the solitude. The snow lay so deep around the cabin that only the top of the stovepipe stuck out. Returning from his traps one day, Jenkins found ski tracks descending from the ridge above the lake and passing right over the cabin. "There was a set of tracks on either side of the stovepipe," he later recalled, "and I knew they never even saw it." Scratching out a living as a trapper when others were skiing for fun, Jenkins felt even lonelier. It's unknown whether he saw the first patrol racers ski by a few weeks later.

The first race was scheduled for March 23, 1930. Two weeks before the inaugural race, Edna Walsh became the first woman to ski the route, accompanied by Paul Shorrock and another man. "Men have always said women couldn't make this trip," Walsh told the *Seattle Times*. "I hope by doing it I've proved their error. I was tired, yes. We were on the way eight hours. But scarcely more tired than I have often been after an unusually active day. I only wish I could have made the trip sooner. I should certainly have organized a woman's patrol to compete in this year's race. Next year, though, just watch us!" Folklore within the Meany ski community speaks of women competing in the Patrol Race in the early years. Unfortunately, I've found no written record of it in Mountaineers files or newspaper reports.

The first race included four teams. The team of Norval Grigg, Robert "Bob" Hayes, and Paul Shorrock started from the lodge around 8:15 a.m., followed a few minutes later by Hans Otto Giese, Andy Anderson, and Fred Ball. As Ball later wrote in the *Mountaineer Annual*,

"We had provided small pouches in which to carry food that could be eaten with one hand and attached them to our packs so we could reach them without stopping to remove the pack. Thus, we were able to munch as we traveled, at little loss of time. . . . Giese, being much the fastest of our team, would race ahead until he came in sight or hearing of the first patrol and would then shout, 'Here they are. Hurry up!' even though Andy and I were too far back to hear him."

On the back side of Tinkham Peak, the Giese-Ball-Anderson team finally overtook the Grigg-Hayes-Shorrock team. They continued in the lead past the Meadow Creek foot-log crossing and up the long climb to Baldy Pass. Ball later recalled the race from this point:

> It had been snowing all this time, and my skis were sticking so at the end of the climb at Baldy Pass we stopped so I could scrape them off. At this point Paul Shorrock came steaming along and passed us by. We did not, of course, know how far behind his teammates might be and so we hastily donned our skis and took off. Coming down the shoulder of the lane I fell headfirst into a crater around a big tree and had a hard time getting out. While I was scrabbling frantically around trying to get my head up and my feet down Andy and Otto were yelling at me to "hurry up!" which didn't help any. I finally got up and crossed the finish line with them while Paul stood and waited for his teammates. They finished second but I do not recall where the other teams finished.

While much of the Snoqualmie-to-Stampede route is on gentle slopes below timberline, it also crosses avalanche terrain. Fred Ball recalled a trip from Meany to the Snoqualmie Lodge with Herbert "Herb" Strandberg and another friend. They planned to meet another party coming from the lodge at the halfway point so each group would have a broken trail for the rest of the trip. After hours of trailbreaking in deep snow, Ball's party reached Mirror Lake at dusk, finding no tracks. "We still had the back side of Tinkham and Silver to climb, including a couple of likely avalanche slopes," he recalled. "As we reached one of them, our lights shone on a wide expanse of fresh snow on a steep hillside unbroken by trees. Someone said, 'What do you think?'" As Ball remembered it, "Herb answered, 'Let's see,' grabbed the top of a little fir tree, and jumped. Without a sound the snow peeled off all across the slope. There was no other way to go, so one by one we gingerly crossed below

Paul Shorrock and Edna Walsh at Meany Ski Hut; Walsh was the first woman to ski from Snoqualmie to Stampede Pass along the Patrol Race route. (Rudolf Amsler collection, The Mountaineers Archives)

the wall of snow at the top. We were still hoping that someone had traveled at least as far as Olallie Meadows, leaving us a broken track. But no! We finally reached the lodge after 11:00 p.m., completely beaten."

Shorrock recalled preparations for the race: "The night preceding one of these grueling tests would be a scene of much activity, speculation, and secret planning at the old lodge. Theories on everything from ski wax to fad diets were discussed with passionate partisanship. There were those who asserted that you raced on the dinner you ate the night before and, according to them, the less breakfast eaten, the better; those of the hearty-breakfast school of thought brought their own lamb chops, steaks, or whatever they figured would best energize them for the long trek across."

Since the early club races were contested between friends, pranks were known to occur. During one race, two skiers completed the course with rocks or bricks in their packs, which had been slipped in, unbeknownst to them, after the official weigh-in. Racer Wolf Bauer recalled, "That one of these victims should turn out to be Paul Shorrock was a more or less foregone conclusion to anybody but him. Hans Otto Giese never did find out whodunit."

THE LATE LIMITED

Another challenge for the Patrol Race skiers was dealing with the trains. Paul Shorrock recalled that during the first attempt at a reverse trip from Martin to Snoqualmie Lodge, he and three friends lost their way and dropped down to the Chicago, Milwaukee, and St. Paul Railroad tracks near Hyak, where they flagged down the Milwaukee's crack train, the Olympian. "We were thrown off at Rockdale," Shorrock wrote, "and I do mean 'thrown'!"

In another instance, he recalled, "the Northern Pacific train started up at Martin before everyone was loaded," stranding fifteen skiers. "It was never clear why." Friends on the train tried to get the conductor to send a car back for the stragglers, but it was considered too dangerous. "We couldn't ski out to the highway," remembered Shorrock, "since most of our skis had been loaded on the train, so we straggled back up to the hut to get what sleep we could. That was not much. The Limited was late, and it was six or so in the morning before we were loaded on the Seattle-bound train. One of the girls asked the conductor if they knew in Seattle that we had been left, and he said, 'Lady, they know in St. Paul you were left, and they are just as unhappy as you are.' We got into town about noon to go to work in our ski clothes with what grace we could. In those Depression days, one was not absent from the job without a better excuse than missing a train."

Several attempts were made to mark the Patrol Race route between the two lodges, beginning with one by Maxwell and Grigg in the fall of 1929. Rumor had it that Grigg made the trip on Maxwell's shoulders while nailing up the markers. Another effort was made by a larger party, but neither was successful in getting the markers high enough to prevent them from being covered by deep snow. Finally, in April 1933, a heavy snow year, a party of nine led by Herbert Strandberg left Snoqualmie Lodge with five hundred orange-colored tin shingles bent and punched for nail holes. The markers were placed roughly every 300 feet so that at least one marker was visible at all times. The task required a day and a half, and the party spent the night around a snow hole at Yakima Pass while their fire slowly sank out of sight.

Club races were held by The Mountaineers from 1930 through 1936, with

March 16, 1936, Seattle Times *article reporting on the victory of the Seattle Ski Club team (Ole Tverdal, Howard Dalsbo, and Roy Nerland) in the first open Patrol Race*

gaps in 1931 and 1934 due to poor skiing conditions. The course record of 4 hours, 37 minutes, 23 seconds was established in 1936 by the young team of Wolf Bauer, Chet Higman, and Bill Miller. "Excitement always ran high at the finish line," Shorrock remembered. "To watch the men at the end of an 18-mile race over the roughest kind of terrain, their legs all but numb from fatigue, try to run the steep 'lane' at Meany and cross the finish line in some kind of an upright position filled the audience with suspense, sympathy, and admiration."

In 1936, as ski clubs were forming throughout the Northwest, the Pacific Northwest Ski Association encouraged each member club to host a tournament. The Mountaineers chose the Patrol Race, since it would be different from the slalom and jumping events typically hosted by other clubs. The open race was scheduled for March 15, a month after the club race won by Bauer and friends. Five teams signed up to race.

Despite 15 inches of new snow, the trail was well broken and the Seattle Ski Club team won with a very respectable time of 4 hours, 50 minutes, 39 seconds. On the Washington Ski Club team, Pat Patterson broke a ski, requiring him to borrow a replacement ski tip from another team. Patterson and teammates Hans Otto Giese and Alf Moystad were disqualified from the race but skied out under their own power. The College of Puget Sound team, which had signed up just for the fun of it, arrived at Meany more than nine hours after starting. The officials, thinking that the team had turned back, had already left for the highway. On being notified of the situation, they returned to Meany to check the team in and give them second place; they were the only other team to finish intact.

The Mountaineers' club race was not held again, but the open Patrol Race was staged every winter through 1941, after which The Mountaineers trustees voted to discontinue the race due to declining interest (see Appendix for Patrol Race winners 1930–41). The biggest year was 1939, when eight teams started the race. On the day preceding the race, the *Seattle P-I* wrote, "It's an odds-on, mortal cinch that the most-tuckered-out gang of ski racers in North America will huddle around a stove in Meany Ski Hut near Martin tomorrow at the close of The Mountaineers' fourth annual patrol race from Snoqualmie Pass. The Mountaineers patrol race is an event unique in Northwest skiing. It's a team affair. There is no such thing as an individual star in a patrol race. There may be . . . and often, too . . . a goat." Writer Mike Donahoe described the series of climbs and descents on the course and concluded, "Boy! Copy! Take it away. Take my skis too! These typewriter trips are killing me."

CHASING HISTORY

When I discovered the "orange-colored tin shingles high on trees" while skiing south from Snoqualmie Pass in 2001, I was inspired. Finding the markers still in place after nearly seventy years made the old stories I'd read about missed trains, rocks slipped inside rucksacks, unplanned bivouacs, and clever telemarks all the more vivid and compelling. I wanted to share those stories with others, so I organized a trip in 2002 through The Mountaineers to repeat the route with a group. Unfortunately, the outing had to be canceled due to avalanche danger. I finally skied the route with a partner two years later, when backcountry enthusiast John Mauro replied to a post I made on Turns All Year, a new website that had transformed how Northwest skiers met and shared stories. I published a report following the trip, and John and I have since become good friends.

In 2005 and 2006 The Mountaineers expressed interest in reviving the Patrol Race, or at least scheduling a group outing as a way to celebrate the club's history and promote the lodges at Snoqualmie and Stampede Passes. The original Snoqualmie Lodge, located at Lodge Lake on the opposite side of the Cascade crest from the highway, had burned in 1944 and was not rebuilt. In 1949 The Mountaineers had acquired property east of the pass, next to the Snoqualmie Summit ski area, and established a new lodge there. But by 2005, that lodge had fallen on hard times after an accident shut down its rope tow, probably forever.

In 2006 I volunteered to lead a Mountaineers tour, open to both members and nonmembers, from the "new" Snoqualmie Lodge to Meany Lodge (no longer called a ski hut). Wolf Bauer, whose 1936 record on the Patrol Race route was still standing, spoke at Snoqualmie Lodge on February 24, the eve of the trip. Fourteen skiers, plus friends and members of the lodge committee, gathered to celebrate Wolf's ninety-fourth birthday and send off the skiers the next morning. After dinner and birthday cake, Wolf—still fit and sharp, with a wry sense

Wolf Bauer celebrates his ninety-fourth birthday at The Mountaineers' Snoqualmie Lodge in 2006.

of humor—entertained us with stories from the 1930s and shared a bit of his life philosophy. "The trick is to die young," he advised, "as late as possible."

After a predawn start the next morning, our group took twelve hours to complete the trip to Meany Lodge, arriving after sundown. The trip satisfied my desire to share the Patrol Race experience with other skiers, and I didn't ski it again for eight years. Sadly, the "new" Snoqualmie Lodge burned down just three months after we celebrated Wolf's birthday there.

In 2014 a new group of Mountaineers revived interest in the Patrol Race. Nigel Steere's family included four generations of Meany Lodge skiers. His grandmother, Dawn Steere, had competed in women's races at the lodge in the 1930s. I helped Nigel with race planning and organized my own team with Seth Davis and Brandon Kern, two younger skiers whom I'd met in ski mountaineering races. My teammates were eager to challenge Bauer's old record, but I was doubtful we could do it, discouraged by too many slow trailbreaking trips in my past. Wolf and his friends in the 1930s were experts at ski waxing. We were not. The modern race allowed the use of either wax or climbing skins. Could a modern skier applying skins to climb and removing them to glide beat an old-school master on waxed cross-country skis? How about rolling terrain, where climbing and gliding intermingle? Would the waxer win there? Where should a skinner make transitions? Experience would teach us the answers to these questions.

Since The Mountaineers' lodges at both Lodge Lake and Snoqualmie Summit were gone, the modern race would start at the base of Snoqualmie's Summit West ski area. This would add about two miles to the course, making comparison of times with the historical race more difficult. It also meant that teams would have to get up earlier to drive to the pass on race morning, rather than spend the night on the mountain. On the evening before the race, after I'd gone to bed, Seth sent Brandon and me a message saying that he'd twisted his knee in a slalom course that day and would have to pull out. Brandon and I decided to ski the route anyway, knowing we wouldn't qualify as a complete team. We made better time during the race than I ever had during my scouting trips, and we began to think that Bauer's record could indeed be broken.

Cody Lourie, Luke Shy, and Jed Yeiser, racing as team R&Ski, won the event in 7 hours, 9 minutes. No women's team was entered, but Anne Brink finished the course (while her two male teammates did not), making her the first woman to ski the route during an actual race. Bauer, who would celebrate his 102nd birthday in two weeks, was eager to hear whether his 1936 record had fallen. It had not. While resting at the Meany Lodge afterward, racers signed a birthday card for Wolf expressing their admiration.

The winter of 2015 brought another snow drought, and the Patrol Race could not be held. The following year, Nigel Steere organized the largest Patrol Race ever run, with twenty three-person teams competing. Brandon, Seth, and I signed up and trained with enthusiasm. We left the parking lot at Summit West at 7:30 a.m. and made our way to the old starting line near Lodge Lake in a little under a half hour. There we started timers to compare our pace to the teams of the past. When the trail conditions were good, we linked ourselves into a train using short tethers. This technique, analogous to the drafting technique used in bicycle racing, was popularized in the 2000s by ski mountaineering race teams. Tethering links individuals into an energy-sharing team. The old Patrol Racers acknowledged that their race was really a contest between the slowest members of each team. Had tethering been known in the 1930s, I think they would have embraced it. Nothing in the rules, then or now, prevents it.

With Seth and Brandon's faster pace and my knowledge of the route, our team moved well and made no tactical mistakes. In the end we completed the route from Summit West

The Mountain Mamas team approaches Checkpoint 1 during the 2017 Patrol Race. (Photo by Rick Meade)

to Meany Lodge in an official time of 4 hours, 52 minutes, 7 seconds. Based on timer and GPS data, our time from the old Lodge Lake start to Meany was 4 hours, 25 minutes, 56 seconds, a little over 11 minutes ahead of the 1936 record set by Bauer, Higman, and Miller. The record had finally been broken, but it had also outlived Wolf: he passed away just a month before, at 103. I knew him well enough to realize that this would have been a great satisfaction to him.

Two all-women teams raced for the first time in 2016. The fastest of these was the Mountain Mavens team of Holly Davis, Stacy McKinstry, and Kari Stiles. Thanks to the success of these teams, the race committee created a separate women's division in 2017. Mixed or all-male teams would compete in a new open division. The 2017 race was held on a cold day with dry powder snow. Trailbreakers were sent out before dawn to establish the track. The Mountain Mamas team of Holly Davis, Heather Kern, and Anne Marie Stonich established the women's division record with a winning time of 6 hours, 9 minutes, 29 seconds. Team Wet & Scrappy—consisting of Seth Davis, Aaron Ostrovsky, and me—won the open division with a new course record of 4 hours, 19 minutes, 23 seconds. This time was faster than the 1936 record set by Bauer's team on a shorter course, finally eliminating the asterisk next to the modern record (see table in Appendix for Patrol Race winners since 2014).

Thanks to the efforts of the Meany Lodge community, local guides, ski patrollers, avalanche forecasters, and many others, one of the oldest ski races in North America was revived and made so popular that a lottery was eventually needed to select the participants. A triumph of skiing skill in the 1930s, the Patrol Race was renewed as a celebration of community and tradition eighty years later. A few teams raced to win; many more raced just for the fun of it. Skis Triumphant: it was a story that could be . . . and ultimately was . . . true.

Opposite: *Skiers above Paradise Inn* (University of Washington Libraries, Special Collections, Dwight Watson Collection)

CHAPTER 4

A MOVEMENT
WITHOUT PARALLEL

As manager of Mount Rainier's Paradise Inn, Thomas Martin recognized a good thing when he saw it. For three winters, from 1917 through 1919, The Mountaineers had made special arrangements with the Rainier National Park Company to stay during the New Year's holiday at Paradise Inn, which normally operated only in summer. Club reports praised Paradise as "a new Mecca for winter sports." Martin and his boss, Park Company president David Whitcomb, apparently took notice: in the fall of 1919 they cached supplies at the inn before snow blocked the roads, so they could return in winter with friends. Thus was born the Tribe of Soyp (an acronym for "socks outside your pants"), an elite club of Puget Sound businessmen,

Agnes Dickert fastens her ski bindings at Paradise. (Othello P. Dickert family collection)

Park Company board members, and National Park officials. Members took Indian-inspired names during what they called "tribal councils." Recruits were called Cheechakos; those who had completed one trip, Papooses; two trips, Tillicums; three trips, Tyees.

Beginning in 1920, the Soyps scheduled a trip to Mount Rainier each February. The earliest trips sometimes involved hiking to Longmire on foot. But by 1924, and every year after that, the Soyps rode to Longmire by bus. Reaching Paradise still entailed a hike of at least six miles and 2,500 feet of climbing on snowshoes. They gathered at night "to relate the incidents of the trail, sing their songs, and discuss the possibilities of The Mountain as a scene for winter sports." Within a year, the Rainier National Park Company was advertising at Longmire a toboggan slide, ski course, four-horse pleasure sleigh, Alaskan dogsled team, sport lounge, and hotel rooms with baths. The company also rented toboggans, snowshoes, and skis.

Paradise was a better winter destination than Longmire, since it was higher, snowier, and more scenic, but lodging was a problem because the Paradise Inn wasn't designed for winter use. So in 1928 the company completed the Paradise Lodge about a quarter mile west of the inn. Winter access to the new lodge still required a long hike from Longmire, however. A planned aerial tramway from the Nisqually River to Paradise was abandoned by the company due to financial problems, so it fell to the National Park Service to gradually extend plowing of the road. In 1930 the road was plowed to Canyon Rim, shortening the hike to two and a half miles. Two years later, plowing was extended to Narada Falls, further cutting that hike by half.

In January 1932 the first Tacoma Winter Sports Carnival was held at Longmire. At the time it was estimated that there were only two hundred pairs of skis privately owned in the Puget Sound area. Four years later, however, the number of skis was estimated at ten thousand and the carnival was staged annually at Paradise. The Seattle Jaycees organized a March ski carnival a few months after the Tacoma event in 1932. The town of Olympia launched a February event a couple years later. From 1929 to 1931, a road was constructed to Yakima Park (or Sunrise), on the northeast side of the mountain. Park rangers, the Soyps, and a few other parties visited Sunrise on skis in the following years, but the road was not plowed in winter, so most skiing remained centered at Paradise.

LIKE THE MEASLES

Ralph Spencer, a Tacoma high school student, wrote in *Scholastic* magazine in 1938 that "skiing is like the measles. I was exposed about three years ago to the most glorious winter sport there is. The craze spread among my friends, just as it is still spreading over the country." Spencer described the climb from Paradise to Panorama Point "with canvas climbers attached to the skis" and "the mighty Tatoosh Range at our backs." Once at the top, he continued, "Goggles are adjusted, harnesses secured, climbers removed and the long-awaited descent begins. Down the face of Panorama, with a snow-tossing stem turn, we are off. With stinging wind taking away your breath, pants whipping in the breeze, the terrain zipping away from under you at a terrifying clip. . . . At last the inn comes into sight and down the draw of Alta Vista we speed. With a screaming christie at the door we stop. It's over—a long time to climb up, a few minutes to speed down."

After a day of skiing, the return to Narada Falls began with a gentle trail descent. Novices gained false confidence as they glided down this primrose path, for a notorious obstacle lurked below. "Two hills," wrote Spencer, "not exceptionally steep, but steep, with a drop between the two and, at the end of a short draw, another sharp drop of about 15 feet and then down around a curve to a trail of 'waves' or bumps. This is the 'Devils Dip' of Paradise Valley, waterloo of many a self-inflated skier. . . . Waiting their turn down the trail are scores of parked skiers. Strewn down the trail are scores of other skiers who failed to make the Dip." For most who made it through the Dip safely, the next weekend could not come soon enough.

Many skiers in the early 1930s were self-taught. A few clubs like The Mountaineers offered ski tests and badges, but it was often up to each skier to learn by watching and experimenting. In a 1936 "ski primer" in *University of Washington Columns* magazine, Proctor Mellquist offered advice for "those hesitant hundreds" who would try skiing for the first time that winter. "You stand at the top of a long snow slope," he wrote. "You have never been on skis before. Somehow you start down. You can't stop. You can't turn. It is problematical if you can even stay on your feet. But if you can you will soon be traveling so fast that your eyes fail you. The oncoming snow becomes a blur, and you realize that roller coasters are child's play and that Sir Malcolm Campbell is a piker. You are skiing." According to Mellquist, one out of every five UW students had tried skiing the previous winter and another thousand would join them this winter. "And each, in that first moment of downhill madness, will become an addict for life—or a never againer."

MOUNT BAKER

In 1911 the Mount Baker Club was formed in Bellingham to promote tourism and development of the Mount Baker region, with the hope of designating the area as a national park. One of the club's early promotional efforts was the Mount Baker Marathon. This grueling race ran from downtown Bellingham to 10,781-foot Mount Baker and back. The race was run three times—in 1911, 1912, and 1913. There were many mishaps, including a derailed train (after colliding with a bull), foul weather, a crevasse fall and rescue, a racer thrown from a horse, broken bones, and near hypothermia. Organizers finally concluded the race was too dangerous.

Bert Huntoon of the Mount Baker Club pushed to build a highway around Baker's north side and a hotel at Heather Meadows, an alpine basin between Mount Baker and 9,131-foot Mount Shuksan. Construction of the lodge began in 1925, and by December, when work was suspended for the winter, skiers from Glacier and elsewhere were already visiting the area. The highway was completed in 1926 and Mount Baker Lodge, a magnificent wood structure costing a half million dollars, opened the following year—but for about a decade the lodge closed every winter.

The Mount Baker Ski Club was organized around this time by a group including C. A. "Happy" Fisher, E. P. "Doc" Spearin, and Erwin Lusby. The initial group of eight to ten skiers possessed only two pairs of skis between them, so they took turns skiing while the others watched. Fritz Koons led the club's first organized ski trip, in January 1929, to Heather Meadows. The party slept overnight at Glacier, then drove as far as they could before carrying skis up the Bagley Creek Trail to the meadows. A year later, on a wet day

Mount Baker Lodge before the 1931 fire (University of Washington Libraries, Special Collections, Dwight Watson Collection)

in April, the first ski tournament—a ski jumping meet—was staged at Heather Meadows. Erling Thomsen of Seattle won with a leap of 125 feet.

Due to an electrical malfunction, Mount Baker Lodge caught fire in 1931. The lodge's oil tank blew up, adding 1,900 gallons of fuel oil to the fire and sending flames 1,000 feet into the air. The main lodge burned to the ground, but the annex and Heather Inn were spared. After the fire, the inn (formerly used by employees) became the guest center and the annex provided accommodations.

In 1934, Twentieth Century Pictures filmed Jack London's *Call of the Wild*, starring Clark Gable and Loretta Young, at Heather Meadows. To accommodate filming, the state highway department kept the road open most of the winter. During breaks in the production, cast members were photographed on skis, helping to popularize skiing in the area. The Pacific Northwest Ski Association held its slalom championship on Panorama Dome in April, and an international downhill race was run from the summit of Table Mountain later that month. As a result of these activities, the highway department decided to keep the road cleared of snow the following year.

Skiing at Heather Meadows in 1931 (Mount Baker Club Records, Center for Pacific Northwest Studies, Western Washington University)

During the winter of 1935–36, the Mount Baker Development Company began operating a cable-drawn sled called a "ski escalator" that carried skiers from Terminal Lake up Panorama Dome. It was the first ski lift in the Northwest, operating for two seasons before rope tows were installed at other ski areas.

Ski clubs established quarters in the area, skiers from Seattle and Vancouver, British Columbia, leased cabins and rooms, and the US Forest Service announced plans to build a public skiers' hut. Walt Little recalled that even the best efforts of the highway department could not always keep up with the massive snowfalls at Mount Baker. The Mount Baker Ski Club had a cabin down the hill along a direct trail route from the lodge. The highway department could usually clear the road to the ski club cabin, but frequently it couldn't keep the road clear from there up to the lodge. Sometimes people at the lodge would get snowed in and couldn't get their cars out, so they'd ski down to the ski club cabin to catch a ride out. With the deep, wet snow, the trail would get packed down and become very fast. Skiers would start out carrying suitcases in their hands and get out of control. Soon "they'd take a dive," recalled Walt, "and a suitcase would fly and hit a tree, emptying the contents and so on. There were a lot of funny sights, like ladies' clothing all over the place."

Skiing became the biggest attraction in the Mount Baker area and a winter obsession for many, as expressed through rhyme in the Mount Baker Club's newsletter in 1937:

Who's the stranger, mother dear.
Look, he knows us, ain't he queer?

Hush, my own, don't talk so wild;
He's your father, dearest child.

He's my father? Why not at all.
Father died away last fall!

Father didn't die, you dub!
Father joined the skiing club.

Now the season's closed, so he
Has no place to go, you see.
No snow left on which to ski,
So home he comes to you and me.

Kiss him—he won't bite you, child.
All those skiing guys look wild.

LEAVENWORTH AND STEVENS PASS

I watched my father compete in veterans-class tournaments at Leavenworth, in central Washington, in the 1960s. It may have been the place where I first put on skis. In the early years skis were not used for sport in this part of the state, but just to get around in winter. By the 1920s and 1930s, kids would sometimes ski on the hill in back of the family orchard. Nahahum Canyon near Cashmere was a popular spot. Wilfred Woods, longtime publisher of the *Wenatchee World*, remembered looking for a wheat field without a fence at the bottom, since no one knew how to stop: "No turns," he said. "Just go."

Walla Walla resident Dorothy Egg recalled that around 1920, her brother had a friend who skied. "He came over to our house on skis one day," she said. "And the bindings were just toe straps. And when he came in the house to visit my brother, he left them on the snow. I think I was, oh, nine or ten years old and I went out and very carefully just stood in them.

Bill Milot throws a pole flip on wooden skis at Stevens Pass in the 1930s. (Wenatchee Ski Club collection courtesy Wilfred Woods)

You know—wow! That was something new and different. That inspired me to learn to ski." Later, an instructor gave lessons at the Buster Brown store in town in the evenings. On weekends Dorothy went to Tollgate in northeast Oregon to ski the sawdust pile and make turns around the stumps.

Walt Anderson, a forest ranger who had competed as an amateur in Cle Elum ski carnivals while living in Easton, moved to Leavenworth, where in the fall of 1928 he wrote a piece for the Leavenworth newspaper suggesting that the community stage its own ski tournament that winter. "We should get together and form an outdoor sport club," he wrote. "Personally, I prefer a ski club. We need to find a good hill not over a mile from town, get permission from the owner of the land to clear a strip for a ski course and toboggan slide and then get busy and clear it before winter advances any farther." A temporary site was found for the winter of 1929, and a year later a better one, about a mile north of town, was secured on government land. This was the beginning of big-time skiing in central Washington. Anderson was voted a lifetime membership in the Leavenworth Winter Sports Club for fathering the ski-course idea.

Magnus and Hermod Bakke, brothers who learned ski jumping in their native country of Norway, moved to central Washington in 1930 and worked to enlarge the Leavenworth ski jump, later named Bakke Hill in their honor. Leavenworth would be the site of several US national ski jumping championships from the 1940s through the 1970s. As an organized sport, ski jumping predated downhill skiing in central Washington, just as it had in the western Cascades.

Around 1935, Walt Anderson took a job as fire assistant in the Forest Service office in Wenatchee. There he founded the Wenatchee Ski Club and served as its first president. Fred Ball of The Mountaineers moved to Wenatchee around the same time and brought with him enthusiasm for alpine skiing. In April of that year, Anderson, Ball, Earl Little, Hermod Bakke, and others visited Stevens Pass to assess it for skiing development. Following this visit, the Everett and Wenatchee Chambers of Commerce encouraged their respective ski clubs to purchase land at the pass from the Great Northern Railway. The purchase was made and the land was deeded to the Forest Service to be developed as a ski area. The Forest Service announced plans to build a public shelter and clear snags from slopes around the pass.

The Stevens Pass highway, US 2, was closed in winter throughout the 1930s. Skiers visiting the pass from Seattle or Everett would take the train to the west portal at Scenic, then through the eight-mile Cascade Tunnel to the east portal, called Berne. From there they could ski, or in later years ride a school bus, west back up to the open slopes at the pass. (The west-side road was not open in winter until 1942.) Years later, Margaret Eilertsen recalled that during her third outing on skis, her husband John's friends suggested they end their day at Stevens Pass by skiing back to Scenic down along the snow-covered highway. By her own account, it was a trial:

> Without knowing what I was getting into, I agreed to tag along. We all started ski-ing off. I was congratulating myself because I managed good on the cross-country trail. Then horrors, we came to the first large slope. Swish—the gang all poled off and disappeared in a cloud of snow. I started off, then fell. Picked myself up. And fell. Et cetera, et cetera. I did more skiing on my rear-end than on skis, and while Johnny was very patient and encouraging, he must have had second thoughts about inviting such a "snow bunny" to tag along.
>
> Breathless and wet, we finally made it to the train and joined our rested friends. For two hours the train had waited for us, and with a blast of their whistle, we were off. I have often thought of that time, when I've rushed to catch a bus, airplane and yes, a train. Never again have I been able to delay their departure. Oh, to be young and foolish again!

MOUNT HOOD

Rodney Glisan, Wesley Ladd, Dr. Herbert Nichols, and several other Portland businessmen organized the Snowshoe Club in 1904 on the north side of Mount Hood. Like the Soyps on Mount Rainier, theirs was an elite group that enjoyed the outdoors, and they began a tradition of winter outings that lasted many years. Most of the men eventually graduated to using skis, but the name "Snowshoe" stuck. In 1910 they built a lodge on the ridge north of Cloud Cap Inn and hired local outdoorsman and guide Mark Weygandt to serve as caretaker. Weygandt is credited with more than five hundred ascents of Mount Hood, and he won what was believed to be the first ski competition on the mountain—a race from Cloud Cap Inn to Kirby Camp organized by the Hood River Ski Club in 1925.

As winter access improved on the south side of the mountain, the focus of skiing moved there. The highway to Government Camp was paved in 1922 and plowed in winter starting around 1927. The Mazamas established their first lodge near Government Camp in 1924 and made their first regular winter outing there over the New Year's holiday.

The Summit ski area at Government Camp, the oldest on the south side of Mount Hood, began development in 1927–28. Around the same time, a ski jump was built on the east side of Multorpor Mountain at the resort community of Swim, where the Mount Hood Ski Club, organized that same year, held its first annual tournament. Hans Otto Giese was invited to fly down from Seattle as a special guest. A year later, the newly formed Cascade Ski Club opened a new ski jump on the northwestern side of Multorpor Mountain. Swiss skier Fritz Bierly appeared on the slopes at Government Camp in 1931 and astounded local skiers with the first christiania turns they had ever seen (see the "Early Skiing Techniques" sidebar in chapter 3). Three years later, the first slalom races on Mount Hood were held at timberline (not yet spelled with a capital T).

By 1935 two ski clubs had built lodges at timberline, and a Forest Service cabin was also in use, but skiing there required a three-mile climb from the highway. The Forest Service and Civilian Conservation Corps (CCC) cleared a long, narrow ski trail—modeled after those in New England—from timberline back down to Government Camp. Just west of Multorpor is a long ridge called Tom Dick and Harry Mountain, where the Ski Bowl winter sports area was developed starting in 1937. It merged with Multorpor in the 1960s and is now known as Mount Hood Skibowl.

CAYUSE AND CHINOOK PASSES

Chinook Pass, at 5,432 feet on the Cascade crest, is located along the eastern boundary of Mount Rainier National Park. The road over Chinook Pass, Mather Memorial Parkway,

James Mount skis toward timberline on Mount Hood in 1935. (Photo by Curtis C. Ijames, courtesy the Mazamas)

took many years to build. Construction began in 1914 but was suspended during World War I. Work resumed in 1921 and was completed in 1931. From the beginning, it was understood that this highway would never be open in winter. The highway travels southeast from Enumclaw, then branches east at Cayuse Pass to cross Chinook Pass toward Yakima. The southern branch at 4,694-foot Cayuse Pass (State Highway 123) descends to Packwood.

Ten miles north of Cayuse Pass (on the Enumclaw side) was the Silver Springs Lodge. Harold Kinkade of Enumclaw remembered skiing there in 1931 on homemade ash-wood skis with toe-strap bindings. There was an informal ski club in Enumclaw as early as 1930. During the 1935–36 season, the Enumclaw Ski Club organized formally with fifty-five members and rented a cabin at Silver Springs as its headquarters.

On the east side of the pass, during the summer of 1935, the CCC built a lodge at a location called the American River (or American Ridge) Ski Bowl. The project trained CCC boys in logging, carpentry, and masonry techniques. Located at 3,000 feet at the toe of American Ridge, above the confluence of the American and Bumping Rivers, the ski bowl became the home grounds of the Yakima Ski Club in the late 1930s. The ski bowl was said to have the largest outhouse in the world—a twenty-holer. Although the area is no longer used for skiing today, the American River Lodge still stands and is managed by the Forest Service for group visits.

Cayuse and Chinook Passes became very popular with skiers in the 1930s. The state highway department kept the road clear to Cayuse Pass in winter over protests from the Park Service. Despite the fact that there was no shelter and no sanitary facilities, more than thirty thousand people used the area in the 1937–38 season. In the late 1930s, Yakima skiers established another ski hill a short distance up Morse Creek east of Chinook Pass. The site was first used for a Pacific Northwest Ski Association (PNSA) ski race during a year when there was not enough snow to hold the event at the American River Ski Bowl. Although the site was located a half mile up Morse Creek from the highway, it was dubbed Quartermile to entice the PNSA to accept the switch.

DEER PARK

During the Great Depression, before Olympic National Park was created in 1938, the Forest Service and the CCC launched a major road-building project in the Olympic Mountains near Port Angeles. Construction on two roads began in the summer of 1933. One road started in the Elwha Valley near Whiskey Bend and climbed just south of Wolf Creek to Idaho Camp, a point on Hurricane Ridge west of today's national park visitor center. The other road climbed from Danz Ranch, southeast of Port Angeles, to 5,400-foot Deer Park, high on the shoulder of Blue Mountain. Both roads were completed by the fall of 1934.

In a stroke of understatement, the Port Angeles paper wrote that "the public will find the Idaho Camp and Deer Park roads not broad highways. But travelers will discover them to be a high type of access into the very heart of a wonderful Olympic mountain region." The roads were steep, narrow, and vertigo-

A skier at Deer Park admires the Olympic Mountains scene. (Olympic National Park Archives)

inducing. "Motorists are advised to be very careful on the Idaho Camp road," wrote the *Port Angeles Evening News.* "As long as they use caution and do not drive fast, they will find the trip one of great pleasure and scenic thrills." The road to Idaho Camp was soon extended eastward along Hurricane Ridge to Obstruction Point. A plan to continue the road to Deer Park was never completed. Today, a seven-mile trail traverses the alpine ridge between the two road ends.

The Deer Park road was graded and widened in 1935 and 1936 to keep it open throughout the winter. Still, it was so narrow that the road was restricted to one-way traffic—up in the morning and down starting around 3:00 in the afternoon. Joy Lucas, a ski instructor who lived with her husband, Jim, at Deer Park for a winter before World War II, recalled that the road had an 18 percent grade near the top. "Many were the chains that were broken trying to climb that road," she remembered. The Forest Service built a lodge at Deer Park to accommodate at least thirty people overnight. Snags were cleared to open up ski runs.

Early in the winter of 1937, the Port Angeles paper reported a Sunday turnout of 200 people and fifty cars, "the largest crowd noted at Deer Park since the visit of Seattle skiers a year ago." A month later, a crowd of 500 was reported, "including 100 Seattle Mountaineers who invaded the region." The paper acknowledged that parking space was "congested." It was estimated that 2,500 people visited Deer Park that winter. Deer Park continued as the principal ski area on the Olympic Peninsula until the winter of 1957–58, when the new Heart o' the Hills road opened skiing at Hurricane Ridge. A few years later the Deer Park facilities were removed (today, there is a ranger cabin at roughly the same location).

SNOQUALMIE SUMMIT

When The Mountaineers built their original Snoqualmie Lodge near Lodge Lake in 1914, densely forested Snoqualmie Pass was inaccessible in winter, due to the seasonal closure of the highway. Neither attribute was very favorable for skiing. The Mountaineers cleared a small hill to open up skiing near their lodge, but their best outings required long tours to reach slopes above timberline. Beaver Lake, about a mile northeast of the lodge (and a few hundred feet higher), was an alpine pond framed by steep forested hills. It was at this location that Reidar Gjolme, winner of the 1916 ski jumping exhibition in Seattle, and several Norwegian friends saw the potential for a major ski jump.

In 1929 the Seattle Ski Club was formed, with Gjolme as its first president. The club leased land near Beaver Lake from the Northern Pacific Railroad and proceeded to clear the trees for a jumping hill. The jump was located on a north-facing slope just west of the lake, shaded from the sun. Because of the hill's steepness, construction of a scaffold was not needed. Access to the jump was from the east, where cars could park near the summit of Snoqualmie Pass.

To reach Beaver Lake in winter required hiking about a mile through deep snow with about 500 feet of climbing. The ski club built a lodge near the pass and held its first jumping tournament in 1930. Although the pass was generally closed that winter, the state highway patrol opened the road specifically for this event. Erling Thomsen of Seattle won first place. Hundreds of spectators endured the snowy road and the tiring hike to see the event.

After the winter of 1929–30, US Highway 10 over Snoqualmie Pass was kept open continuously. This encouraged other clubs to locate there, and within a few years the Washington Alpine Club, the Commonwealth Ski Club (later renamed Sahalie), the Washington Ski Club, and others had established ski lodges near the pass.

In the spring of 1933, William J. Maxwell of The Mountaineers drummed up support for the idea of public ski grounds at Snoqualmie Pass. It's not clear where the idea originated, but within a few months he was working with Ben Evans of the Seattle Park Board on the project. In December, under the auspices of the Depression-era Civil Works Administration, forty loggers and a few carpenters from North Bend began clearing a slope on Forest Service land at the pass and building a shelter. Known as the Seattle Municipal Ski Park, it was to be operated by the city, despite the fact that it was more than 50 miles from Seattle. Opening ceremonies were held on January 21, 1934, with Seattle mayor John Dore

Seattle mayor John Dore crowns Marguerite Strizek queen during the opening of the Seattle Municipal Ski Park. (Seattle Municipal Archives)

presiding and more than a thousand ski fans present. In an omen to future generations of Snoqualmie Pass skiers, a light but steady rain fell throughout the day.

The year 1934 marked an inflection point in Northwest skiing: the beginning of mass appeal of the sport. Six weeks before the opening of the Municipal Hill, the *Seattle Times* began publishing an eleven-part weekly series of ski lessons, written and illustrated by Ben Thompson. Through these short articles, *Times* readers were introduced to the finer points of stemming, crouching, christies, telemarks, jumping, waxing, and more (see the "Early Skiing Techniques" sidebar in chapter 3 for definitions of these terms). More and bigger ski events were staged before the snow melted that season.

In the *American Ski Annual* two decades later, Fred McNeil wrote about skiing in the Pacific Northwest: "One year, we'll say, there was no skiing. The next year—and that was when programs of winter road opening had been launched—hundreds were skiing, or learning to. The following year, thousands were on the snow, and easily within a decade, winter sports enthusiasts were trooping by the hundreds of thousands to the fast-developing skiing centers. It was a movement I believe without parallel in any American sport. Opening of the roads was the key."

Two weeks after the Municipal Hill celebration, the Pacific Northwest Ski Association held its first alpine skiing race, a slalom, on the forested slope on the opposite side of Beaver Lake from the jumping hill. Alpine skiing and racing arrived at Snoqualmie Pass and would dominate skiing at Snoqualmie from that day forward. But the pass would also remain a center for ski touring and exploration, and skiers of the 1930s discovered trips that would be enjoyed well into the next century. Granite Mountain, Red Mountain, Snoqualmie Mountain, and Kendall Peak were all skied by 1933, and Mountaineers skiers completed the circuit of Chair Peak, which they described as "the finest trip in the Lodge country."

Veida Morrow, a well-traveled skier from Seattle, fondly recalled the "most intriguing ski trip" she ever made, over several days with her brother and friends in the early 1930s. They skied from Snoqualmie Pass over the saddle between Red Mountain and Snoqualmie Mountain and down to a cabin at Goldmyer Hot Springs on the Middle Fork Snoqualmie River. Of the descent to the cabin, Morrow wrote, "Then for four miles downhill running, carefree and as happy as the winds that flew with us. Gone and far behind—the noise and clamor of the city. Not even the beasts of the forests trespassed upon this ground we were skimming. Forgotten all the petty sordid things that ever surround one in this greedy rush to exist among the smokestacks of the city, for here, in the covert of the towering, unchanging mountains, for a few brief days, we *lived*."

Opposite: *Mount Rainier ski climbers below Little Tahoma in 1928 (from left): Bill Maxwell, Fred Dupuis, Andrew Anderson, Otto Strizek, Hans Otto Giese, Walter Best* (Giese Archives)

CHAPTER 5

THE SKI CLIMBERS

The earliest skiers in the Pacific Northwest fit largely into two groups. First were the immigrant Scandinavians who grew up jumping and cross-country skiing in their native countries. Second were the members of mountaineering clubs, already drawn to the hills, who found in skiing a way to continue enjoying Northwest mountains in winter. Members of The Mountaineers and Mazamas tried skiing as early as 1910, but being self-taught, they were limited to relatively easy terrain. It was not until the arrival of European skiers such as Rudy Amsler, Hans Otto Giese, and Fritz Bierly that locals learned the skills needed for bigger mountains. That occurred in the late 1920s and 1930s.

Before that, Northwest skiers found inspiration through a visit by three French mountaineers in the winter of 1922. Jacques Landry, his brother Jean Landry, and Jean's brother-in-law, Jacques Bergues, had experience climbing in Europe,

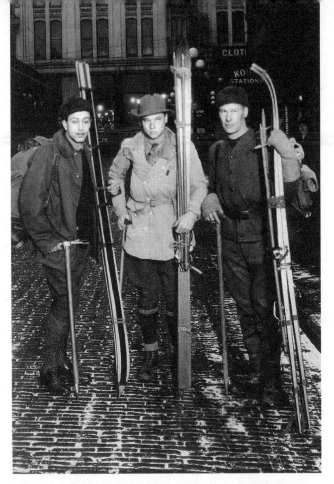

Members of the 1922 Rainier winter ascent party: Jacques Bergues, Jean Landry, Jacques Landry (Photo by Jean Landry)

including midwinter ascents of major peaks in the Alps. Drawn to Mount Rainier, the trio planned a ski ascent of the mountain via the Emmons-Winthrop Glacier. But after viewing pictures of the mountain and talking with local members of The Mountaineers, they switched to the Gibraltar Route, where they could take advantage of shelter cabins at Anvil Rock (9,584 feet) and Camp Muir (around 10,100 feet).

The Landrys' plan garnered support from the Park Service and US Army, as well as fanfare from local newspapers. On February 5 they made a reconnaissance from Paradise toward Anvil Rock while army signal corpsmen laid telegraph wire. Captain Cansler of the Signal Corps declared, "Those Landry chaps are the goods. I never saw such skill on skis as they exhibit and they are apparently old mountain men. I have no doubt that they will make the top."

Around this time, Charles Perryman, a Selznick newsreel cameraman, arrived at Paradise to film the ascent. After delays due to weather the climbers, accompanied by Perryman, climbed to Anvil Rock, abandoning their skis due to the icy, wind-hardened snow. On the 11th, they scouted the route across the Gibraltar Ledges, with Perryman shooting 450 feet of film of their reconnaissance climb. They left Anvil Rock at 4:00 a.m. on February 13 and climbed to the summit in a little over eight hours. Despite having no previous climbing experience, Perryman accompanied them to the top, shooting more film while carrying a movie camera and tripod weighing more than fifty pounds. "Perryman performed as if mountain climbing had always been his principal hobby," Jean Landry later wrote. The climbers descended Gibraltar at dusk and reached Anvil Rock after nightfall.

Following the climb, Jean Landry was disappointed that Perryman's film was distributed by Selznick News without compensation to the climbers for the extra effort they made to produce it. Writing to Mount Rainier historian Dee Molenaar more than forty years later, he explained, "It was agreed that if the film was sold, each member of the party would receive an equal share of the proceeds. We had hoped in this way to earn funds with which to finance other winter climbs in North America." The film passed out of knowledge until 2003, when Steve Turner, Perryman's grandson, emailed me after reading notes about the 1922 climb on the Alpenglow Ski Mountaineering History Project website (see Resources). Turner wrote that he had his grandfather's newsreel footage from the climb.

Over a period of eight years, Turner and I exchanged emails, with long gaps between correspondence. In 2009 he offered to donate the film to The Mountaineers in exchange for a copy on disk. In 2011, I received the film, which was then digitized; a copy was mailed to Turner, and the original donated to Special Collections at the University of Washington Libraries (see Resources). Finding and preserving the 1922 film of the Mount Rainier climb is one of the more memorable and significant episodes of my journey in writing this book.

"OUR NEAREST LARGE HILL"

Of The Mountaineers club members who took up skiing in the 1920s, William J. "Bill" Maxwell was one of the most enthusiastic. In 1926 he made the first recorded ski ascent of Denny Mountain, site of today's Alpental ski area and one of the earliest peaks skied near Snoqualmie Pass. "Finding that skiing on small hills was extremely pleasant and that higher hills were even more alluring," he wrote in 1927, "our ambition was aroused to ski as high as possible on our nearest large hill, namely, Mt Rainier." With his friend Andy Anderson, Maxwell was convinced that it would be possible to ski to the summit of the Northwest's greatest mountain. They set plans for an attempt in April 1927—the winter climbing season was then considered to extend from October until Memorial Day.

Maxwell knew about the Landry party's climb of Mount Rainier in 1922. He reckoned that the Emmons Glacier would be better for skiing than the routes above Camp Muir, since it was gentler and less rocky. But in 1927, roads on Rainier's northeastern side were still under construction, and in winter the plowed highway ended at Silver Springs. Between there and Glacier Basin, base for an ascent of the Emmons Glacier, lay 16 miles of walking, skiing, or (perhaps) coaxing a car up a partially melted-out road. With friends, Maxwell and Anderson made two attempts in the spring of 1927, both thwarted by wintry weather. Turned back at 12,500 feet on their second try, they found compensation in a

Mount Rainier and its Emmons Glacier were a magnet for early ski mountaineers (The Spring Trust for Trails)

thrilling descent of the Inter Glacier below Camp Curtis (at about 8,700 feet). Maxwell later described the experience:

> *Chilled from the breeze which usually prevails at Curtis Ridge, you point your skis downhill. Swiftly they rush, and perforce you fight to keep up with them. Your blood warms with the struggle, and for a moment your whole effort is concentrated on the idea of balance; . . . a spray of snow fluffs behind; your muscles relax somewhat as you grow accustomed to the swift descent; your mind blots out the idea of fear and telegraphs to every nerve the sheer joy of living; the thrill of speed exalts you and every petty worry fades away—this, indeed, is life.*

Maxwell and Anderson returned to Rainier in 1928 with a strong team. Fred Dupuis had been on the first ski attempt in 1927. Norwegian Lars Lovseth had been one of the most experienced skiers in The Mountaineers for a decade. Walter Best had been a varsity crewman on the 1925 University of Washington rowing team. Otto Strizek, a dentist and son of the Czechoslovakian consul in Seattle, had just won the Harper Cup as the most improved new skier in The Mountaineers. Finally, Hans Otto Giese was regarded by many as the best skier in the Northwest.

The climb from their igloo near Steamboat Prow on April 8 started out badly. Strizek had spent most of the night jumping in place because his feet were freezing. As they ventured onto the Emmons Glacier, Anderson, in the lead, plunged into a hidden crevasse. He swung a ski pole across the chasm to check his fall, then dangled for a moment before his friends pulled him out. After the men rescued Anderson and regained their composure, they tied into their safety ropes to continue the climb. As they zigzagged up the glacier, some of the men used sealskin climbers strapped to their skis to grip the frozen snow. Others used a sticky wax rubbed onto the ski bases. Most of them climbed with two ski poles, but Maxwell skied with a single pole, holding a long ice axe in his other hand to fashion a belay if needed.

After a few hours of climbing, alpenglow tinted the summit dome and the sun began to rise behind them. As they neared the 12,000-foot level, still 2,400 feet below the summit, lack of food and water added to their fatigue. The snow became so hard that their climbing skins and wax would no longer grip. None of the men's skis had metal edges, and their bindings, made of iron lugs bolted through the skis with leather straps to secure their boots, gave only limited control as they stamped their feet for purchase. Reluctantly, Maxwell, Anderson, Lovseth, and Dupuis decided to turn back at 12,000 feet. Best, Giese, and Strizek

April 1927: Fred Dupuis, Andrew Anderson, Lars Lovseth, and William J. Maxwell at the Mount Rainier National Park entrance (University of Washington Libraries, Special Collections, Mountaineers Collection)

abandoned their skis and continued to the summit on crampons. After a short summit celebration, the three men returned to their skis and skied back to Glacier Basin, descending in two and a half hours what had taken two days to climb. "It was marvelous," Giese later recalled. "We skied past our igloo so fast we couldn't stop."

Bill Maxwell was surely disappointed to have been turned back again by Mount Rainier but proud of his friends who had made what was regarded in those days as the second winter ascent of the peak. Although they failed to ski all the way to the top, Giese, Strizek, and Best had established a milestone in Northwest mountaineering. They had demonstrated that skis could be tools of mountaineering, full-fledged complements to crampons and an ice axe. Skis had carried the party higher than nearly all the mountains in the Northwest and promised one day to conquer the highest of them all. Their climb of Mount Rainier ushered in a new sport to the Pacific Northwest: ski mountaineering.

IN NO SENSE A STUNT

Born in Germany in 1902, Hans Otto Giese immigrated to the United States in 1923. In Seattle he worked as secretary at the German consulate, studied law at the University of

Washington, and competed in ski tournaments in his spare time. A family scrapbook entry from the 1920s indicates that Giese was winning an average of three prizes per month for his prowess in skiing. He was also an ardent mountaineer, and his experience on Mount Rainier sparked his interest in more ski mountaineering adventures.

Mount Baker was the next logical step. In 1925 the Mount Baker Club had built a sturdy log cabin near 5,000 feet on the north side of the mountain. Kulshan Cabin, an ideal base for mountain climbs, was just below timberline near Heliotrope Ridge and a 10-mile hike from the town of Glacier. The cabin cost $2,000 to build, a lot of money in those days. The cost and effort of constructing the cabin so drained the Mount Baker Club that they reorganized in 1928 as an outing club, their days of lobbying and development over. In December 1925, four club members took advantage of the new cabin to make the first winter climb of the volcano, on foot. The cabin remained a landmark on the approach hike to Mount Baker for more than sixty years. Climbing parties were still using it regularly in 1975, when I made my first climb of the mountain. The cabin was closed and removed after 1984, when Mount Baker became a federally designated wilderness area.

Built by the Mount Baker Club in 1925, Kulshan Cabin served as a base for climbers on Mount Baker for sixty years. (University of Washington Libraries, Special Collections, Mountaineers Collection)

Nearing the saddle during the first ski ascent of Mount Baker by Edwin Loners and Robert Sperlin with John Booth (C. F. Easton's Mount Baker Collection, Whatcom Museum, Bellingham)

Hans Otto Giese made plans with Robert "Bob" Hayes, another Mountaineers skier, to climb 10,781-foot Baker on skis on Christmas Day 1929. A Seattle newspaper announced their plans the day they left for the mountain. "If we succeed, it will be the first time that a major Western peak has been conquered with skis," said Hayes. They drove from Seattle to Glacier on the evening of December 23, then climbed 4,000 feet to Kulshan Cabin the following day. Rain fell during the approach, and slushy snow made the skiing difficult. On Christmas Day the storm grew to a blizzard. The two skiers labored to a point near the Black Buttes but were forced back. Hayes later said, "I am sure Mount Baker can be climbed with skis under favorable weather conditions."

Giese and Hayes were not alone in hoping to make the first ski ascent of Mount Baker. A week later, on January 3, 1930, three University of Washington students left Glacier for Kulshan Cabin. Robert Sperlin, Edwin Loners, and Ernie Pugh climbed into a blizzard on the Coleman Glacier during their summit attempt and failed to get beyond the Black Buttes. Conditions on January 5 were so bad that it took the men ten hours to ski 10 miles *down-hill* back to Glacier. Two weeks later, another group of UW students gave it a try. Arnold Campbell, Ned Cunningham, Bert Heinz, Donald Norbeck, and William Sweet attempted to ski the mountain on a clear but bitterly cold January 18–19. The temperature at Glacier dropped to minus 6 degrees Fahrenheit, and the skiers estimated that it was 20 below zero at Kulshan Cabin. The party abandoned the climb due to the extreme cold. Cunningham froze his left foot but managed to get back safely.

Each of these attempts was reported in local newspapers, and the series of efforts ignited quite a rivalry. The Giese-Hayes attempt also caused a scandal within The Mountaineers. Mountaineers club historian Stella Degenhardt found the following entry in the February 6, 1930, minutes of the board of trustees many years later: "Upon the request of Mr. Hayes and Mr. Giese it was voted to insert an item in the *Bulletin* which will make it clear to the membership that their attempted climb of Mount Baker on skis on New Years was in no sense a 'stunt' climb; that ski mountaineering is a new phase of mountaineering, and in many respects safer than summer climbing; that their plans had been carefully made, that it was a feasible trip, and they turned back only on account of weather conditions." A statement to this effect was published in the club's March *Bulletin* "to modify or correct the recent criticism" aimed at Giese and Hayes.

In early May, Robert Sperlin and Edwin Loners of the Washington Alpine Club returned to the mountain to complete the first ski ascent. The morning of their success-ful climb was crystal clear. Snow conditions were good as they zigzagged up the Coleman Glacier. "We stopped often to enjoy a view which was beautiful beyond description," recalled Sperlin. "Before us were the Black Buttes and the peak itself, glorified by a fresh fall of snow."

Above the Coleman-Deming saddle, however, conditions became icy. The third member of their party, John Booth, left his skis there and continued on crampons. The two skiers worked slowly up the slope above the Deming Glacier. "Here we were very cautious, as a slip might mean a drop into one of the many crevasses below," Sperlin recalled. "By stamping our skis down hard they would break through enough to give a comfortable hold." Eight hours after leaving the cabin, Sperlin and Loners reached the summit on skis. Due to the icy snow, they decided to carry their skis while returning to the saddle on crampons. Conditions improved below and they enjoyed fine skiing back to Kulshan Cabin. "It was one fast run after another," wrote Sperlin.

This climb by Sperlin and Loners was heralded as the first ski ascent of a major Cascade peak. Interest in skiing Mount Baker grew after this milestone. Ski mountaineers realized that unlike Mount Rainier, which was nearly 4,000 feet taller, Mount Baker might offer reasonable ski conditions near the summit on a fairly regular basis. In 1933 Hans Otto Giese and Don Fraser made the first complete ascent and descent on skis.

THE ADVENTURES OF MILANA JANK

In 1930 ski instructor and accomplished alpinist Milana Jank was sponsored by her native Germany to come to the United States as a goodwill ambassador of skiing. She had previously made a winter ski crossing of the main chain of the Alps from Vienna to Mont Blanc over a period of 146 days, covering some 1,300 miles. Born in Bavaria in 1902, Jank learned to climb with her brothers as a teenager. "Twelve years ago my friends in Europe called me 'ski crazy,'" she wrote in 1932. "And they were right—still are."

After arriving in America, Jank sought adventures in various parts of the United States in the company of local experts. In January 1931 she made a winter ski traverse of New Hampshire's Presidential Range with Fritz Wiessner, topping several of the main peaks along the way. "It proved to me the possibilities for advancing the white sport in the United States," she wrote. "And to which region in the West should I go later? To the Cascades of the Pacific, I decided. Soon various different mountains of the Cascade Range saw for the first time this modern weapon, the ski, conquering the steepest and most difficult approaches." Jank tirelessly promoted the virtues of skiing. A ski, she wrote, is a "wing of wood" that "leads the adventuresome to thrilling victories over great white steeps high above the plains and plateaus where man has built his villages and cities."

In the spring of 1931, Jank became the mountain sports director at the Mount Baker Lodge, where she taught skiing and guided outings. In early summer she joined mountain guide Ben Thompson and others to attempt a ski ascent of the volcano from the lodge. This scenic route travels above timberline for more than 10 miles, traversing Ptarmigan Ridge and passing through Epley Portal to the massive Rainbow and Park Glaciers. The way had been followed to the summit of Baker by the Mazamas on their summer outing of 1906 but had never been traversed on skis. Following an attempt foiled by bad weather, Jank and Thompson were joined by Robert Hayes and Otto Strizek to complete the climb on June 28. At the steep headwall of the Park Glacier, the party abandoned their skis, crossed the bergschrund, and reached the summit on crampons twelve and a half hours after leaving the lodge.

Jank repeated the climb solo a few weeks later. "When, after my victory, I descended the seven-hundred-foot ice wall," she later wrote, "there were my trusty skis waiting for me like restless chargers eager for the speedy race to the valley." The Rainbow Glacier, which had required four hours to ascend, was descended

Milana Jank was mountain sports director at the Mount Baker Lodge in 1931. On June 28 she made a ski-climb of the volcano via the Park Glacier with three companions. On July 15 she repeated the ascent solo. (From *Game & Gossip* magazine, February 1932, courtesy Ingrid Wicken)

in just twenty minutes. The approach and ascent from the lodge had taken her fifteen hours, but the return took only two. "Past was the first and only solo ski ascent made by a woman to a majestic peak in the United States," she wrote. "Before me lay the snowy land which the ski had now to conquer." Near Table Mountain, Jank encountered her ski students, and they joined her on the final slopes back to the lodge. She later wrote, "Mount Baker has been the zenith of my ski experience."

When the Mount Baker Lodge caught fire on August 5, 1931, Bert Huntoon, a key figure in developing the lodge, awoke Jank in her room. She escaped safely along with all twenty-seven guests. During the following winter, Jank shifted her attention to California's Sierra Nevada, and in March 1932 she completed the first ski crossing of Tioga Pass from Mono Lake to Yosemite Valley with Dennis Jones.

Jank saw herself as a prophet of skiing, descending from the mountains to inspire American men and women to take up the sport in their own country. Of the mountains of the West Coast, she wrote, "I have tried and scaled them all with my skis, and I have sped down from their wind-swept summits to tell you who dwell in this amazing region that you have in your mountains one of the world's grandest winter playgrounds." To those who would follow her, Jank promised, "You all may see the majesty that with me is constant in memory, if you will learn to ski, and other benefits will be yours in measure as you turn your faces to your mountains." Jank, who returned to Germany in July 1933, was one of a kind.

GUARDIANS OF THE COLUMBIA

Records of skiing in Oregon go back farther than in Washington. The John Craig Memorial Ski event in central Oregon honors a mail carrier who lost his life in 1877 while attempting to deliver the mail on skis over McKenzie Pass. Skis arrived on Mount Hood early as well, spurred by the development of the railroad along the Columbia River. As roads were improved on the south side of Mount Hood, interest in winter sports grew there. A spur road was constructed from Government Camp to timberline in 1930–31, but it was not plowed in winter until 1937.

In the 1930s there was informal competition for the fastest time from the Portland city limits to the top of Mount Hood and back. On April 26, 1931, Hjalmar Hvam and Arne Stene of the Cascade Ski Club joined with Swiss skier Andre Roch to set a new record. With driver Harald Lee, the party left Portland at 6:03 a.m. and returned at 2:52 p.m., for a roundtrip time of 8 hours, 49 minutes. They started skiing halfway between Government Camp and timberline. Their ascent was remarkable not only because of their fast time, but because they kept their skis on continuously to the 11,240-foot summit and back. Hvam wrote in the Cascade Ski Club yearbook that they had sidestepped up the summit chute to the lookout cabin on top. After pausing to take a few pictures, they sidestepped and sideslipped down the chute, then boomed down the Palmer snowfield back to timberline. Even today most mountaineers leave their skis at the Hogback below the summit gullies and continue to the top on crampons. In 1931, it would have been much trickier to ski from the summit with leather boots and skis that probably lacked steel edges. But this was no ordinary ski party.

Born in Norway in 1902, Hjalmar Hvam moved to Portland in 1927. In the mid-1930s he emerged as the top all-around skier in the Northwest. Hvam won the US national

Andre Roch, Hjalmar Hvam, and Arne Stene below timberline after skiing Mount Hood in 1931 (Oregon Historical Society)

championship in Nordic combined at Lake Tahoe in 1932. His best year was perhaps 1936, when he won twelve straight contests, including the Silver Skis on Mount Rainier. In May of that year, Hvam entered a four-way tournament at Mount Baker, consisting of cross-country, slalom, downhill, and jumping events. He took first place in every discipline against stiff international competition. Hvam's partner, Andre Roch, born in Switzerland in 1906, later made difficult first ascents in the Alps and pioneered the route to the South Col of Mount Everest in 1952. In his career as director of the Swiss Avalanche Research Institute in Davos, Roch was regarded as the world's foremost expert on snow and avalanches. He was also a first-rate ski mountaineer.

The April 1931 ski ascent of Mount Hood was no fluke. In December of that year, a ski party including Elsa Hanft of Spokane repeated the ascent. (It's unknown whether the party skied all the way to the summit.) Formerly a guide at Mount Baker Lodge, Hanft was probably the first woman to scale Mount Hood with the help of skis. By the mid-1930s, ski mountaineering on Hood was becoming quite popular. In the 1935 *American Ski Annual*, Boyd French wrote, "It is an almost weekly occurrence for skiing parties to reach

Hans Otto Giese, Walter Mosauer, and Sandy Lyon rest during Mosauer's 1932 visit to the Northwest, which culminated in the first ski descent of Mount Adams. (Giese Archives)

the summit at an altitude of 11,225 [sic] feet." This was written before Timberline Lodge opened or the road was plowed in winter.

Walter Mosauer was a native of Austria, where he learned the Arlberg style of skiing popularized by Hannes Schneider. After receiving his PhD at the University of Michigan, he came to the University of California–Los Angeles in 1931. Mosauer looked for skiing opportunities in Southern California. He met Pomona College students with whom he formed a little community of skiers. In June 1932, after the Southern California ski season ended, Mosauer recruited student Sandy Lyon to accompany him on a ski vacation in the Pacific Northwest. Mosauer and Lyon skied to and from the rim of Crater Lake in Oregon, ski-climbed Mount Hood, made several trips to Camp Muir and Burroughs Mountain on Mount Rainier, and skied around Mount Baker Lodge. These trips were made in the company of local skiers such as Bill Maxwell, Hans Grage, Robert Hayes, Ben Thompson, and other members of the Seattle Mountaineers.

During his ski trips on Hood and Rainier, Mosauer admired the majestic bulk of Mount Adams standing on the horizon. At 12,276 feet, Adams is second in elevation only to Rainier among the Pacific Northwest volcanoes. The south route on Mount Adams is one of the simplest climbs on any major Northwest peak. During the 1930s, pack trains climbed the mountain to extract sulfur from the summit. Covered with snow in spring and early summer, and lacking crevasses, the south route offers an ideal ski descent.

Local skiers knew of no previous ski ascents of Adams, so a plan was hatched to ski the peak as the climax of Mosauer's 1932 vacation. The party would include Mosauer and Lyon along with Hans Otto Giese, Hans Grage, and Otto Strizek of Seattle. On July 16, the five men left a camp at Cold Creek (around 5,500 feet) and climbed to the summit of Mount Adams in about seven and a half hours. Mosauer later wrote, "Since an ice-cold gale converted the snow into hard ice, skis were used only occasionally during the ascent, while in other places crampons were indispensable. Thus, our trip cannot be considered a 'ski ascent' proper, which in my opinion is a meaningless classification anyway. The descent, however, was a full, continuous ski-run from 12,307 [sic] to below 6,000 feet, delightful in spite of difficult snow conditions."

Upon returning to Southern California after his Northwest tour, Mosauer wrote, "I unloaded my boundless enthusiasm for skiing on anybody who was willing to listen." He founded the ski mountaineering section of the Sierra Club and started (and coached) the UCLA ski team. Tragically, Mosauer died in 1937 of a tropical fever contracted on a zoology expedition in Mexico. Today he is regarded as the father of alpine skiing in Southern California.

Giese and Strizek made the first ski descent of 9,677-foot Mount St. Helens, the last of the "Guardians of the Columbia" to be skied, the following June. Their trip received only the tiniest mention in the August 1933 *Mountaineer Bulletin*, so tiny that it was overlooked for nearly seventy years. Giese recalled the ascent for journalist Tim Thompson in the December 1969 issue of *Seattle Magazine*. Giese had just gotten his first pair of steel-edged skis. As the two men skied down Mount St. Helens, Giese decided to show off his new skis. "I'd say, 'Lean out, Otto' but, of course, I had the advantage," he recalled.

Mount St. Helens before the 1980 eruption (The Spring Trust for Trails)

As they zoomed down on opposite sides of a small ridge, Giese slipped, and at nearly the same time—unknown to him—so did Strizek. They slid for hundreds of feet, unable to see each other. "I tried to stop with my bamboo poles, but I was going too fast," Giese recalled. Finally, he slid over a crevasse and went "*Bam!*—like a ball hitting a mitt—right into the lip on the opposite side," he said. The same thing happened to his companion. "It was foggy and we couldn't see each other," Giese recalled. "He yelled, 'Otto, Otto' and I yelled, 'Otto, Otto.' Oh what a mess!" The men finally found each other and rejoined their girlfriends, who had been waiting at the bottom of the mountain. With six bottles of homemade beer, the group drove to Cannon Beach in Oregon for a night swim in the ocean. "Ha! Marvelous," Giese remembered. "That was quite a day, quite a day!"

AN UNLIKELY PARTNERSHIP

In 1938, the first ski ascent of 10,541-foot Glacier Peak was made by Dwight Watson and Sigurd Hall. The two men were very different from each other, yet they formed a complementary pair. Watson was born in Seattle in 1900. Quiet and deeply religious, he strongly opposed the theory of evolution as taught in public schools. Watson briefly studied engineering at the University of Washington and became interested in the outdoors after working on a hydroelectric project near Mount Rainier. He began skiing relatively late in life, in his early thirties.

In 1926 Watson was descending from a snowshoeing trip at Indian Henrys Hunting Ground near Mount Rainier when a pair of skiers passed by. "They took off their skis and put on snowshoes!" he recalled with surprise. "There was probably fifteen inches fresh snow. That unsold me on skiing for a long time." Pioneer climber Hermann Ulrichs, who was not a skier, introduced him to the North Cascades. Watson eventually fell in love with the sport, especially skiing high, remote mountains. He was never much interested in the competitive or social aspects of skiing.

Sigurd Hall (originally Hoel), born in 1910 on his family's farm in the Sunndal valley of Norway, was an outstanding young athlete in skiing and soccer. As a farm boy, he never had a lot of fancy equipment and was known to show up at ski competitions with poles made out of the farm's curtain rods. When Sig was twelve, he broke one of his skis a few days before a competition. The family had no money to buy skis and there was no time to make another, so he patched the ski with a piece of sheet metal. The city boys teased him about his shabby equipment, but he nevertheless won the event. His victories were the subject of many articles in the local newspaper.

Hall was a free spirit and an adventurer at a time when rural Norwegian society was quite conservative. As the oldest boy, he was in line to inherit the Hoel family farm. But

RECONQUERING OLD MAN MOUNTAIN ON SKIS

Toward the end of 1932, Art Winder wrote an article for *The Mountaineer* that highlighted club skiing for the year. The Mount Adams ascent was the outstanding achievement, which Winder recognized as part of a larger trend. "Mountaineers are re-exploring their alpine domain," he wrote. "But instead of going in the plodding manner of preceding years, afoot, slim skis that dart like lightning over the white blanket of snow carry the enthusiast into the wilderness he loves."

Winder made a prediction with confidence: "Much still remains for the Mountaineer to do. Not only is he confronted yet with the vast task of completing the exploration of his own Northwest mountains afoot, but he has as yet but scratched the surface of the possibilities of re-conquering old man mountain's domain a-ski. But the fever is growing rapidly and the next few seasons will see the track of grooved ski firmly implanted beside the mark of nailed boot on the summits of many of our beloved mountain monarchs."

Dwight Watson in 1939 (University of Washington Libraries, Special Collections, Dwight Watson Collection)

times were hard, so in 1929 at age nineteen he left for America with the intention of staying a few years to earn money to help the farm. But he arrived at the start of the Great Depression and found hard times here as well. He worked as an electrician, a skill he had taught himself, but his real passions were climbing and skiing.

Hall met Watson through The Mountaineers. Watson's knowledge of the local mountains and Hall's passion for skiing led to an unusual partnership for exploring the Cascades backcountry on skis. Their ascent of Glacier Peak began on a cloudy afternoon at the end of Suiattle River Road. They hiked and carried skis a few hours up the Milk Creek Trail, then camped under a tarp in light rain. The next day they continued to a campsite above Mica Lake, stashed equipment, and scouted the route ahead in clouds and fog. On the morning of July 4, 1938, the pair started early, skiing past Milk Lake and following a spiral route up the northeastern side of Glacier Peak across the Ptarmigan, Vista, Ermine, and Dusty Glaciers. Light rain fell at times.

The shoulder above North Guardian Rock proved to be the crux of the route. "Now the ridge narrowed and steepened," Watson wrote, "and ahead was a vertical pinnacle several hundred feet high. It looked like defeat for the fog lay thick and baffling and it is not socially correct to ski on steep slopes with visibility nil especially when terrain is new." They removed their skis and jabbed them into the snow like ice axes to climb up and around rock walls to the saddle south of the Rabbit Ears. From there they skied easily to the summit.

When the clouds parted, they noticed a route west of the Rabbit Ears that offered an easier descent. They skied onto the upper Kennedy Glacier, then removed their skis briefly to cross pumice and rocks to Kennedy Ridge, from which they could see their morning tracks. Watson shot 16-millimeter movies during the climb, with an especially memorable descent. "I've got a beautiful shot of Sig," he later told historian Harry Majors. "He must have been doing sixty miles an hour here.... Oh, tremendous speed." They packed up and hiked out around 7:00 p.m. Darkness fell halfway down the 10-mile trail as they stumbled along with a single flashlight. They arrived at their car after midnight, Hall passing out in the passenger seat while Watson drove, stopping a couple of times to snooze. They arrived home at 5:00 a.m., cleaned up, and headed for work.

Watson and Hall were keenly aware that the 1928 ski-climb of Mount Rainier by Walter Best, Hans Otto Giese, and Otto Strizek was incomplete from a ski mountaineering standpoint. Because of icy conditions, Best, Giese, and Strizek had abandoned their skis at 12,000 feet and continued to the summit on foot. Skis had not yet reached the summit of Rainier, and Watson and Hall hoped to be the first to ski all the way to or from the top. "On several weekends in the fore part of the summer," Hall wrote, "we had had a party ready for the assault, but Saturday would come with dark clouds and rain, calling off the trip."

Watson decided to try a midweek attempt on the mountain, on June 28, 1939. He teamed up with Erick Larson, a Swede who had come to the United States as a youngster in the 1920s, and alpinist Andy Hennig, who'd recently emigrated from Austria to become a ski instructor at Sun Valley, Idaho. Their attempt started well, but the group was repelled around 12,000 feet by gathering clouds. Watson's short film of the trip is held in the University of Washington Libraries' Special Collections.

Sigurd Hall near the summit of Glacier Peak during the first ski ascent, July 4, 1938 (University of Washington Libraries, Special Collections, Dwight Watson Collection)

Three days later, Hennig returned with Hall for another try. With Watson and Larson unable to go, the two skiers joined forces with a climbing party led by Larry Penberthy. "When we checked in at the White River Ranger Station," wrote Hall, "the ranger looked with some distrust at our skis. However, as we also had crampons and ice axes, he checked us through." After a four-mile hike to Glacier Basin, the party skied up the Inter Glacier using klister wax. A member of three winning teams in The Mountaineers' Patrol Race, Hall was an expert waxer. At Camp Curtis they changed to skare wax, anticipating hard crust in the morning. A gale blew off the mountain, and they went to bed with doubts about the climb. They left their bivouac at 3:00 a.m. on July 2. The weather was unchanged, but they hoped for the best. Around 12,000 feet, Hennig had trouble with one of his bindings, so he removed his skis and switched to crampons. This left Hall as the only skier.

"The last two thousand feet were the most difficult," Hall wrote. "The slope was too steep and the snow too hard to use the climbing surface of the ski. I had to jab in the steel edge two or three times, take a step and do it all over again. However, the edges proved their usability. Not once did they slip." Near the summit, the surface was hard ice with a trace of new snow. "Progress was very slow the last three hundred feet," Hall wrote, "but finally we arrived at the rim and looked over the crater. The mountain had been conquered on skis!"

As they rested and ate lunch near a steam vent in the crater, a cloud cap formed over the summit. Recognizing this warning sign, they began their descent on crampons. The snow was rock hard, making skiing impossible. "Even metal edges wouldn't hold," Hall wrote. The cloud cap grew and descended toward them, preventing the snow from softening as they had hoped. The party descended to about 12,000 feet before exchanging crampons for skis. Visibility was near zero, and they reached Camp Curtis in driving rain. "In spite of the weather we had a fine run down Inter Glacier to Storbo," Hall wrote. "We waited for the rest of the party and reached the cars at White River Camp—tired but happy."

Speaking to the *Seattle Times* a few days later, Hall offered condolences to William J. Maxwell, the enthusiastic ski fiend who had inspired so many attempts on Mount Rainier. "I can tell Bill Maxwell," said Sig, that "skiing in the crater isn't worth the climb. Bill tried three times to get there on skis, and he told me he'd give anything to be able to ski in the crater on top of the mountain. But it was wash-boardy and hard as stone." Thus the group had not been able to ski down. "It's too precipitous," Hall conceded, "and even metal edges wouldn't hold. I'm glad I made it, but I never want to try it again."

Opposite: *Don Amick and Bruce Kehr ski fresh snow above Paradise in 1936.* (University of Washington Libraries, Special Collections, Dwight Watson Collection)

CHAPTER 6

A WINTER PARADISE

As skiing spread throughout the Cascade Mountains in the 1930s, the Rainier National Park Company sought to establish Paradise as the premier ski destination in the Pacific Northwest. In the fall of 1932, the company began leasing accommodations on the mountain to skiers for the entire winter season. In the early years of the Great Depression, more than two hundred housekeeping cabins had been built at Paradise for summer tourists. During the first season of leasing, fifteen cabins were made available, along with nearly forty rooms in Paradise Lodge. Rates were as low as thirty dollars for the whole winter.

A year later, the number of cabins for lease nearly tripled, and the new Paradise Winter Lodge opened with thirty-five more rooms. Virginia Boren wrote in the *Seattle Times* in 1933, "There's dancing in the lobby at night, there's skiing on the side-hills in the gleam of a big searchlight that plays on the snowbanks, giving the whole scene the effect of a tinseled Christmas postcard." In the fall of 1935, the Paradise Inn opened to winter guests after being retrofitted for year-round use. Nearly a hundred cabins were available by then for winter lease. The Park Company advertised overnight accommodations for nine hundred people in Paradise Valley. Writing in the 1934 *Eastern Ski Annual*, Veida Morrow described the lively winter scene:

> A familiar sight was to see people tunneling down into their cabins that had been buried beneath the snow. On one occasion, a party of three, after digging for about an hour, discovered that they had miscounted the mounds, and had tunneled into someone else's cabin. The underground city has become an established thing at Paradise, and by the end of the season there is a network of tunnels about fifteen feet below the surface of the snow, connecting individual cabins, and leading to the main Lodge. Frequently, even the chimneys were buried, and from a distance it was quite a sight during the dinner rush hour, to see tiny spirals of smoke emerging from innumerable mounds of snow, for all the world like a miniature Valley of Ten Thousand Smokes.

Shafts and tunnels became commonplace at Paradise. As Hans Otto Giese recalled, "One inventive skier constructed a high shaft at the entrance of his cabin with ladders on the inside and outside and a tight cover on top so that he would not have to dig a tunnel to his door and shovel snow to clear it."

Such efforts didn't entirely solve the challenges of a Saturday-night arrival. Jane Stoddard Mayer recalled that after one's cabin was reached, "you would tap forever on the stove pipe while your pals pressed their ears to the snow someplace above you until the stove pipe was found and you could build a fire." Tunnels were equipped with "Sceva traps," named for Park Company manager Paul H. Sceva, Mayer remembered, "to warn illegal overnighters should the park management come to check you out. A spy wouldn't be hurt, but could be scared to death by the pots and pans that clattered down over his head."

Canned food was brought up in autumn, when you could still drive to the cabins, and stored for the winter. But, as Joy Lucas recalled, "by the time winter came, four-footed marauders had torn the labels off the cans so it was anyone's guess what you ate for dinner." Although several of the lodges at Paradise prohibited cooking, coffeepots were allowed. "Ah, the many fragrances of coffee that came from those coffee pots!" Lucas remembered fondly. "Sauerkraut and weenies, stew, soup or other pungent odors—all cooked in the coffee pot! The understanding ranger, Bill Butler, turned his head." Mayer remembered less

From 1933 through 1936, housekeeping cabins like these were available for lease throughout the winter season at Paradise. (Mount Rainier National Park Archives)

fondly "the horrible condition of the bathtub in the annex after all the dishes and cooking utensils had been cleaned there over the weekend. Never knew anyone who bathed there."

During the long winter, the Paradise Inn and Paradise Lodge were engulfed by Mount Rainier's massive snowfalls. Lucas remembered climbing in and out of third-floor rooms at the lodge and wondered, "Who ever used the lobby?!" Mayer recalled coils of rope stored inside upper-floor windows to be used as fire escapes. But when a window was opened, "there was only darkness and an air space as the snow went all the way up to the roof." Hugh Bauer, brother of Wolf Bauer and a longtime Paradise skier, recounted a particularly exciting late-night arrival:

> One of the permanent renters wanted [Paul] Gilbreath and me to help dig a tunnel
> to his front door (about twenty feet long and three feet wide). As we got closer and
> closer to the door, we kept hearing more and more strange clattering noises, like

someone throwing dishes and chairs around. We finally got to the door, unlatched it, and turned on our flashlight. At that moment, the door opened outward with a bang, and a brown bear pressed me into the snowdrift as it charged by to get out of there. The inside of the cabin was a mess, but nothing major was broken. It looked more like a picture show robbery where everything was on the floor.

The underground city thrived for four winter seasons. By 1935–36 the park was welcoming sixty thousand visitors in winter. The next fall, the Park Service ruled that housekeeping cabins would be leased only during the early part of the snow season. Once the snow depth exceeded the height of cabin doors and windows, requiring tunnels or shafts, use of the cabins would be suspended due to concerns about fire safety and sanitation. The new rules crowded skiers into other lodgings at Paradise, including the inn, Paradise Lodge, Tatoosh Lodge, Sluiskin Lodge, and Guide House. The road was plowed to Paradise throughout the winter for the first time in 1936–37: no more hiking required. Private cars were still parked at Narada Falls, but a bus delivered skiers to Paradise from there. Skiers began using the bus as a ski shuttle, making the one-and-a-half-mile run from Paradise to Narada several times a day.

The route along the Paradise River took skiers down the notorious Devils Dip. A column in the *Seattle Times* in 1937 prodded, "How about a gentle suggestion to the Rainier National Park Service about that Devil's Dip trail? The Timer's neck crawls every time he spills in the Dip, doubles up into a horrified knot and peers out of the self-imposed huddle to see what straight-running demon is going to ram a ski clear through him. A wider trail might help." Joy Lucas remembered the Dip: "It was a marvelous mess of wild holes and bumps in the trail caused by skiers who did not know how to ski—and fell, and fell, and fell—creating hundreds of bathtubs as no one filled in his holes. There is an old 8-millimeter movie taken during this time, showing the skiers making literally hundreds of falls, piling one on top of another, some even hanging upside down from the tree branches. No, it was not staged. It was just the way it was!" Photographer Ira Spring described Paradise as the "Valley of Ten Thousand Sitzmarks."

Although the closure of the housekeeping cabins ended a unique era in Paradise skiing, the consolidation of lodging enhanced the social scene. New floodlights were erected on the lower slopes of Alta Vista, expanding the opportunity for night skiing. A new dance floor was installed at the Paradise Inn, an orchestra was engaged, and Saturday-night dances were scheduled every week at both the inn and the lodge. With thirty new rooms at the inn and all-season road access, Mount Rainier was touted by Park Company manager Paul

Schussing from the roof of Paradise Inn in the 1930s (Mount Rainier National Park Archives)

H. Sceva as a "complete winter resort." Weekly ski races were organized for both beginners and experts. Ski champion Hjalmar Hvam recalled a memorable afterparty:

> *I had won a race and was invited to celebrate with friends who were staying on the second floor in the lodge. After a few aquavits I thought I had better go to my lodgings in another building, and being a bit befogged I thought I was on the first floor and could put my skis on and ski out. I found myself on the stairs and was under the impression that the stairs would not be slick. I decided to go down. They were wet from skiers' boots, and I really picked up speed, made the turn, and sailed out onto the crowded dance floor. I was so embarrassed, I just looked down at the floor and skied out. Needless to say, I didn't hear the end of that one for quite a while.*

Maurita Shank, queen of the 1937 Tacoma winter carnival at Paradise (University of Washington Libraries, Special Collections)

Winter carnivals were hosted at Paradise each month by Seattle, Tacoma, and Olympia ski boosters, with snow queens, costume parades, obstacle courses, and races. One year the winner of the Paradise costume race was an outhouse, with the door open, Joy Lucas recalled, showing the skier sitting on "the pot" as he skied down the course. "I don't think there was any group of people who ever had more fun," Walt Little recalled wistfully when I spoke with him in 2001. "Lots of people who skied at Paradise before World War II are firm friends still today."

CHASING SILVER

By the winter of 1934, Mount Rainier had nearly everything a skier could ask for—open slopes, deep snow, comfortable lodging, and a lively social scene. But for Hans Otto Giese and a few friends, the mountain lacked one thing: a true skiing spectacle. Giese was a pro-ponent of the alpine disciplines of slalom and downhill racing, having gained knowledge of and enthusiasm for them in Europe. He helped organize the first Pacific Northwest Ski Association slalom race at Snoqualmie Pass in February 1934, two weeks after Seattle Municipal Ski Park opened there. A couple days before the Snoqualmie Pass slalom was held, the *Seattle Post-Intelligencer* announced sponsorship of a "Thrilling Downhill Ski Race" to be staged on Mount Rainier later that spring. Giese was the race's leading booster. The race would run from Camp Muir to Paradise, a distance of about three and a half miles with 4,600 feet of descent.

For two months leading up to the race, the *P-I* pumped up the event, soon dubbed the Silver Ski Championships by the paper. Royal Brougham, an old-school sports writer who didn't worry much about the difference between reporting the news and making it, por-trayed the race like a Kentucky Derby on snow. Three separate races would be held, all ending at 5,500 feet, just above Paradise Inn. All three races would employ a simultaneous start, with the men's, women's, and junior races staggered by twenty to thirty minutes. (See course diagram on page 306.) The men's course would employ just four control gates between the start at Camp Muir and the finish at Paradise. Racers would line up across the slope and begin racing at the sound of a gun. A beautiful trophy was commissioned for the men's race. Fashioned by Norwegian skier and silversmith Carl Zapffe, the solid silver award was nearly two feet tall, with a column supporting two skis outfitted with downhill racing bindings. The skis were detailed down to the buckles on the binding harnesses and the screws fastening them to the skis.

After weeks of newspaper promotion, one hundred racers climbed from Paradise toward the start of the three events on Sunday, April 22, 1934. Sixty men gathered at 10,100-foot

Skier and master silversmith Carl Zapffe created the Silver Skis trophy. (From American Ski Annual, *courtesy New England Ski Museum)*

Camp Muir. The women and juniors converged at 6,500-foot Panorama Point and 7,300-foot McClure Rock, respectively. The weather was ideal, clear with light wind. Racers were worried about soft, sticky snow, so many had worked for days on their skis—not with wax but with shellac. They applied one coat after another on the ski bottoms. They sandpapered it carefully, applied another coat, sandpapered some more, and applied again. Then they rubbed wax over the shellac for the cold snow expected near the top of the course.

At Muir the racers sported a motley assortment of gear. A few chose long, heavy jumping skis for the race. Others nailed lead strips atop their skis for added weight and stability. Some skis had metal edges, but many did not. Racer Emil Cahen wore a football helmet, the only participant with head protection. Friends recalled that he took a lot of kidding for it. As the starting time approached, Otto Sanford raised a red flag high above his head and eyed the official watch in his left hand. At precisely 1:30 p.m., Sanford dropped the flag and someone fired a pistol, sending the men on their way. Spectator Harry Webster, watching from far below, recalled, "It looked like someone had poured a bottle of ink on the snowfield below Camp Muir."

Racer John Woodward remembered that a dry, cold wind had frozen the snow near the start. "It was like little ball bearings of ice," he said. "It's the fastest snow you could ever have. We all got in a crouch, and all of a sudden the wind was screaming and the fronts of the skis are vibrating and sort of flying in the air." Racers faced daunting choices—whether to continue in a deep crouch toward a likely crack-up, attempt to turn with racers hurtling on either side, or stand up to brake using wind resistance. Woodward chose the third option. "I'd never tried it at that speed, so I didn't lean forward far enough, so when I stood up a little too quick, it was like fifteen pillows hit my chest and *boom*. When I stopped tumbling one of my ski tips was gone. Busted clear off."

Other racers remembered similar spills. "I had gone into Spartan training doing deep knee bends during weeks of preparation in order to prevent the cramping effects of a deep crouch position against expected headwinds," all-around mountaineer Wolf Bauer recalled. "The extra speed cost me both poles, goggles, and a broken ski still hanging precariously together with a steel-edge fastening—result of a somersault at near sixty miles per hour." As he remembered, "Most of us had waited too long to check speed and change course because of the traffic on all sides. When checking became imperative, the smooth snow surface suddenly changed to shingled windrows and waves, bringing about a fearsome explosion of cartwheeling humanity. It was not until the race was over that I learned how others behind me had spilled at the same time and place. Somewhat dazed I picked myself up, deciding not to waste time looking for my poles and goggles, and immediately got under way again."

Skiers practice for the geschmozzle start of the 1934 Silver Skis race. Hans Otto Giese is third from the right. (University of Washington Libraries, Special Collections)

Don Fraser avoided the worst. "Fortunately, I was soon out in front of the mob headed for Little Africa," he said, "so I didn't witness the terrible collisions that took place just behind me." One of the most serious involved Ben Thompson, chief climbing guide on Mount Rainier, who collided with another skier who'd cut in front of him. Thompson woke up minutes later with a broken jaw and two teeth knocked out. He walked down from Anvil Rock to the foot of Panorama Point, where he was put on a toboggan and taken to Seattle to have his jaw set. The youngster that Thompson hit suffered torn shoulder ligaments. Another had a broken collarbone.

Fraser stayed near the front of the pack. Near McClure Rock and above Panorama, he recalled, "there were large mounds (like small jumping hills), and one was airborne 100 feet or more on each one. The speed, at this point, was far more than any of us had ever gone before—even on a jumping hill. Tired legs took their toll. Many skis and poles were broken and some god-awful falls took place." Below McClure Rock, Fraser said, "the shellac was clear off my skis and they were sticking. You'd suddenly be thrown forward when you hit sticky spots. I didn't fall, though." At the Panorama Point control gate, Fraser led, followed closely by Carleton Wiegel, then Alf Moystad, Bauer, and Giese.

On the sticky snow below Alta Vista, Fraser and Wiegel were running over the snow, pumping with their ski poles and striding as much as their leather boots would allow. Loudspeakers were set up at Paradise, and sports editor Royal Brougham called the action. "My knees were shaking," Fraser recounted. Wiegel poled frantically to catch up, but fell short at the finish line by about a ski length. Fraser crossed first to win in a time of 10 minutes, 49.6 seconds. Following Wiegel by a few minutes were Moystad, Tom Heard, Bauer, and Giese. Racers continued to arrive for another half hour.

Even the officials were not necessarily safe. Mel Borgersen, who was monitoring the race, somehow got hurt. "I'm sure it was Mel," John Woodward recalled. "The ski patrol was bringing him down in a toboggan. They weren't trained in those days, and they both fell down and the toboggan got away. He's strapped in and it's heading for the top of Edith Creek basin. Right below Panorama, those cliffs there. He was heading right for that and he knew it, so he rocked himself back and forth and finally rocked and turned himself upside down and skidded to a stop, with him underneath the toboggan."

Thirty minutes after the men's start, while a couple of those racers were still on course, the junior race started from McClure Rock. Paul "Sonny" Sceva Jr., son of the Park Company manager, took the lead and held it, finishing in 6 minutes, 7 seconds, with Kjell Qvale nearly a minute behind. Otis Lamson was third. Finally, the woman's race started, after a brief delay because several racers had jumped the gun. Marguerite Strizek won with a time of 3 minutes, 9 seconds. Racing on a previously injured leg, Strizek ran most of the course in a telemark position, with her left leg bent beneath her and the right leg extended forward. Grace Carter came in second, and Ellis-Ayr Smith finished third.

Racer Ed Newell noted that the lead skier in the men's race had covered the first two miles of the course from a standing start in just 1 minute, 57 seconds. Wendell Trosper, who guided on Mount Rainier during the 1930s and finished near the middle of the pack, remembered, "We picked up things all summer on Muir Glacier—knives, a few coins, bits of cloth, straps, parts of bindings and ski wood (in splinters), and parts of metal edges. I imagine there is still a certain amount of debris that is still there." Indeed, during the summer of 2007, Mount Rainier guide Seth Waterfall found a broken and splintered ski tip high on the Muir Snowfield. The ski was of unlaminated wood,

Marguerite Strizek, 1934 Silver Skis women's champion (Museum of History and Industry, Seattle P-I collection)

without metal edges, with shellac residue still clinging to the base. Seth gave the ski tip to me, and it is now held in The Mountaineers' archives in Seattle.

Nearly three thousand spectators witnessed the 1934 race. The *Seattle Times* reported the next day: "On the steep ski course from high Camp Muir to warmer Paradise today were tracks—scores of tracks; a broken ski tip here and there; holes dug by spilling skiers; control flags still marking a stretch of ski terrain where yesterday was run as astounding a ski race as America ever saw."

THE US NATIONAL ALPINE CHAMPIONSHIPS

The Silver Skis race became an annual event. In the spring of 1935, the Washington Ski Club hosted the first US National Alpine Championships on Mount Rainier. The championships doubled as tryouts for the 1936 US Olympic team, which would compete in the first Winter Olympic Games to include downhill, slalom, and women's ski races. The winners of the men's and women's downhill races on Mount Rainier would also be dubbed the Silver Skis champions. The event was open to both American and international competitors, and to the surprise of many, the Austrian Ski Federation sent Hannes Schroll, a top European skier, to participate. Although he was not eligible for the US Olympic team, Schroll was allowed to compete for the national championship title.

The Dartmouth ski team from New Hampshire arrived with their coach, Otto Schniebs. During informal competition before the championships, Dartmouth racer Dick Durrance impressed Northwest skiers with his brilliant skiing. He had attended school in Germany, had raced in the Alps, and was the best American alpine skier of the time. Two days before the Mount Rainier downhill, several of the Northwest's best skiers, including Don Fraser and Carleton Wiegel, were injured in practice runs. It was speculated that they were overstretching their limits trying to emulate Schroll's aggressive skiing style.

Hannes Schroll runs the slalom in the 1935 US National Alpine Championships. (Mount Rainier National Park Archives)

The men's downhill was held on April 13, starting at Sugar Loaf and ending in Edith Creek basin. The women raced first on a shorter course, and Ellis-Ayr Smith won by 30 seconds over second-place finisher Grace Carter. The *Tacoma Ledger* reported that "most of her competitors were somersaulting five to fifteen times in their do-or-die races against time." In the men's downhill, Schroll won handily, overtaking five racers who had started ahead of him at one-minute intervals. Durrance placed second, over a minute behind Schroll. John Woodward, who finished eleventh in the downhill, was impressed by Schroll's run. "At Edith Creek basin," he recalled, Schroll "was going so fast, had enough speed up, he took off in the air and . . . took his Tyrolean hat off and yodeled and threw his hat back on, right in the middle of the race."

Remembering the course, Woodward said "that was a tough hill. Near the finish line you could see where people tried to turn to make the finish gate and spilled. So I thought, 'Turn as little as you can and just don't push too much on that outside ski, trying to get through.' So I got right down near the finish. It was coming up right there and I thought, 'Now you've got it.' Then I pushed hard and it flipped me. I did about two somersaults and landed up against the finish post. 'Throw your skis across!' they shouted. So I threw my skis across and they said, 'You're in.'"

Schroll was awarded the Silver Skis for his downhill victory. The following day brought fine weather and an estimated seven thousand people to Paradise to watch the slalom events. Ellis-Ayr Smith's younger sister Ethlynne (known as "Skit") won the women's slalom, with Grace Carter finishing second. Schroll dominated the men's slalom, with Robert Livermore of Boston taking second. Schroll was named the US National Champion for the men and Ellis-Ayr Smith was the women's champion.

LATER RACES

For the 1936 Silver Skis, the starting point of the men's race was returned to Camp Muir. The simultaneous (or *geschmozzle*) start was abandoned, never to be used again. The finish line was moved up to Edith Creek basin at around 5,700 feet to minimize sticky snow near the end of the race. Hannes Schroll, now working as a ski instructor in California, foreran the course but was not allowed to compete, since he was no longer an amateur. Hjalmar Hvam won the men's race despite a crash near the hard-left turn below Panorama Point.

"There was a whole row of flags—right there in front of me," Hvam recalled. "People had gathered to stand on that shelf. To the right was an outcrop of rocks. I was going too fast to turn, so I put my hands in front [and yelled], 'Gimme way, gimme way!'" The spectators cleared out, "but there was a little bump I hadn't figured on. I broke through that bump and somersaulted right in front of them. I yelled back, 'Did I hit anybody?'" Luckily he hadn't, so

Don Fraser, men's champion, and Gretchen Kunigk, women's champion, after the 1938 Silver Skis race (Museum of History and Industry, *Seattle P-I* collection)

"I got up and kept skiing." Despite losing at least 10 seconds in the tumble, Hvam won with a time of 5 minutes, 38 seconds, just 4 seconds behind Schroll's forerunning pace. Peggy Harlin of Vancouver, British Columbia, won the women's race that year.

The Pacific Northwest Ski Association sanctioned an open race for the Silver Skis in 1937. This enabled both amateurs and professionals to compete, but the event was cancelled due to bad weather. The following year brought Schroll back as a competitor, and with him came controversy. Snow and weather conditions in 1938 were variable and challenging. Following a run in what he thought was an unbeatable time, Schroll declared, "I would give ten bottles of champagne . . . *good* champagne . . . to the man who comes down there faster than me. Why, I am flying!"

Don Fraser beat Schroll's time by 3.1 seconds, despite a spill near Panorama Point. Upset, Schroll couldn't believe he'd been beaten. His countryman Otto Lang, who operated the ski school at Paradise at the time, offered an explanation. Lang and Fraser had worked on Fraser's skis for hours, waxing them thoroughly for the race. "Hannes waited until he got to Camp Muir to put on his wax," Lang explained. "He couldn't wax properly there, it was so cold. . . . He ran a beautiful race. He didn't fall. But he didn't go as fast as Don, who had a fall at the top of Panorama, but who had faster wax."

The 1938 women's race was won by nineteen-year-old Gretchen Kunigk, whom Lang had tutored since arriving in the Northwest the previous winter. Through Lang, Kunigk had landed a role as the skiing double for Sonja Henie in the 1937 Hollywood film *Thin Ice*. Kunigk got to know Fraser through their skiing experiences, and the two were married in 1939.

Austria-born Peter Radacher, a Sun Valley ski instructor, won the 1939 race with a record time of 4 minutes, 51.4 seconds from Camp Muir to Edith Creek basin. Nine racers broke the previous course record set by Schroll in 1936. Dorothy Hoyt won the women's race, which started near McClure Rock (see Appendix for a complete list of Silver Skis winners during 1934–48).

EXPERIENCING GESCHMOZZLE

Any skier who is familiar with Mount Rainier and aware of the Silver Skis race wonders what it was like to schuss from Camp Muir to Paradise with sixty other skiers in 1934. After reading many accounts of the race and talking to several of the original racers, I wanted to do more than just imagine the race. I wanted to experience it.

In the spring of 2005, I posted a note on the Turns All Year (TAY) website looking for like-minded backcountry skiers to stage a reenactment of the race. I guessed that a formally organized race would not be welcomed by the Park Service, and I didn't want to focus too much on competition. Fortunately, several TAY respondents were receptive to the idea and seemed to share my attitude. On May 1 we skinned to Camp Muir under blue skies for our agreed-upon 1:00 p.m. starting time. The participants were a diverse lot, from twentysomethings eager to go all-out to fortysomethings wondering if this was a smart thing to do after a poor snow year with little skiing under their legs. We were bound by curiosity and a shared admiration for the pioneers whose tracks we hoped to follow.

Tightening our boots at the Camp Muir shelter, we traded excuses. "I've hardly been downhill skiing at all this season," said one. "I don't know if I can even ski this without stopping, let alone race it," said another. With butterflies swirling, we spaced ourselves across the snowfield below the shelter and gave a final wave to the camera. "Geschmoz-zle!" we cheered. The starter shouted, "Fifteen seconds!" and began counting down at ten. Adrenaline surged through the group. Finally, a shout of "three, two, one, *bang!*" and seventeen pairs of skis (plus one snowboard) hit the fall line.

Earth jerked into motion as I began my plunge. Blurred figures accelerated both left and right of me. With the Muir Snowfield rushing toward me and a line of racers surrounding me, I felt like I was riding an avalanche or surfing a human wave. I tried to imagine what it was like in 1934, with more than sixty skiers starting in a line. Out of the corner of my eye, I saw climbers on the hiking trail suddenly look up, as if to mouth, "What on earth . . . ?"

I was using light touring skis, a far cry from the heavy eight-foot-long jumping skis some of the racers had used in 1934. I stood up tall and let the wind slow me down a bit. Ahead, the gung-ho skiers pulled away in racing tucks. Some made it from Camp Muir to Pebble Creek, almost 3,000 feet below, without a single turn. The snow could hardly have been better—soft and cushiony but not sticky. I straight-lined the slope longer than I had expected to, then began weaving gently back and forth, watching out for skiers doing the same thing on either side of me. My thighs burned and I tried to stretch and relax my legs between turns. Anvil Rock swept by, and soon McClure Rock was gone. Near Pebble Creek I passed a colorful wreck without recognizing what it was. I later learned that my brother Carl had flown off a wind-formed ridge, nearly landing on Jason Hummel—they had both crashed. Carl took several minutes to collect himself, but Jason was soon under way again.

At Panorama Point we took different routes through the rock-studded thin snow. A few of the leaders made wrong turns here, enabling those of us who actually turned on the upper snowfield to catch up. Near Alta Vista, I snuck up on Jason and his twin brother, Josh, on the boot-packed trail—old age and treachery nearly (but not quite) overcoming youth and strength. We poled furiously, seesawing our positions as we alternately hit slippery and sticky spots. We reached the parking lot within feet of each other, the Hummel twins just ahead of me and Bill Frans just behind. Matt Kuharic and Jan Kordel were already there, and over the next twenty to thirty minutes the rest of the crew trickled in. Everyone was safe and sound, and everyone finished with a smile.

With all the excitement, I had forgotten to run my stopwatch. Jan timed himself at 9 minutes, 15 seconds and estimated that Matt, who arrived first, made the run in about 8 minutes, 30 seconds. Bill said that he, I, and the Hummel twins finished at around 10 minutes, 40 seconds. I was thrilled to have skied as fast as Don Fraser, the 1934 Silver Skis winner, who'd done it in 10 minutes, 49.6 seconds, but humbled thinking of his feat in much tougher conditions, with much more primitive gear.

We lingered at the edge of the parking lot, laughing and sharing stories. A visitor from Chicago took a group picture—and like a saint patiently repeated the process with the dozen cameras we pushed in front of him. Finally we drove out of the park and stopped for dinner near Ashford. Before we finished eating, it started to rain hard—the perfect ending to a day that had fulfilled one of my oldest skiing daydreams.

MASTERING GRAVITY: THE EMERGENCE OF INSTRUCTION

Early skiing in the Northwest was mostly associated with local outdoor clubs. The Mountaineers, the Soyps, the Mount Baker Ski Club, the Cle Elum Ski Club, the Mount Hood Ski Club, and others offered skiers the opportunity to learn from each other, often at lodges

Otto Lang greets skiers upon his arrival at Mount Rainier for the winter of 1936–37. He was welcomed by Park Superintendent O. A. Tomlinson (left), Park Company manager Paul H. Sceva (center), and instructor Ken Syverson (right, on skis). (Courtesy Crystal Mountain Alpine Inn)

built for club members. The emergence of skiing on Mount Rainier began to change this pattern. There was no "club hill" at Paradise, and in the 1930s more skiers were trying the sport without going through a club apprenticeship. The opportunity emerged for independent ski teachers to play a role.

Swiss-certified instructor Hans Thorner came to the United States in 1933 and was teaching skiing at Lake Placid, New York, when he saw a picture of Mount Rainier in the rotogravure section of the *New York Times*. He inquired by telegram to the Rainier National Park Company and landed a job as winter sports director. After he moved west with his wife, Florence, during the 1934–35 season, the mountain had a dedicated ski instructor for the first time. "When we arrived at Paradise Valley," Thorner recalled, "there must have been a ten-foot base of snow, at least. A tremendous mountain that looked as good and as promising to me as the Jungfrau. I was thrilled. This was my kind of mountain. It was beautiful. And from Monday to Friday it was all ours! We were all alone! On weekends there was some activity but, my God, I had seen more ski traffic at midnight in the cemetery of my hometown. The ski lessons were practically nonexistent. We starved!"

Thorner was at Paradise during the US National Alpine Championships in 1935 and his wife, Florence, competed in the women's events. The couple moved away the following year, and local skier Ken Syverson took over as the Rainier Park Company's ski instructor. When the Pacific Northwest Ski Association began certifying instructors in 1939, Syverson earned badge number 1, and he continued to teach for decades thereafter. But the world's best-known ski instructor in the early 1930s was Hannes Schneider of Austria, who came to America in December 1935 to teach skiing in New Hampshire. Schneider had written several books, including *The Wonders of Skiing*, published in 1933. The book described equipment and technique with hundreds of photographs showing every maneuver of the Arlberg ski progression. Working with filmmaker Arnold Fanck, Schneider was also the star of several groundbreaking ski movies, including *The Chase* (1921) and *White Ecstasy* (1931).

Otto Lang was an assistant to Hannes Schneider. In 1935, Lang published his own instructional book, *Downhill Skiing*, and in the spring of 1936 he traveled west with Jerome Hill, grandson of James J. Hill, the Great Northern Railway "Empire Builder," to make a film of the Arlberg ski technique called *Ski Flight*. The film, shot at Mount Baker and Mount Rainier, premiered at New York's Radio City Music Hall alongside Walt Disney's *Snow White and the Seven Dwarfs* in 1938. Lang had witnessed the excitement of the 1936 Silver Skis race on Mount Rainier, won by Hjalmar Hvam. Impressed by the mountains of the Northwest, he decided to move to Washington, and in the winter of 1936–37 he opened

Chauncey Griggs rides the Paradise rope tow in the 1930s. (Tacoma Public Library)

Hannes Schneider ski schools at Mount Rainier and Mount Baker. At Paradise, Ken Syverson became Lang's assistant, while at Mount Baker Lang had help from Millette O'Connell. A single-day lesson at Paradise cost a dollar and a half, and for a weekend lesson, with Saturday-night instruction under the floodlights and Sunday daytime instruction, the fee was two dollars and fifty cents.

AHOY SKIERS!

In January 1934, three days before the *Seattle P-I* announced the "thrilling downhill ski race" that would become the Silver Skis, the paper published a tiny notice in its sports section under the headline "Ahoy Skiers! Read This!" The first rope tow in the United States had opened that week, at Gilbert's Hill near Woodstock, Vermont.

"The device consists of an endless rope," wrote the *P-I*, "which runs over a guide pulley at the top of the hill and over a motor at the foot of the incline. It takes skiers up 900 feet in one minute. The fun in skiing is in going down the hill, thought the engineer, so he eliminated the climbing up." Rope tows didn't appear in the Northwest right away, and for two years the only uphill lift was the barge-like "ski escalator" that operated at Mount Baker in 1936 and 1937.

Rope tows popped up at most of the popular ski areas after Jim Parker moved to the Northwest in 1937. Parker had experience with rope tows in the east and enlisted the financial acumen of Chauncey Griggs to form Ski Lifts Inc. in Tacoma. Their goal was to install rope tows at Paradise, Snoqualmie Pass, and Mount Baker. David Hellyer, a renaissance man with interests ranging from skiing to medicine to wildlife conservation, became the group's operating partner.

Hellyer worked in 1937 to build the Paradise rope tow, setting poles, constructing the engine house, devising safety gates, and figuring out how to manage the system that Parker had designed to adjust the tow for huge changes in snow depth during the season. The tow was powered by a Ford V-8 engine and capable of hauling 250 skiers per hour. The lift fee was ten cents a ride or a dollar a day. Because it was in a national park, the tow, including the engine house, had to be removed in spring when the snow melted.

Walt Little recalled that the Paradise rope tow ran pretty loose and dragged in the snow. It had a manila rope with some kind of waterproofing in it. "It was supposed to be water-proof," he remembered, "but as the rope got wet—it was always wet—it dripped water and waterproofing on your pants. You could tell anybody who'd ridden on the Paradise rope tow because they had this big patch of waterproofing and goo on their pants. No kind of cleaning would ever take it out."

The Snoqualmie Pass rope tow was similar in design to the one at Paradise. The Mount Baker tow was a more challenging design. The most popular run at Mount Baker, below Panorama Dome, ran onto a small lake. The tow's bottom tower was mounted on a raft in the lake, which became frozen in place during autumn. The engine house was at the top of the lift, and blasting was necessary to clear its foundation and set poles in the hard rock of the area.

During a work party before all the poles were set, Hellyer and two helpers arrived on a rainy evening and settled into a Forest Service cabin. They unloaded their gear, started a fire in the cabin's wood-burning cookstove, and prepared dinner. Not long after they closed the firebox door (which should have sent all the smoke up the chimney), Hellyer noticed an odd smell of charred wood coming from the stove. He opened the oven door. "There," he recalled, "with wooden sides blackening and smoldering, was our nearly full case of dynamite sticks, caps, and wire that someone had either hidden there or stored there to keep dry. We looked at one another with horror."

Hellyer piled the group's sleeping bags on the floor as a cushion, grabbed a fireplace poker, and carefully slid the box out of the stove until it plopped onto the sleeping bags with a thud. Then the men doused the box (and sleeping bags) with water and rushed out into the night. Peering around the cabin door a few minutes later, as Hellyer later recalled, "[we] poured ourselves huge rations of bourbon and collapsed cursing the perpetrator of this insanity." Jim Parker later acknowledged that he should have left the men a note so they would have no trouble finding the dynamite when they needed it.

Otto Lang teaches a young student at Timberline Lodge on Mount Hood. (Otto Lang collection, courtesy John Forsen)

THE UP-SKI REVOLUTION

During the winter of 1937–38, Don Adams and Bruce Kehr installed a rope tow at Stevens Pass, around the same time the Forest Service and Civilian Conservation Corps were completing a $10,000 ski hut there. The hut burned down, but the tow and ski area flourished, despite unreliable plowing of the highway from Berne. A writer in *Western Skier* magazine described five hours of trailbreaking along the road that was rewarded by just two hours of fun on the rope tow. Nonetheless, the skier returned home with "a strong desire to get back there."

At Hyak, near the east portal of the Snoqualmie Pass tunnel, the Chicago, Milwaukee, St. Paul, and Pacific Railroad opened the Snoqualmie Ski Bowl (later renamed the Milwaukee Ski Bowl). The railroad built a lodge and a 1,400-foot rope tow. The ski bowl offered an experience, unique in the Northwest, of riding to the ski slopes on a train scheduled expressly for that purpose. A train on Saturday was reserved for Seattle high school students and sponsored by the Parent Teacher Association. Two trains on Sundays were open to the general public.

During his second season in the Northwest, Otto Lang opened another ski school, on Mount Hood. The school was at timberline, where the Works Progress Administration

(WPA) was busy finishing construction of Timberline Lodge. The lodge was a museum for the work of Oregon's artisans, with carved wood furnishings, wrought-iron detailing, hand-woven draperies, and tile murals. Timberline Lodge was dedicated by President Franklin D. Roosevelt in September 1937 and opened to the public on February 5, 1938. The Mount Hood ski patrol, the nation's first organized volunteer patrol, was also formed that year. A rope tow was built at Government Camp during that winter, and a portable tow was installed at Timberline the following year. In the spring of 1939, the US National Alpine Championships and Olympic Team Tryouts were held on Mount Hood with 125 racers competing. The selected team never competed due to the outbreak of World War II.

In the Olympic Mountains, the Forest Service built a ski lodge at Deer Park in 1937. Deer Park became the principal ski area in the Olympics before World War II, and a rope tow was installed during the winter of 1939.

A highway had been completed in 1938 to Spirit Lake at the foot of Mount St. Helens. Around the same time, the Longview Ski Club constructed a cabin to accommodate thirty people near timberline on the north side of the mountain, below the Forsyth Glacier. During winter, club members hiked several miles to the cabin from the end of the plowed road near Spirit Lake. They built their own rope tow using donated rope and a Briggs and Stratton engine purchased by club members. The engine was kept in a shed and the tow was set up each weekend before club members arrived. The cabin was used every winter until 1980, when it was destroyed in the eruption of Mount St. Helens.

Otto Lang taught skiing in the Northwest for a third and final winter in 1938–39. The 1937–38 season on Mount Rainier saw eighty-three thousand visitors pass through the Nisqually entrance to the park between December and May. Boosters predicted one hundred thousand skiers in 1938–39. The November 1938 issue of *Ski Illustrated* looked forward to a banner year and predicted that Otto Lang, recently married, would soon be sounding the familiar cry, "Ze clawss will meet in front of ze Inn wiz in a few moments!"

Opposite: Ed Kikendall drives a dogsled to the Azurite Mine during the 1930s. (Shafer Historical Museum)

CHAPTER 7

THE LAST MOUNTAIN MEN

As skiing for recreation spread along both sides of the Cascades, there were places in the mountains where men and women continued to experience winter in more traditional ways. Earning a living or just getting by dominated the concerns in many communities, particularly east of the Cascade divide. This was especially true in the Okanogan Mountains near the US-Canada border. One of the most remote and rugged mining areas in the Northwest is the Slate Creek region, 30 miles northwest of Winthrop, Washington. Prospecting in the area began in the 1870s, and by the 1890s the small town of Barron had grown up around gold claims between Slate Creek and 6,257-foot Windy Pass.

New Light Mine buildings above Barron in the mountains north of Harts Pass (Photo by Mel Gourlie)

In 1895, Colonel Thomas Hart hired Charles Ballard to survey and build a road from the Methow River to Barron over what became known as Harts Pass (6,198 feet). The finished road was just three feet wide. One portion of the road was built across a cliff on wooden platforms supported by steel rods driven into a rock wall 1,000 feet above the valley floor. Around 1900, Frank Willis was leading a pack train over this section. A young boy followed at the back of the line. Ahead of the boy was a colt carrying a light load—one loosely tied steel washtub. The colt paused for some reason, and the boy threw a rock at the animal to get it moving. The rock missed the colt but hit the tub with a loud bang. The colt bolted up the trail, wedging between the other horses and the rock wall. As the panicked colt pushed his way through, the packhorses peeled off into space one by one. Though the road was improved by the CCC in the 1930s, Deadhorse Point remains to this day an unsettling place to drive, walk, or ski.

In 1915, Ballard filed claims in Mill Creek, one valley west of Slate Creek over 6,000-foot Cady Pass. He formed the Azurite Copper Company, later reorganized as the Azurite Gold Company after Ballard found that the primary metal in the vein was not copper but gold. In 1930 the company improved the road from Lost River to Slate Creek and constructed a crude road over Cady Pass to the mine site. The road was restricted to low-geared narrow vehicles and was passable for only five to six months a year.

In 1934 the American Smelting and Refining Company (ASARCO) leased the claims and agreed to share profits with Ballard. During that summer, equipment was installed, supplies were shipped in to sustain operations through the winter, and mine buildings were constructed near the foot of Majestic Mountain. The buildings were designed with sloping roofs to allow avalanches to pass over them without damage. Some of the men were joined by their wives during the summer, but by the end of October, as snow began piling up at the mine, the women were sent home, grudgingly, to the valley below.

The year 1935 was a huge snow year, and although the mine was occupied, production was delayed. Writing to his wife on January 31, superintendent Ray Walters described his experience:

> *Dearest Jessie:*
> *I am ready to believe some of the stories they told about winter in the Azurite. As one of our old timers said, "If any of you boys are alive the first of March, you will know I was telling the truth about the weather here."*

View of the Azurite mine camp (looking west) from near the mill in 1936 or 1937 (R. B. Austin photo courtesy Okanogan County Historical Society)

We had a long cold spell, 29 below and froze our water pipe up and we have to carry our water from the creek uphill through the deep snow. We nearly froze to death and I put my boots and pants under the bed clothes to keep them from freezing stiff.

It turned warm and started to snow. I never saw anything like it—seven feet fell in two days. It then started to rain and poured down for three days. The old snow was packed hard and conditions were just right for snowslides. They started at once and hell was popping for five days. There was hardly a five-minute interval that you couldn't see a slide running in the daytime or hear one roar at night. Some of the big ones filled the air with snow so you could hardly see. Little slides ran between and against the camp buildings and bigger ones stopped just a few feet above them. Some of the boys got panicky and went to the tunnel and root house to sleep.

Our mine building was demolished and had to be dug out and rebuilt. Another building we are not using was knocked down. The roof on our sawmill caved in from snow load.

Charley Graves, the cook's helper at the mine, stepped out of the kitchen to fetch water one evening and was buried in a slide. He later recalled the experience:

I had just stooped down, filled the buckets, and straightened up when—whoosh— here it came.

It came in solid to up around my waist—I couldn't move my legs at all. Around my chest and overhead it wasn't quite so dense. I managed to claw it away from my face a little. I could still breathe, what little air there was to breathe. I yelled, but it was like hollering into a pillow.

Scared? I was away past that. I knew that if they didn't come and dig me out of there right away, I was through. All I could do was wait. It was pitch black and I began to get a little groggy for lack of air. I had a big cud of tobacco but no place to spit.

Men at the mine kept track of each other, and Graves was missed almost immediately. The crew grabbed shovels kept handy for just such an emergency and began digging out the path to the spring. Twenty-two minutes after the slide came down, the rescue party found Graves. "It seemed I was there an hour when I suddenly saw it was getting light above my head," he recalled. "I hollered but wasn't heard, and the next thing I knew a shovel hit me

Ed Kikendall assembles his dog team outside one of the Azurite Mine buildings. (R. B. Austin photo courtesy Okanogan County Historical Society)

on the right thigh. They sliced the snow away and I fell out sideways." Graves still had the cud of tobacco in his mouth and spat enormously before thanking his friends. The next morning, he was back at work.

Four deaths occurred in the Harts Pass–Slate Creek region that winter, though none of the lost were Azurite workers. Near Barron, a man was buried by an avalanche while going to fetch water. On the south side of Harts Pass, two CCC boys were buried in a cabin they were using while trapping. An eighty-year-old prospector named Johnny Young died after his cabin near the mouth of Mill Creek was crushed by a snowslide. Young survived the slide but collapsed in the snow while trying to reach another cabin one and a half miles away.

During the summer of 1935, the road to the Azurite Mine was widened to accommodate small automobiles. Tunneling and other work continued, and in the fall of 1936, ASARCO put the mine into production. The company hired Stonebreaker Brothers of Orofino, Idaho, to supply the mine. Stonebreaker in turn hired Charles and Ed Kikendall of Winthrop to transport supplies in winter by dogsled. The Kikendalls made weekly trips to the

"MEN AND DOGS WIN DEATH RACE"

In January 1937, Fred White, a twenty-five-year-old shift boss at the Azurite mill and son of the manager of the ASARCO smelter in Tacoma, was stricken by appendicitis. This began a race against time, as Dr. E. P. Murdock of Okanogan, Washington, was transported to the mine by dogsled, equipped with a complete surgical kit and drugs. After assessing his patient and the conditions on-site, Murdock decided that performing the surgery at the mine was too risky. His decision was supported by White's father, who urged that the surgery be performed at a hospital rather than at the mine.

The drama played out for week. White was given opiates to fight the pain, then wrapped like a mummy in blankets and lashed to a dogsled layered with a hundred pounds of hot bricks. As White steeled himself for the ride out to the Okanogan hospital, he said, "I'll be glad to get there. This waiting and waiting and never knowing what's going to happen next is worse than the pain. Everything is under control now though, I guess."

On January 21 the front page of the *Wenatchee World* declared, "MEN AND DOGS WIN DEATH RACE." The dogsled had taken nearly twelve hours to travel over Azurite Pass to the road at Robinson Creek. This was followed by a six-mile ride by horse-drawn sleigh to a waiting ambulance at the town of Mazama. White reached the hospital in Okanogan about seventeen hours after leaving the mine. He was thought to have an even chance of surviving the surgery.

The following day, the Wenatchee paper reported grim news. Despite the best efforts of his rescuers, White had died a few hours after the operation was completed. His father made arrangements to return his son's body to Tacoma for a funeral.

Two other men at the Azurite Mine, Howard James and Chris Weppler, fell ill that winter with symptoms similar to Fred White's. The race to transport Weppler out by dogsled stretched mushers Charles and Ed Kikendall to their physical limits. "It was the nearest I ever was to absolute exhaustion," Ed recalled. "I slept for two days and nights before waking up. The mailman came by, saw Chuck and I asleep and determined that we indeed were not dead or anything. So he just fed the dogs for us and let us sleep." Both James and Weppler survived their ordeals.

mine either by the snow-covered road over Harts Pass and Cady Pass or by a winter route over Azurite Pass. The latter route went along the West Fork Methow River, up a steep headwall to Azurite Pass, then three and a half miles down Mill Creek to the mine. Wash Vanderpool, one of the mine workers, once skied from the pass to the mine in just eight and a half minutes.

The Kikendalls preferred the Azurite Pass route because it was shorter, had only one pass to cross, and avoided the hazards of Deadhorse Point. But after the south-facing slope below Azurite Pass melted out in March, the mushers and dog teams switched to the Harts Pass–Cady Pass route. When that route started to melt out, the men and dogs carried freight on their backs over stretches where the sleds could not be used. Richard R. Smith, one of the Azur-

The Gourlie family cabin near Windy Pass in the 1930s (Photo by Mel Gourlie)

ite miners, recalled, "If it was clear and cold you could hear the sled dogs barking for hours before they arrived. Their noise was a welcome sound. One never knew, maybe someone loved you enough to send you an epistle of warmth and tenderness." In good conditions, the trip by dogsled could be done in a single long day, but an overnight stop along the way was not unusual. Between those weekly trips, communication with the mine was only by short-wave radio.

SOME SACRED PLACE

The old mining town of Barron was abandoned in 1907. Later, a few prospectors continued to high grade for gold in the old claims. In 1920 Leon and Florence Gourlie had a son, Mel, in the tiny northeastern Washington town of Orient. When Mel was in grade school, the family moved to an apartment in Wenatchee and began spending summers in the mountains near Barron.

Mel Gourlie displays a silver fox caught in one of his traps.
(Photo by Mel Gourlie)

The Gourlies had little money. "We three seemed to own nothing from my point of view," said Mel, "except for what clothes we wore and the very few necessities needed to keep a person going from day to day." The family lived in a tent near Barron over several summers in the 1930s, trapping and high grading in nearby prospect holes. They returned to Wenatchee in autumn, where Leon looked for short-term jobs and Mel attended school and sold newspapers to buy day-old bread and sandwich spread.

Around 1935 the New Light Mine reopened to work the "glory hole" that the Gourlies had been exploring near Barron. Mel and his father got jobs with the mine. That summer, Leon proposed that the family build a cabin about a mile from the reopened mine, near Windy Pass. This enabled the Gour-lies to live year-round in the area, and Leon took a job as winter caretaker of the New Light buildings and equipment. The cabin was tiny, just over 12 feet square, with walls of spruce logs and crossbeams and rafters of tamarack. They scrounged lumber and sheet metal for the roof from an old mill house nearby. There were two windows, a fifteen-gallon barrel stove for heat, and a small cookstove for baking. After the mine workers left the area in early September, the family was alone again. "It was a strange feeling to me," Mel wrote, "knowing that in a short time we would be snowed in on Windy Pass and that our activities would be controlled mostly by the weather."

Since the Gourlies had no money to buy skis or snowshoes, they made their own snow-shoes from spruce limbs and strips of deer hide. "They didn't look so good," Mel remem-bered, "but they sure kept our buns out of the deep snow when they were needed." For skis, they scrounged floorboards from old mine buildings, shaped them with an axe, then steamed the tips in a tub of boiling water and bent them over a rafter in their cabin. They had to re-bend the tips a couple times a winter because the skis would gradually lose their shape. For bindings, they took belts from old mine equipment and tacked them on the sides of the skis. They didn't have ski boots, just work boots. They made half-length climbers out of deerskin that extended from under the foot to the tail of the ski. The long hairs on the deer hides were trimmed to grip the snow while climbing. They taught themselves to ski, sitting on a single five-foot tamarack pole to control their speed on steep slopes. For turns in soft snow, they did telemarks. They never read any books about how to ski.

The Gourlies had a 15-mile trapline from their cabin up the West Fork Pasayten River toward the Canadian border. They trapped pine marten, ermine, fox, and anything else they could catch. They would ski over Windy Pass and down the Pasayten periodically during the winter to check their traps. They'd dig a snow hole, build a fire, and spend the night out during those trips. Mel later wrote about the animals they trapped: "I felt sorry for them, really I did, but it was either they live or us. There were lots of them and only one of Mom, Dad, and I."

Once or twice a month, Mel would ski 18 miles out to Lost River where the road was plowed. He'd leave at 10:00 p.m. by moonlight if possible or by flashlight when necessary. Hitching a ride with the mail carrier, he'd travel to Winthrop to buy fresh vegetables and pick up lessons for a radio and electronics correspondence course he was taking. The return trip was grueling, with 12 miles of uphill skiing. Mel recalled crossing Deadhorse Point carrying his skis over his shoulder and using a hand axe to chop steps in the snow.

"Looking back on it," Mel said, "I realize how lucky we were, miles and miles from civilization, no one to call on for help if we needed it. We could have broken a leg, fell in the Pasayten River while crossing, or frozen while camping overnight in the snow. We had no sleeping bags, just the garments we had on." Yet the mountains around their cabin left an impression more lasting than the hardships they faced. "It made me feel as if I was intruding on some sacred place," Mel recalled, "and yet I wanted to be here and enjoy all of this. It was meant to be seen by someone; why not Mom, Dad, and I along with our faithful dog."

In late January 1940, Florence awoke one morning with terrible pains in her side. For three days, the pain grew steadily worse. "We decided that I should ski out and get help," Mel recalled. "There was a Mr. Kikendall in Winthrop who had a dog team and sled. Our two dogs and sled wasn't big enough, so out I went." Mel's parents left the cabin on skis a few hours later. "My ski tracks made it easier for them to travel." Florence took it as easy as she could, moving slowly to reduce the pain and stopping frequently to rest. She and Leon

Mel Gourlie (left) and William A. "Bill" Long pause on skis on the shoulder of Tamarack Peak in December 1940. (Photo by Mel Gourlie)

skied 11 miles in eleven hours, encountering a half dozen snowslides that had crossed the trail since Mel had passed through. About five miles from the end of the trail, they were met by Mel with Ed Kikendall and his sled dogs. Florence was loaded onto the sled and rushed to Deaconess Hospital in Wenatchee, where she underwent gallstone surgery. The *Wenatchee World* later reported, "She Skis to Scalpel" and published photos of Florence resting after her surgery. Doctors said that if she'd arrived twenty-four hours later, she wouldn't be recovering.

The Gourlies weren't always alone at their Windy Pass cabin. In December 1940, Mel's school friend Bill Long visited the family for three weeks before Christmas. Bill and Mel explored the area together, visiting nearby mines and basins, skiing powder snow from the summit of Tamarack Peak. Long later wrote that this experience had the greatest influence on his life, other than being in combat during World War II. He taught high school science and math and worked summers for the US Forest Service as a geologist. Longs Pass near Mount Stuart in central Washington is named for him.

Many years later, I met Mel Gourlie at his home in Wenatchee, almost by accident. The day was September 11, 2001. I'd made an appointment to meet Bill Long's widow,

Kathleen, after finding a photo by Bill of skiing on Tamarack Peak in a 1940 edition of the *Wenatchee World*. I arrived to find Kathleen glued to the television, as images of the burning Twin Towers in New York City filled the screen. During that visit, Kathleen suggested that I meet Mel Gourlie, and she called him to introduce us. I drove across town that very afternoon and had a short but memorable conversation with Mel. Later I returned to copy some of his photographs and journals. His stories were written in longhand. Despite never finishing high school, Mel had the most perfect penmanship I have ever seen.

Following his father's death in 1975, Mel felt that the last link to the experience he shared with his parents had been broken. "There would be no one to talk over the many hardships, happy times, trips together, et cetera, during our years in the hills," he wrote in his memoir, "just me now and some old photographs. Soon we will be gone and forgotten just like all the ones before us. Until then, all I can do is tell the kids and grandchildren some of the tales of what happened way back when, just like all the grandparents do, and hope that the stories will be remembered for a few years to come. What fun we had together, searching for our pot of gold, yet never finding it."

THE BEAR AND THE BADGER

A lifelong outdoorsman, Walt Anderson was born in 1896 on his family's homestead in the Cascade Mountains near Easton, Washington. His Swedish parents had immigrated to the United States, and he was skiing around his home in wintertime before the age of ten. As a young man, Anderson signed on with the Forest Service as a part-time firefighter. In winter he entered some of the early Cle Elum ski tournaments (see chapter 2, The Big Snow), where he won the amateur trophy in 1924. Later that year, he launched his career with the Forest Service as a fire guard.

Around 1928, Anderson moved to Leavenworth, where he encouraged the community to form a ski club and build a ski course near town. This began Leavenworth's long tenure as the capital of ski jumping in Washington. The enthusiasm generated by the sport encouraged Leavenworth and Wenatchee skiers to scout and develop Stevens Pass as a downhill ski area during the 1930s.

Anderson was named fire control officer of the Wenatchee National Forest in 1930. He saw skiing by the public as a positive influence in reducing forest fires. "Winter sports make for rosy cheeks that are natural, smiles that stay put, and eyes that sparkle with the joy of living," he wrote. "Enjoyment of the woods throughout the year also builds up the necessary appreciation of those woods so that they still receive proper consideration when

Dale Allen hiking in the North Cascades, circa 1950 (Robert Woods collection)

they are dry and inflammable during the summer months." He founded the Wenatchee Ski Club around 1935.

Anderson transferred to the Chelan (now Okanogan) National Forest, where he became chief of fire control in 1936. He oversaw the development of a new breed of firefighter, one who could be dropped by parachute into remote and inaccessible fires. He coined the name "smoke jumper" for these elite firefighters and made three jumps himself during the feasibility phase of the program. During the off-season, Anderson founded another ski club, in Okanogan, prompting the *Wenatchee World* to write that he had been instrumental in organizing "practically all ski clubs in North Central Washington." Okanogan skiers were soon exploring 8,200-foot Tiffany Mountain and developing a ski hill nearby at Salmon Meadows, nine miles northwest of Conconully.

Walt Anderson's friend Dale Allen was born in 1910 on a homestead up the White River road from Lake Wenatchee. As a boy Allen roamed the Cascades constantly. He traveled to and from school on horseback or snowshoes, depending on the season, and graduated from high school in the middle of the Great Depression. "When those banks went broke, I stayed in the mountains," Allen told historian Harry Majors. "There was no work. I'll tell you, I could eat by trapping." In the early 1930s, he started working for the US Forest Service. With Nels Bruseth of Darrington, Allen surveyed the route of the Cascade Crest Trail from the Little Wenatchee River to Cascade Pass in 1935. Allen eventually left the Forest Service out of frustration with the paperwork and took a job as a game protector with the newly organized Washington State Game Department. When Anderson was based in Wenatchee, Allen did winter game surveys with him.

Their partnership was solidified in 1940 when Allen was transferred to Okanogan, where Anderson was also stationed. Both old-school woodsmen, they made long winter ski trips together solely for enjoyment. Traveling without a stove or tent, the pair organized their equipment so they carried packs of only twenty to twenty-five pounds each for up to ten days in the woods. In a 1970s conversation with Chester Marler, Allen observed that a light pack was essential for skiing. "Helps keep the spirit up," Allen espoused.

The men would overnight in cabins whenever possible but could sleep out in the open when necessary. Sometimes they would cover as much as 20 miles in a day. On his earliest trips Allen used a blanket for sleeping, but he acquired a four-and-a-half-pound down bag in the early 1940s. Everything else was 100 percent wool. They carried dried food, mostly hardtack, oatmeal, raisins, chocolate, powdered eggs, milk, chicken or vegetable bouillon, and lots of concentrated pea soup. "I got awfully tired of pea soup," Allen confessed. He carried a regular-size axe, slid between the packboard and his body. Even in subzero

Walt Anderson dressed in an Inuit parka, circa 1928 (Stevens Pass collection, courtesy of Chester Marler)

temperatures, Allen traveled without a coat, saving it for warmth when he stopped.

"We would have just enough food to keep body and soul together," Allen said. "Always carried the lightest possible pack; after all, we were up there for the fun of it—that's what we went for. We knew we could do without certain things—we just left them." Each man would ask the other how he felt as the day progressed, Allen recalled. "We would have no goal when traveling—no rush," he said. "That old mountain won't run away."

Though no longer acceptable with modern equipment and "leave no trace" ethics, the techniques used by Allen and Anderson were admirable for their display of backwoods skill. Before camping, the men would look for an old fir snag and dry standing trees for fuel. "Don't pass this up when darkness is only a couple of hours away," said Allen. "Stop to make camp early. In the center of the fir snag you will find pitch to start your fire. If there is no fir snag, break off the fine dead branches, which you will find low down on all standing green trees in the high country. These fine branches will always burn regardless of weather conditions and will kindle your fire. Melted snow will furnish you with water."

Sometimes they would back off if conditions were bad. They'd stop in the afternoon while their spirits were high and they had time to prepare camp. "If we found a good spot with fuel, we sometimes stopped earlier," Allen recalled. "Each of us would tramp a hole in the snow, cut the top out of a tree, and put boughs on the top and bottom of the hole.

Nature herself would insulate us from the cold. We would start very early in the morning, sometimes at first light—when avalanche danger was at a minimum. We would time our trip so that we would cross avalanche areas early in the morning. Sometimes this meant that we might travel only a few hours out of a certain day."

The men adopted the nicknames "Bear" (Allen) and "Badger" (Anderson), inspired by incidents on the trail. Allen's name originated during a descent to the Pasayten River, following Anderson on skis. Rounding a clump of trees at high speed, Allen suddenly saw Anderson beating his ski pole in the snow and shouting, "Jump!" Allen did, clearing a deep washout just in the nick of time. Anderson laughed, remarking that with his pack on, Allen looked like a bear flying through the air.

Anderson's name originated during a trip through Indian Pass, where they dug a 12-foot-deep snow shaft into a cabin with a one-gallon bucket. With no stove, they started an open fire at the base of the shaft. But with a storm blowing outside, the smoke refused to go up the hole and instead filled the cabin. Allen rushed out of the hole choking, and before he knew it, two packs came flying out behind him. Anderson soon followed, wearing a cap with a couple of white stripes on it. He looked like a badger emerging from his den. In a worsening blizzard, they fled the cabin, which "looked like a volcano," and retreated to another shelter a couple miles away.

In early February 1941, the two left the Methow River near Robinson Creek with Roy Roberson, a Game Department man who had never skied before. After a night in a cabin near Harts Pass, the trio descended Slate Creek toward Barron, where Roberson sprained his ankle. They split up on their third day, with Allen and Anderson heading for Windy Pass and Roberson attending to his game protector duties in the area. Allen recalled that Roberson was left behind "with his skis, klister wax, triangular bandages, and blue streaks of something or other about skiers in general."

At Windy Pass, Allen and Anderson met the Gourlie family at their cabin. "Mrs. Gourlie put on the frying pan and coffeepot without even asking us if we were hungry," Allen later recalled. "We have skied for many winters without a miss, and those fried potatoes and bacon, coffee, homemade bread and butter, and home-canned pears were even better than any skiing we ever enjoyed."

The Gourlies advised the two men of the best route over Windy Pass, and the following day they descended the West Fork Pasayten River to Three Forks Cabin. On the fifth day of their trip, they skied past the snow-covered Pasayten airstrip to the East Fork Pasayten River, just two miles south of the Canadian border. They turned southeast the next day and fought difficult snow conditions past Hidden Lakes to the Ptarmigan Creek cabin. Over the succeeding days, they traveled down Lost River, crossed over Lucky Pass and Eightmile Pass to the Billy Goat Mine, then glided most of the 17 miles down Eightmile Creek to the Chewuch River, where they caught a ride on a CCC fuel truck to Winthrop. They called this nine-day adventure their "Pasayten trip" and returned home enchanted by the country.

Later, Allen and Anderson made an equally long trek they called the "Ashnola." This ten-day trip began at the Eightmile Ranch, the last residence up the Chewuch River and the end of the plowed road in the 1940s. This was the same place where they had finished on skis during their Pasayten trip. They skied up the Chewuch to Lake Creek and followed that drainage to Ashnola Pass, then down the Ashnola River and up Spanish Creek to Bald Mountain. They enjoyed telemarking in the area for a day or so, then continued northeast to the Tungsten Mine cabin. They traversed Bauerman Ridge and made their last camp in a snow cave north of Windy Peak. On their final day they descended as directly as possible toward the Middle Fork Toats Coulee road. The moon was out, so the men forsook their usual rule about stopping early and pressed on for nearly 20 miles to the town of Loomis, arriving at 9:00 p.m. Two fellows at the gas station said it had been minus 30 degrees Fahrenheit in town the previous night.

Despite the rigors of this outing, the Ashnola was their favorite long trip, and the pair skied it three times during their lifetimes. When asked by Chester Marler decades later why they did these trips, Allen replied, "For the simple pleasure of going, just being out in nature . . . there is the beauty of the country . . . I'm not sure exactly what being in the mountains does to you, but it does something, and it's wonderful." His advice to other winter travelers was both practical and inspiring: "Avoid taking unnecessary chances. If you do have bad luck, keep cool and avail yourself of the resources at hand. Remember that going ahead cheerfully is the most worthwhile when it is the toughest. In other words, let adversity find you at your best."

Opposite: "Clouds were boiling up." Darroch Crookes and Don Henry circling Mount Baker in 1932. (Photo by Ben Thompson, American Ski Annual)

CHAPTER 8

INTO THE RANGE OF GLACIERS

At the US National Alpine Championships on Mount Rainier in 1935, Nathaniel Goodrich, editor of the *American Ski Annual*, stood atop Panorama Point with local skier Ben Thompson. Turning to Goodrich, Thompson asked, "So what do you think of the Pacific Northwest?"

"A great country," said Goodrich. "A great country. What a place for high altitude skiing. A skier could make long tours, staying out day after day without coming back to timberline every night."

"What a great place it *is* for high altitude skiing," said Thompson. "Let me tell you about a trip three of us made to Mount Baker three years ago . . ."

Thompson's story, later published in the 1935 *Annual*, described an eight-day trip that presaged a new wave of ski exploration in the Northwest. By the mid-1930s, Northwest skiing was already established at centers that would thrive into the twenty-first century. Mount Baker, Stevens Pass, Snoqualmie Pass, Mount Rainier, and Mount Hood were popular before rope tows arrived, and the introduction of tows around 1937 only reinforced their popularity. Early on, ski mountaineers were attracted to the landmark peaks of the Cascades, and by 1939 all the volcanoes from Mount Hood to Mount Baker had been surmounted on skis. These major peaks and passes have remained the centers of Northwest skiing. But taken together, they represent just a fraction of the mountainous terrain in the Northwest. As rope tows, ski schools, and races came to dominate the sport, a few adventurers chose to explore peaks and glaciers far from the well-known ski centers.

Thompson's 1932 crossing of Mount Baker with Darroch Crookes and Don Henry was one of the most ambitious of these early adventures. The men were enjoying a three-month skiing vacation at Heather Meadows when they got the idea of a five to six day trip across the glaciers of Mount Baker, hoping to completely encircle the mountain and return to their starting point. The trip would be a much longer outing than the Park Glacier ski-climb Thompson had made the previous year with Milana Jank. That climb had been completed in a single day from Mount Baker Lodge. Thompson's proposed orbit of the mountain would require food and equipment for nearly a week, with snow camps above timberline. The men packed a lightweight silk tent for three, eiderdown sleeping bags, a Primus stove, dehydrated foods, ice axes, crampons, and 100 feet of climbing rope for glacier skiing. Their packs weighed about forty-five pounds each.

Over three days, they skied from Mount Baker Lodge to Kulshan Cabin on the northwest side of the mountain, their progress delayed by deteriorating weather. The pair spent two days at the cabin in storm and on their sixth day crossed Heliotrope Ridge and descended to a camp on the Thunder Glacier. The next day they circled the west side of the mountain below the Black Buttes and crossed the canyon holding the Deming Glacier to a camp near the Easton Glacier. Nearly out of food, they hoped to traverse the south and east flanks of the mountain to Mount Baker Lodge in a single day. They started out on the morning of their eighth day, but before noon a lightning storm was upon them.

"Hear that sound?" yelled Crookes through the wind.

"Sounds like a bee," replied Henry. "Look!" He pointed at Crookes's ice axe, tied to the back of his pack. A fine blue flame was dancing all over the steel—St. Elmo's fire.

"Let's get out of here!" said Henry. The men fled from the storm, descending to the Middle Fork Nooksack River and walking 14 miles to the nearest road.

Encircling the volcanic peaks seemed a logical step in exploration after the summits had been reached on skis. In April 1934, Ralph Calkin and James Mount of the Wy'east Club made the first ski encirclement of Mount Hood. They left Cloud Cap Inn at 8:20 a.m. and returned at 6:00 p.m., after encountering fog and small avalanches on the Reid Glacier. During the spring of 1937, Joe Leuthold and Everett Darr repeated the circuit to join the select group of what were known as "Side Hill Gougers."

On Mount Rainier, just a week before the 1934 Silver Skis race, Otto Strizek, Orville Borgersen, and Ben Spellar traversed the east side of the mountain from Paradise to the White River. Their route climbed to Camp Muir then crossed Cathedral Rocks to the Ingraham Glacier, which Strizek described as "a snow park built of ice blocks in a modernistic design." Crevasses, seracs, and swirling clouds hampered their crossing of the Emmons Glacier, and at times they exchanged skis for crampons. They finally reached Steamboat Prow, skied the Inter Glacier, and hiked out through Glacier Basin, traveling more than 20 miles in about twelve hours.

In the center of Washington's Olympic Mountains, 7,969-foot Mount Olympus is one of the most glaciated

Ome Daiber at the Deer Lake forest cabin in the Soleduck Valley, Olympic Mountains, 1933 (Daiber family collection)

peaks in the Northwest, rivaling the Cascade volcanoes as a stronghold of snow and ice. Yet Olympus is also among the most remote summits in the region, and this was particularly true in the 1930s. One of the earliest ski ventures in the Olympics took place in the spring of 1933, when Wendell Trosper joined Ome Daiber on a five-day expedition starting from Sol Duc Hot Springs. Their objective was a ski-climb of Mount Olympus. The men hiked and skied to Deer Lake, where they slept in a Forest Service cabin buried under 10 feet of snow. The next day they skied over Bogachiel Peak and descended to the Hoh Valley, pitching their tent on a bough bed on snow near the river. Snowy weather continued during their third morning, so the two men reluctantly returned to Deer Lake. The weather cleared overnight, and they enjoyed fine ski conditions the next morning on the slopes around the cabin. Daiber returned to Seattle enthusiastic about skiing in the Olympics, although he acknowledged that "it will be even more attractive when the roads are extended."

Dwight Watson visited the Olympics in the spring of 1935. With John Bissell, he hiked and skied from Olympic Hot Springs to the headwaters of the Soleduck River near Appleton Pass. The pair scouted the Soleduck divide on skis, impressed by distant views of Mount Olympus and the Bailey Range. The following year, Watson returned alone to traverse the Bailey Range over two weeks in June. He started the trip carrying short summer skis. Unfortunately, there was much less snow than in 1935, so he abandoned his skis on the High Divide near Cat Peak, removing the bindings and carrying them with him. Watson was unaware of the 1930 traverse of the Bailey Range on foot by Herb Crisler, who later gained fame filming *The Olympic Elk* for Walt Disney Productions. Some years later, during an event hosted by The Mountaineers in Seattle, Crisler mentioned that he had found skis in the Olympics left by "some crazy skier" in the Bailey Range country. "That's me!" confessed Watson.

The finest ski route established in the Olympics during the 1930s was the high traverse from Deer Park over Obstruction Point to Hurricane Ridge. Max Borst, caretaker of the Deer Park lodge, led a group of fourteen skiers over this route in April 1938. Their goal was to survey cross-country skiing possibilities and likely sites for ski huts. A Civilian Conservation Corps (CCC) truck met the skiers on the Elwha–Hurricane Ridge road twelve hours after they started their trip. Borst returned enthusiastic about the ski terrain and "thoroughly convinced" of the need for huts along the way. Three Port Angeles boys—Dick Owens, Guy Montgomery, and Frank Herron—had made a "preview" trip over the same country the day before Borst's trip. It's unknown whether the route had ever been skied before either of these ventures.

Skiing Mount Gladys above the Flapjack Lakes cabin in 1940; Mount Skokomish rises in the distance. (Spring Trust for Trails)

While Deer Park served as the center of skiing in the northern Olympics in the 1930s, skiers farther south on the Olympic Peninsula hoped to find a ski area closer to home. The Bremerton Ski Cruisers organized their club in the winter of 1935–36 and searched for a local ski area. In April 1937 they found a ski bowl on the northeastern side of Mount Gladys, approached via Flapjack Lakes. With the Shelton Ridge Runners, the Ski Cruisers built a cabin at the lakes during the summer of 1938, around the same time Olympic National Park was established. The cabin required a six-mile hike from the Staircase Ranger Station, a lot of work when packing in provisions for a winter weekend.

Though the Flapjack Lakes cabin yielded many fond memories, Ira Spring recalled that more time was spent building the lodge than was ever spent using it. Olympic National Park was expanded to include the cabin location in 1939. A special-use permit for the cabin was issued by the Park Service in 1941, but by that time many club members preferred skiing at Mount Rainier and the cabin was little used in winter. After 1948 the Park Service reclaimed the cabin and removed it. The Bremerton Ski Cruisers built a lodge at Stevens Pass, which they still use at the time of this writing.

THE LOOKOUTS

Skiers and hikers born after World War II have little notion of how much "civilization" there was in the Cascade and Olympic Mountains during the 1930s. The Forest Service and CCC developed trails, shelters, and lookouts at a pace unequaled since that time. While many roads were pushed into the mountains after the war, the number of lookouts dwindled as other methods of fire detection took their place. In their 1981 book *Lookouts: Firewatchers of the Cascades and Olympics*, Ira Spring and Byron Fish tallied nearly two hundred lookouts built in western Washington before the end of the 1930s. The lookouts were connected by miles of telephone wire, long since gone.

Since most lookouts were built for fire detection, they were unstaffed in winter and spring and difficult to reach during the snow season. It was more common for early ski parties to use forestry or mining cabins below timberline, of which there were many more in the 1930s than there are today. One exception was Mount Pilchuck, 20 miles northeast of Everett on the western front of the Cascades. A scenic and strategically located lookout was built on its summit in 1918. In April 1933, a party of Everett Mountaineers climbed to the lookout, finding excellent skiing just below the summit. Pilchuck was developed as a ski area in the 1950s, and it remains a popular ski-touring destination today. The lookout is still in place.

Clearly visible from Mount Pilchuck is a triple-summited peak known as Three Fingers. It, too, features a fire lookout, one of the most striking in the Cascade Range. The south peak of Three Fingers towers above a nearly vertical 2,000-foot wall on its eastern flank. The northwest face rises steeply for 400 feet above the Three Fingers Glacier. Only on the southwestern side is the summit easily approachable. Snow slopes lead to the base of the summit tower, where a 50-foot chimney splits the shoulder of the final rock spire. In the 1930s, Three Fingers was a 15-mile hike from the nearest road. In 1931, Harry Bedal and Harold Engles used twelve boxes of dynamite to blast the top off the south peak of Three Fingers. A lookout cabin was built on the resulting platform and lashed to the rock with steel cables. Ropes and ladders were installed in the chimney and on the final smooth slab near the top. The lookout cabin was ready for occupancy by the end of summer in 1932.

Harold Weiss staffed the lookout in 1935—a cool, wet year with no major fire or lightning storms. The following summer, the job was taken by Harland Eastwood, accompanied by his new wife, Catherine. At six feet, four inches and 210 pounds, Eastwood was a powerful and skilled outdoorsman. In high school he excelled in track, basketball, and football. After being hired by Harold Engles, Eastwood worked for the US Forest Service at Verlot and staffed the Mount Pugh lookout in 1935. He started the Harland Eastwood Company in the early 1930s, making and selling ski wax. Later Eastwood's product line grew to include packs, ice axes, crampons, pitons, climbing skins, outdoor clothing, and more. He also participated in ski patrol and mountain rescue.

Eastwood accomplished all of these things despite the loss of his right arm, at age sixteen, in a duck hunting accident. His feats in the mountains were regarded by his peers with amazed respect, and in 1936 Eastwood landed what was considered the toughest job of any lookout in his forest district. That year, Eastwood and his bride, Catherine, moved into a log cabin at Goat Flat, a 5,000-foot shoulder about two miles below the top of Three Fingers. They lived in the cabin through the Fourth of July, as Eastwood and others ferried supplies to Tin Can Gap, the highest point accessible by packhorses. From there, it was necessary to backpack loads across the Three Fingers Glacier and up the final slopes to the summit. Eastwood was assisted in supplying the lookout by Bob Craig, the Mount Higgins lookout (who took over at Three Fingers the following year and occupied the lookout every summer from 1937 through 1940).

It was mid-July before the lookout was ready for use. Bob Craig returned to Mount Higgins, and the Eastwoods packed the last few things to move into their home in the sky. After crossing the glacier, they climbed a permanent snowfield on the south shoulder of the mountain. "From the base of this icefield I got my first good view of 'home,'" wrote Catherine. "Still two or three hundred feet above us, the lookout cabin seemed to be peering over at us from its granite perch. The shutters standing out over the glass windows, and the peaked roof above, gave it a distinctly Oriental appearance. It was as though we had come to some mysterious lamasery high in the Himalayas."

Harland recalled, "We never got lonely. We were just happy as larks up there. When the weather was good, we'd sometimes go on hikes. Catherine and I had some short skis and with those things on, boy, you could get over to Tin Can Gap in a hurry." Bob Craig continued using the skis during his four summers on the mountain. The Eastwoods stayed in contact with the lookouts on Mount Pugh, Mount Higgins, and French Point. "One night," Harland

Harland Eastwood waxes his ski one-handed. Note the use of the ski pole for support. (Photo courtesy Harland Eastwood Jr.)

remembered, "three lookouts on three different mountains tried to sing harmony on a song over the radio. Some evenings we'd be entertained by harmonicas or ukuleles."

During electrical storms, Harland said, you could see the electricity dancing up and down the cables that held the lookout on the mountaintop. Catherine vividly recalled one such storm: "I sat up sleepily, feeling very strange. There was something wrong. I raised my hand to my head. My hair was standing on end, literally. I pushed it down and it jumped right up. Wind and rain beat against the windows. Every time the lightning flashed the telephone rang. The room glowed with a strange light. I peered outside and saw that every guy wire looked like a neon sign. Electricity crackled up and down the cables. The very rocks shone with a weird illumination. This was St. Elmo's fire."

During the storm, the Eastwoods rearranged items in the lookout to minimize damage in the event of a direct strike. Catherine was too busy to be afraid. Harland had to keep watch through the entire storm, recording which way it traveled, how much it rained, when and where the lightning struck, and more. Just before dawn, the dark clouds moved on and the lookouts were finally able to get some sleep. With the arrival of September, there were clouds around the peak nearly every day. It was impossible to spot fires from the summit of Three Fingers, and Harland soon received orders to come down. The Eastwoods packed

Catherine Eastwood climbs to the Three Fingers lookout in 1936. (Photo courtesy Harland Eastwood Jr.)

what things they could, left the rest, and battened down the lookout for the winter. They descended with memories of sunsets and distant mountains, of skimming down the glacier on their skis, of a honeymoon in the sky.

Years later, Catherine acknowledged feeling homesick when thinking of their time on the peak. She knew she could never go back. After the Eastwoods' summer on the mountain, the Forest Service passed a ruling that no woman could stay in a government lookout unless it could be reached by auto road. There would be no more honeymoons in the clouds.

SKI SCOUTING

As a skilled photographer, Dwight Watson often visited a photo lab in Seattle near the Cornish School (now Cornish College of the Arts) in the 1930s. It was on one of these errands that he met Hermann Ulrichs, a piano teacher at Cornish. Ulrichs was a climber with experience in the Sierra Nevada, the Selkirks, the Canadian Rockies, and Switzerland. In the early 1930s, inspired by new Forest Service maps that filled in blanks in the North Cascades for the first time, Ulrichs made twenty-one first ascents in the range, many of them solo. He wrote about the North Cascades in the *American Alpine Journal* and *Sierra Club Bulletin* in 1937, bringing national attention to the mountaineering potential of the range.

Although Ulrichs was not a skier, his enthusiasm for the North Cascades inspired Watson, and they did some climbs and winter rambles together on foot. In July 1936, not long after Watson's hike through the Bailey Range in the Olympic Mountains, he joined Ulrichs for a trip from Image Lake to Kaiwhat Pass in the North Cascades—an area Watson called the Hanging Gardens. After Ulrichs returned to Seattle, Watson continued wandering the range for six weeks, logging around 480 miles of rambling and 125 miles of backpacking between camps. He later credited Ulrichs with introducing him to the North Cascades. During the next five years, he would return on skis to scout many of the places he saw during his 1936 summer trek.

One of Watson's earliest ski partners was Walt Hoffman. Hoffman had proposed a trip to the Winter Olympics at Garmisch-Partenkirchen, Germany, in 1936, but Watson instead spent two months skiing and photographing at Paradise for the Rainier National Park Company. In May 1937, Watson recruited Hoffman to scout Eldorado Peak in the North Cascades, a glacier-clad summit he had admired during his rambles the previous summer. They approached Eldorado from Sibley Creek, the end of the road in the 1930s. After a couple tries thwarted by weather and other obstacles, Watson and three friends skied the slopes of Eldorado (though probably not the summit) in mid-May 1938. His movie of the trip is now in the University of Washington Libraries' Special Collections. One of Watson's partners on that trip was Sigurd Hall, whom he had met through The Mountaineers (their adventures on Glacier Peak and Mount Rainier are described in chapter 5).

Watson and Hall did many other trips together. In May 1937, with Walt Hoffman, they made a ski-climb of 9,415-foot Mount Stuart in the central Cascades. Though most of the peak was climbed and descended on foot during this trip, they reported conditions favorable for a 4,000-foot ski descent. Later that spring, with Ralph Eskenazi, Watson and Hall skied from Cayuse Pass over Governors Ridge and through the Cowlitz Chimneys to Summerland, traversing some of the most rugged country on the eastern side of Mount Rainier National Park. With Hall, Watson also skied White Mountain near Glacier Peak and Mount Daniel that spring. In 1944, Watson skied Daniel's western satellite, Mount Hinman.

Watson's most productive year of ski scouting was 1938. In addition to his May trip to Eldorado Peak, he skied Old Desolate in Mount Rainier National Park and North Star Mountain near Lyman Lake on successive weekends. The Lyman Lake trip was a classic Memorial Day adventure. It started with a flat tire on a Saturday morning, after camping overnight at Lake Wenatchee. Following a detour to repair the tire, Watson, Hall, and Eskenazi (then known as Sam) drove up the snowy Chiwawa River road, cutting branches and using tire chains to get within three miles of the old Red Mountain Mine at Trinity. The

Skiers in the 1930s view Eldorado Peak from near Sibley Pass. (University of Washington Libraries, Special Collections, Dwight Watson Collection)

trio walked on snow to Phelps Creek, then skied the valley to Phelps basin, sleeping in an old cabin there. The next morning, they skied over Spider Pass in fog and made their way, placing willow wands for the return trip, down the Lyman Glacier to the lake. They rested at the Washington Water Power Company cabin, hoping for the weather to clear a bit.

Watson and friends had originally planned to ski Plummer Mountain and complete a 30-mile loop back to Trinity via Buck Creek Pass, but they lowered their sights due to the many obstacles already encountered. Later that afternoon, they skied up North Star Mountain, reaching the summit just as the clouds dissolved to reveal the Cascade crest gleaming from Dome Peak to Glacier Peak and beyond. From the top, Watson could appreciate his friend Ulrichs's description of the North Cascades as printed in the 1936 *American Alpine Journal*: "There is something different about the light in the Cascades from any other range of my experience, perhaps because it is so close to the ocean and has a relatively moist atmosphere. The hard, diamond-clear light of the inland ranges is replaced by a light equally clear, but so softened that the mountains have almost a dream-like quality."

In the evening light, Watson, Hall, and Eskenazi skimmed refreezing snow back down to Lyman Lake. "Never to be forgotten," wrote Watson, "was the run of Sig and Sam from the shoulder above the pass, silhouetted in the sunlight and scorching down the hill like a couple of frightened antelope." The next day, they returned easily over Spider Pass and skied down Phelps Creek to their car. Watson continued his run of scouting trips that spring, skiing Ruth Mountain, Glacier Peak, and Echo and Observation Rocks (near Mount Rainier) before setting his skis aside for the summer.

One of Watson's finest trips was a novel idea, a ski traverse over the summit of Mount Baker in 1939, starting at Kulshan Cabin and finishing at Mount Baker Lodge. Watson's partners on the trip were Erick Larson and Andy Hennig, both of whom would join him a month later in his attempt to ski Mount Rainier. When I spoke to Larson in 2001, some sixty years after this adventure, he remembered that Watson had planned the trip meticulously. Watson was known to telephone at midnight if a trip was in the works and conditions suddenly looked good. After a night spent at Kulshan Cabin, the trio started their ascent of the Coleman Glacier at 4:00 a.m. on May 13. Watson carried a 16-millimeter camera and filmed scenes of the climb. Skiing to the summit around noon, he theatrically unfurled an American flag for the camera.

Next they descended the opposite side of the mountain. After skiing along the ridge toward the Cockscomb, the men roped up and down-climbed to the bergschrund, then jumped over the gap. They descended through Epley Portal, traversed the north side of Coleman Pinnacle, and reached Mount Baker Lodge a little after 8:00 p.m. "Andy's most

Dwight Watson (left) and Andy Hennig celebrate atop Mount Baker during the 1939 summit ski traverse. (University of Washington Libraries, Special Collections, Dwight Watson Collection)

famous accomplishment was finding the lodge manager and persuading him to drive us twenty-two miles to our car at Glacier Creek," Watson recalled, "a delightful and friendly gesture which we all appreciated but most of all Erick who had to be at work next day."

Perhaps the finest adventure of the prewar period was the 1941 ski ascent and descent of 9,131-foot Mount Shuksan by Dr. Otto Trott and Hank Reasoner. Born in Berlin in 1911, Trott left Germany in 1937 when the Nazis refused to let him practice medicine. He dreamed of finding a residency in Seattle, which German travel books had called "the most beautiful city in the United States." When Trott finally arrived in the Northwest in 1939 and saw Mount Rainier towering in the distance, he recalled, "tears came to my eyes—I had reached alpine country again." Trott learned about The Mountaineers and visited their club room, where he met "a wiry-looking man" who introduced himself as Dwight Watson. Watson invited Trott to join him on a filmmaking climb of Mount Shuksan a few weeks later. Sigurd Hall and Andy Hennig, who had made the first ski ascent of Mount Rainier earlier that summer, were also on the trip. During the climb, Trott fell in love with the Mount Baker area and joined the Mount Baker ski patrol the following winter, where he met Hank Reasoner, a founding member of the patrol. The two men admired Mount Shuksan and decided to try skiing it in the spring of 1941.

On the afternoon of March 27, Reasoner and Trott skied from Mount Baker Lodge to a bivouac on Shuksan Arm. The next morning, they descended into White Salmon basin and skied up the White Salmon Glacier. After removing their skis to climb the 45-degree

Otto Trott brought mountaineering skills acquired in Europe to the Northwest in 1939. (University of Washington Libraries, Special Collections, Dwight Watson Collection)

slope of Winnies Slide, they put the skis back on and carefully zigzagged up Hells Highway to the base of the summit pyramid. They scrambled to the summit at dusk and flashed a signal to their friend Gage Chetwood at Mount Baker Lodge. Chetwood blinked his car's headlights in response. Reasoner and Trott spent the night beneath the summit in a bivouac tent, then skied the route back to the lodge the following day.

Recalling their adventure many years later, Reasoner said that the conditions were perfect during their climb. He and Trott had similar attitudes about safety, and they didn't try to use skis where they weren't appropriate. "I like to remember what an old Swiss once told me," Reasoner said. "You climb the mountain in the mood it's in, not in the mood you're in. Otherwise, the mountain will kick your butt." Trott was more wistful. "I feel close to Mount Shuksan," he said. "I'd heard about it while I was still in Germany, but from the first time I saw it, I could never move far away."

THE LEGEND OF SIGURD HALL

Dwight Watson's friend Sigurd Hall was one of the Northwest's most accomplished ski mountaineers during the 1930s. His pioneering ascent of Mount Rainier in 1939 with Andy Hennig made him the first person to ascend or descend on skis every Cascade volcano from Mount Baker to Mount Hood. Hall was also a top competitive skier. His team won The Mountaineers' open Patrol Race three years in a row, from 1937 through 1939 (see Appendix). Hall was what was known in those days as a "four-way" skier, competing in downhill, slalom, cross-country, and jumping events. In the 1940 Four-Way National Championships held at Mount Baker and Snoqualmie Pass, Hall won the downhill race and placed third in the overall standings, behind Alf and Sverre Engen of Utah. As a top participant, in both ski mountaineering and ski racing simultaneously, Hall occupies a place in Northwest skiing history that may never be filled again.

The 1940 Silver Skis race on Mount Rainier was scheduled for Sunday, April 13, one month after the Four-Way Nationals. With his recent downhill victory at Mount Baker, Hall was a favorite to win the Silver Skis. But the day of the race presented challenging conditions on the mountain. Camp Muir, the starting point for the event, was above the clouds with good visibility, but there was a cold wind. In the 1940 *American Ski Annual*, Fred McNeil wrote, "The course was described as hard, icy and exceedingly fast in the opening stretches and tremendous speed was possible." Lower on the Muir Snowfield, clouds and fog reduced visibility. Several competitors declined to race due to these conditions. Observers reported that the red advisory flags, which marked the course, were visible from one to the next, but some early racers still strayed from the course, although all managed to regain it. Paul Gilbreath, the eventual winner, was one of those who got off course but regained the "groove" of the main track.

Racing three spots behind Gilbreath and wearing bib number 16 was Sigurd Hall. Just below Anvil Rock, near a formation known as Little Africa, Hall strayed from the course to skier's left and sped toward a wedge of rocks that extend out into the Muir Snowfield. "His skis were heard banging along at speed," wrote McNeil, "indicating he was 'wide open.'" At the last moment, Hall saw the danger and tried to veer to the right. His skis shattered on some isolated rocks and he hurtled headfirst into the wedge. "Such was his speed," wrote McNeil, "that he was thrown entirely across this wedge and into the snow beyond." A spectator trained in first aid hurried to Hall, but he had died instantly.

Sigurd Hall racing for the Seattle Ski Club, circa 1939 (Courtesy Matt C. Broze)

Four days before the race, Hall's native country of Norway had been invaded by German armed forces. Mail to the Hoel family farm in the Sunndal valley was disrupted, so although news of Sigurd's death reached his family, the details were sketchy. As the oldest son, he would have inherited the farm if he had returned to Norway, but the property went to his younger brother instead. Sigurd's memory passed into family legend. Conventional armed resistance to the invasion ended two months after the invasion, and Norway remained occupied until the surrender of Germany in May 1945.

Odd Hals, born in Norway shortly after World War II, grew up with the legend of his uncle Sigurd Hall. An athlete himself, Odd was puzzled by some aspects of the story of his uncle's death. For more than fifty years, the Hoel family legend said that Sigurd had won the 1940 Silver Skis race. The accident, it was said, took place after the race, during a "lap of honor." This never made sense to Odd, and his curiosity about the circumstances of his uncle's death grew over the years. Odd's cousin Gunnar Rekdal shared his curiosity. Gunnar had inherited the Hoel family farm and, in keeping with tradition, had changed his last name to Hoel. Gunnar and his brother Kristen nurtured the idea of coming to America and visiting Mount Rainier.

This smoldering idea caught fire in 2002, when Judy Earle, a Seattle-area cousin of the Hoel family, traveled with her husband, Dick, to Norway to explore her Scandinavian heritage. Judy learned about the legendary Sigurd Hall and, upon returning to Seattle, tried to find out more about him. An internet search led to my ski history website (see Resources), and a brief email led to me. I mailed Judy photos, articles, and 16-millimeter movies of Sigurd Hall, which she forwarded to the family in Norway. Just two months after our first contact, Judy told me that Sigurd's youngest sister (Gunnar's mother) had passed away in Norway at age ninety. A month before her death, however, Gunnar had showed her the films of her brother skiing in the Cascades in the 1930s. She said that, after more than sixty years, it was like bringing Sigurd back to life again.

In Norway, planning for the journey to America continued. During the winter of 2006, Judy informed me that Gunnar, Odd, and Odd's son, Endre, had scheduled a guided climb of Mount Rainier for July of that year. Judy's sons, Jeff and Doug Earle, planned to join them, and Gunnar's nephew, Jon Rekdal, made arrangements to fly out from New York to join the expedition as well. At the last minute, Doug Earle had to withdraw from the climb, and I was able to take his place in the party.

We all converged in Ashford on Saturday, July 22, for a one-day climbing school conducted by Rainier Mountaineering Inc. (RMI), one of the guide companies authorized by the Park Service. The next day, we hiked from Paradise to Camp Muir with three RMI guides and two other clients. We made a special stop near Anvil Rock, at the formation known today as Moon Rocks. Based on information provided by Karl Stingl, a former Silver

Odd Hals, center, and other members of the Hoel family climb toward Camp Muir in July 2006.

Skis racer who knew Sigurd Hall, plus written accounts, we concluded that this was the approximate location of Hall's death. It was impossible to exactly match the terrain described in McNeil's 1940 article, probably due to melting of the Muir Snowfield. We felt satisfied that we'd found the right area even if we couldn't precisely pinpoint the accident location.

From Camp Muir, we started our climb of the Disappointment Cleaver route very early on July 24 because of hot weather, leaving around midnight. Stars filled the moonless sky. We craned our necks as we watched the first rope teams, the lights of their headlamps seemingly suspended in air, snaking their way toward the summit. One of our party had been fighting a stomach ailment for several days, and at "High Break" (13,500 feet), the guides decided it would be best for him to stop. They skillfully made him comfortable in a sleeping bag on a quickly constructed snow platform. The rest of the party climbed to the summit crater, and several continued on to the register book at Columbia Crest.

Odd produced a small banner bearing the Norwegian colors, which we signed in Sigurd Hall's memory. I scattered the last of the ashes I had been keeping since the funerals of two family members the previous winter. With photos and memories secured, we made our way back down the mountain, to Camp Muir and, finally, Paradise. Near Alta Vista, we were greeted by Judy Earle and her sister, Odd's sister Gunvor and her family, and more members of the extended Hoel clan.

Later seventeen of us, including Gunnar's sister Olaug from Sweden, gathered for dinner at Alexander's Inn near Ashford. I asked Judy whether the family often gathered like this, and she said it had never happened before. She passed out lyrics of a song, "Nar det blomster I Hardanger" in Norwegian, that she had written for the occasion; it was sung to the tune of "Springtime in the Rockies." We joined together to sing about Sigurd Hall and his home in Norway.

So ended one of the most memorable climbs of my life.

"THE ORCHARD BLOOMS AT HOEL"

When the orchard blooms at Hoel
Well, it's like a sea of foam.
And if fate were not so cruel,
It could light Sig Hall's way home.

But the Mountain was capricious
On that day he went to Muir.
And she sent the fog to claim him,
But his spirit's still up there.

They've been training in the mountains,
They've been training on the sea;
And they've come across the ocean
All for Sig Hall's memory.

So we've all been brought together,
And whenever we're apart
We'll remember Sigurd Hoel
And the places that held his heart.

When the orchard blooms at Hoel,
And the snow's on mountain domes
In America and in Norway
Sig Hall's mem'ry's safely home.

—Judy Earle, July 2006

Opposite: Men of the eighty-seventh Mountain Infantry Regiment train on skis at Paradise in 1942. (US Army Signal Corps)

CHAPTER 9

MOUNTAIN SOLDIERS

The invasion of Norway in April 1940 was just one more step in the tragic development of the Second World War. As Adolf Hitler and his Nazi party rose to power in Germany in 1933, fascism was on the rise in Italy as was aggression by the Empire of Japan. In 1936, both the Winter and Summer Olympic Games were held in Germany, and the Nazis exploited the Olympics for their propaganda value. Several nations, including the United States, considered boycotting the games, but after Avery Brundage, president of the American Olympic Committee, ruled out a US boycott, most other countries fell in line.

Lt. John Woodward with the US Army's Fifteenth Infantry patrol in 1941 (Denver Public Library, Tenth Mountain Division collection)

Twenty-eight teams competed at the Winter Olympics at Garmisch-Partenkirchen, more than in any previous winter games. The propaganda benefits from this event were short-lived, however. In March 1938, Germany annexed Austria. World-renowned ski-meister Hannes Schneider was imprisoned during this time. Fortunately, influential friends in America managed to secure his release and passage to the United States about a year later. Germany occupied Czechoslovakia in March 1939 and a few months later partitioned Bosnia. Otto Lang, who grew up in Bosnia, was in Yugoslavia with his wife at that time, hoping to rendezvous with his parents and sisters. Warned in a telegram from his father that war was about to break out, they canceled their plans and caught a train to Paris. Lang and his wife arrived there on September 1 to news that Hitler had invaded Poland. Great Britain and France declared war on Germany two days later. After a few tense days, during which Lang was at risk of being interned because of his German passport, he and his wife boarded a ship to New York.

Prior to the invasion, Germany and the Soviet Union, although sworn enemies, had agreed in secret to partition Poland, the Baltic Republics, and Finland between their two spheres of influence. This set the stage for the Russian invasion of Finland, which was launched on November 30, 1939. The Winter War, as it came to be known, inspired newspaper readers around the world. The Finns, outnumbered more than thirty to one in some battles, held off the Russians for more than three months. In the woods of central Finland, squads of Finnish skiers, cloaked in white and following hidden forest paths, launched daring "road cutting" operations against the invading Russian columns. As the fighting continued, the Finnish defense gradually lost ground to an enemy whose reserves were effectively inexhaustible. Finland signed a peace treaty in mid-March 1940, ceding key territory to Russia while retaining independence. The Winter War had cost Russia a half million men killed or wounded. Four weeks later, Germany invaded Norway and Denmark.

In America, members of the National Ski Association and National Ski Patrol lobbied the US Department of War to organize and train a US mountain fighting force. The US Army was already pursuing experiments in this direction. As early as the winter of 1939, one thousand soldiers of the US Third Infantry Regiment, dubbed the Arctic Regiment, were training on snowshoes and skis in subzero weather at Fort Snelling, Minnesota. News stories reported that the drills were "part of the Army's program for preparing for campaigns in extreme climatic conditions."

By the next November, the War Department had agreed to an arrangement in which the National Ski Patrol would organize volunteers to become familiar with mountainous terrain throughout the United States. These volunteers would serve as guides to the army for training or operations in local mountains, in effect extending civil defense warning capability into these rugged areas. A separate directive ordered the creation of ski patrols in six army divisions stationed in northern states. This marked a significant shift in army thinking about the value of ski troops, a topic that was debated with greater urgency after the Russo-Finnish war began. As Colonel Muir of the Twenty-Sixth Infantry observed, "I believe ski training is an asset. Like the Texan's six-shooter, you may not need it, but if you ever do, you will need it in a hurry, awful bad."

"WE'LL HUNT YOU DOWN"

Response to the War Department's directive was swift. On December 7, 1940, a ski patrol unit from the Third Division, Fifteenth Infantry Regiment, was formed at Fort Lewis, Washington. The patrol was made up of about twenty enlisted men and two officers. Although the commanding officer, Capt. Howard Crawford, was not a skier, the unit's technical adviser, Capt. Paul R. Lafferty, was both an experienced skier and an expert mountaineer. Lt. John Woodward, former Pacific Coast alpine ski champion, was ordered to active duty and assigned as the unit's ski instructor. The Fifteenth Infantry patrol moved into Mount Rainier National Park headquarters at Longmire and began daily training.

Sgt. Reese McKindley of the Fifteenth Infantry patrol on the cover of *Life* Magazine, 1941

Around the same time, another ski patrol of twenty to thirty men was formed in the National Guard's Forty-First Division, stationed near Fort Lewis at Camp Murray, Washington. This patrol was under the command of Lt. Ralph Phelps, who would rise through the ranks after the war to become the commanding general of the Forty-First Division. The Forty-First patrol was made up mostly of experienced Northwest skiers. Sgt. Karl Hinderman, an expert skier from Whitefish, Montana, was the group's ski instructor. While the Fifteenth Infantry patrol was billeted at Longmire, the Forty-First Division patrol commuted weekly to Rainier from Camp Murray and spent Thursdays and Fridays training on the mountain.

The glamour of army ski troops training on the slopes of Mount Rainier proved irresistible to the press. On January 20, 1941, the cover of *Life* magazine featured trooper Reese McKindley with his rucksack and rifle at Paradise, accompanied by a short piece describing equipment and techniques used by the Fifteenth Infantry patrol. In a letter to the editor, Samuel Hadden of Westminster, South Carolina, wrote, "No finer picture of the typical U.S. Army man has ever been published. In characteristic American fashion this soldier coolly sucks his homemade cigarette, but one knows almost instinctively that when he takes his last draw from it, he is ready to 'go into action.'"

As the men gained experience, Lafferty and Woodward tested them on longer patrols. In February the patrol made two 20-mile trips from Paradise to Ohanapecosh, overnighting at the Nickel Creek shelter and crossing the Cowlitz Divide on skis. Two straight days of rain tested the waterproofness of the men's clothing. Now the patrol was ready for a tougher exercise. Later that month, Lafferty, Woodward, and about a dozen enlisted men

Lt. John Woodword guides the Fifteenth Infantry patrol across the north flank of Mount Rainier in 1941.
(Rainier National Park Archives)

were joined by Assistant Chief Ranger Bill Butler to traverse the north flank of Mount Rainier from Yakima Park to Mowich Lake. This five-day trip took the men from the White River to Sunrise, over Burroughs Mountain and St. Elmo Pass, then across the Winthrop, Carbon, and Russell Glaciers to Spray Park. Butler had traversed part of this route the previous spring with Ome Daiber to evaluate the area's potential for winter ski development, but it's unlikely that the entire route to Mowich Lake had ever been skied before.

Buoyed by this success, the Fifteenth Infantry patrol prepared for the final test of their winter training. A few days after returning from Mowich Lake, they were trucked to Snoqualmie Pass, with the objective of a 55-mile ski traverse along the Cascade crest from Snoqualmie Pass to Naches Pass. The first 20 miles took the route of The Mountaineers' Patrol Race to Stampede Pass. From there, the men would follow the watershed divide to Naches Pass, finally descending snow-covered roads toward Greenwater, where they would be met by army trucks.

The trip began in fine weather as the men left behind the rope-tow slopes of Snoqualmie Pass. Lafferty was testing prototype skis that were so stiff they wouldn't float in the soft snow. He constantly had to pull up the ski tips while breaking trail. After a day of this with a sixty-five-pound pack, Lafferty developed painful shin splints and had to leave the patrol around Stampede Pass, placing Woodward in charge.

The patrol carried no radio during the trip and communication with headquarters at Fort Lewis was difficult. Woodward recalled that before the patrol set out, they were told, "You've got to learn how to hide your tracks and hide from the airplane. We're going to come and hunt you down. They'll be able to find you." Laughing, Woodward recalled, "Hell, they couldn't find us for nothin'!" About a day into the trip, near Yakima Pass, the men left a message for their aerial reconnaissance plane. "We had some black panels and we had this manual . . ." Woodward said. "So we put the panels out, and wrote what we wanted to say. . . . The plane . . . was a biplane, a big fighter. It swooped down and . . . pretty soon they came right over where we had a group standing and they dropped an aluminum tube with a little streamer. We ran over and opened it up and took out the message and read, 'You have the only manual in Fort Lewis on ground-to-air signaling, so we don't know what you're telling us!' It shows you how prepared we were."

The following day, near Stampede Pass, the patrol came to a small lake with a clear view of the sky. "I went out and stomped an *O* and a *K*," Woodward said, "and my gosh they spotted it. So they took a picture of it and they turned it over to the papers. And the papers printed it with a caption like 'Ski patrol believed safe.'" He recalled, "There was a holiday of some sort and they dropped a message down there that said, 'Gee, if we knew what you guys wanted, we'd have dropped you some stuff.' 'Thanks a lot,' we thought."

The Fifteenth Infantry patrol returned to Mount Rainier during the last week of February and boarded trucks back to Fort Lewis. The Forty-First Division patrol led by Phelps moved into quarters at Longmire shortly after the Fifteenth Infantry patrol departed. Woodward was loaned to the Forty-First Division patrol as a technical adviser. The skiing skills of the Forty-First Division patrol were demonstrated during The Mountaineers' open Patrol Race on March 9. During this, the last patrol race of the prewar period, the Forty-First Division team of Donald Brown, Ray Osborn, and Lee Zerba finished second behind the Washington Alpine Club patrol. The Mountaineers team took third. Four weeks later, Osborn and Sgt. Karl Hinderman participated in the Silver Skis race on Mount Rainier; Lt. John Woodward finished fourth in that race.

Phelps and Woodward led the Forty-First Division patrol on trips that were the equal of those completed by Fifteenth Infantry. In March the patrol crossed the Olympic Mountains from east to west, skiing over Anderson Pass from the Dosewallips River to the Quinault River, a distance of about 40 miles. In April the patrol crossed the northern Olympics from Deer Park to the Elwha River. From there they were trucked to the Soleduck River, where

Harold Peebles skis above Paradise with pack and rifle in 1942. (Denver Public Library, Tenth Mountain Division collection)

they hiked to Deer Lake and skied across Seven Lakes Basin to Heart Lake, eventually returning down the Soleduck to their starting point. These efforts were just the beginning of the army's long task of preparing mountain troops to join the war effort.

"OH, GIVE ME SKIS"

In mid-November 1941, the US Army authorized formation of the First Battalion of the Eighty-Seventh Mountain Infantry Regiment at Fort Lewis. Several of the officers, including Lafferty and Woodward, were transferred into the new unit from the Fifteenth Infantry. Lt. Col. Onslow Rolfe was named regimental commander. On the morning of Sunday, December 7, 1941, Lafferty and others were on weekend leave to ski at Paradise when music on their car radio was suddenly interrupted by news of Japan's attack on Pearl Harbor. The Tacoma Ski Club had planned a race that day with the Rokka Ski Club of Seattle, formed in the 1930s by skiers of Japanese ancestry. "Most of us just sat around most of the day," recalled Tacoma club member Howard Clifford. "No one felt like skiing." Lafferty and the men with him at Mount Rainier returned to Fort Lewis to find the base blacked out, its gates barricaded by barbed wire and guarded by machine-gun nests.

Recruiting and transfers into the new Eighty-Seventh Regiment accelerated. The War Department authorized the National Ski Patrol to recruit men for the mountain troops, and many of the early recruits had significant experience on skis. By mid-February 1942, the Eighty-Seventh Regiment had secured the Paradise Lodge and Tatoosh Lodge on Mount Rainier for the use of 350 men over an intensive eight-week training period. Lafferty selected a nucleus of around thirty men to serve as the instructional cadre, training soldiers in military skiing for six days a week, six to eight hours a day. The troops claimed full use of the rope tow above Paradise Inn on weekdays and yielded the ground to visitors on weekends.

Lt. Charles Bradley, eldest of seven skiing brothers from Wisconsin, discovered the challenge of skiing with a heavy pack. "When we were finally carrying rifles," he recalled, "a common misjudgment of speed and control could end in the load lifting the skier off the snow, rolling him forward in the air, and driving him headfirst back into the snow. The rifle, lagging slightly, would now catch up and deliver the coup de grace by whacking the skier on the head and driving him still deeper into the snow."

One evening, after a long tour with much bitching by the men, Lafferty strolled into the lodge, set his pack down, and shed his outdoor clothing. He'd been trying out a new rucksack and said to Bradley, "Why don't you try it on and see how it feels?" At first Bradley thought the pack had been nailed to the floor. "It was all I could do to get it onto my back," he remembered. "What do you have in there?" Lafferty explained that he always added a few rocks to train for carrying combat loads. He knew Bradley would share that with the rest of the company. "The bitching faded away on the night wind," Bradley recalled.

In early April, the men were tested on a ski march with thirty-pound rucksacks starting from Paradise Lodge, climbing 4,000 vertical feet to Sugar Loaf before descending the Paradise Glacier and climbing over Mazama Ridge to return to the lodge. It was the fifth day of a five-day series of tests. There were no accidents, and every man completed the march.

The annual Silver Skis race was held on April 12 over the full course from Camp Muir to Edith Creek basin. Matt Broze of the Seattle Ski Club won the race in a time of 4 minutes, 57 seconds. Walter Prager, a former world downhill champion serving in the mountain troops, finished two seconds behind Broze. Seven of the top ten finishers were members of the Eighty-Seventh Regiment. Broze and the women's champion, Shirley McDonald,

THE SINGINGEST OUTFIT

The Latrine Quartet (Charles Bradley, Glen Stanley, Charlie McLane, and Ralph Bromaghin) performs for Seattle's KVI Radio in 1942. (Denver Public Library, Tenth Mountain Division collection)

Lt. Charles Bradley wrote, "Perhaps the best measure of the spirit of a group of men can be found in the music that comes from them." He described the Eighty-Seventh Mountain Infantry Regiment as "one of the singingest outfits to ever shoulder an army pack." With Ralph Bromaghin, Dick Look, Charlie McLane, and Glen Stanley, Bradley gathered almost every night to sing and compose lyrics to popular tunes. A favorite was "The Ballad of Sven," a song about a skier named Oola and his snowshoeing cousin Sven, sung to the tune of "He was a Bold Bad Man, He Was a Desperado." The song had this chorus:

> Oh, give me skis and some . . . poles and klister,
> And let me ski way up on . . . Alta Vista!
> You can take your snowshoes and . . . burn 'em, sister,
> And everywhere I go I'll give my war whoop!

The A and B Companies of the Eighty-Seventh Regiment returned to Fort Lewis in mid-April 1942 and were replaced on Mount Rainier by C and D Companies. Company D, a heavy weapons unit, soon added to the ballad:

> The Eighty-Seventh had a Heavy Weapons Company.
> It spent six weeks in Paradise but never learned to ski.
> The reason for this tragedy as you can plainly see
> Was everywhere they went they wore their snowshoes.
>
> *Chorus:* "Oh, give them skis . . ." etc.

received their trophies from Colonel Rolfe, commander of the Eighty-Seventh Regiment. Morale during the Mount Rainier training was high.

BUILDING THE TENTH MOUNTAIN DIVISION

Veterans of the US mountain troops remembered the winter of 1942 on Mount Rainier as the "song and story" phase of their training. But a long road lay ahead before they would be ready to contribute to the war effort. Using training films from Mount Rainier, public relations officer Capt. John Jay created the recruiting film *Ski Patrol*, which toured around the country the following year. Applications to the mountain troops were distributed after every screening, and 75,000 people viewed the film. The War Department designated the National Ski Patrol (NSP) as the official recruiting agency for the mountain troops; the NSP was authorized to furnish applicants with a letter that would be honored by all reception centers to send men directly to Camp Hale, Colorado, for basic training. In December 1942, the first battalions of the Eighty-Seventh Mountain Infantry Regiment began arriving. Camp Hale had a unique culture. Unlike other army outfits that featured pinup photos of pretty swimsuit-clad woman in their newspapers, the paper for the Tenth Mountain Division—the *Ski-zett* (later renamed the *Blizzard*)—printed photos of snowcapped mountains under the heading "Pin-Up Mountain of the Week."

The Eighty-Seventh Mountain Infantry Regiment completed moving from Fort Lewis to Camp Hale in January 1943. Training problems became apparent during a two-week maneuver on Homestake Peak in February. Due to inadequate training, 260 men, or about 30 percent of the command, became casualties of the elements—a result of frostbite, dehydration, and exhaustion. Woodward thought the most important mountain training they received at Camp Hale was in winter survival and winter hygiene, since trench foot had knocked out a lot of troops in Europe during World War I. The US mountain troops were taught to dry their socks out in their sleeping bags at night and to go slower and take short breaks to keep from sweating too much while on the move.

Duke Watson recalled the rigorous maneuvers his platoon completed on foot and by ski in the Colorado Rockies during the winter of 1943. They included a ski ascent of Homestake Peak with seventy-five-pound field packs, a ski traverse from Camp Hale to Vail Pass and back, and a nine-day traverse from Camp Hale to Aspen, with full army packs. In July 1943, as its ranks grew, the Tenth Infantry Light Division (Pack, Alpine) was created, with more than 10,000 men. Three regiments—the Eighty-Fifth, Eighty-Sixth, and Eighty-Seventh—ultimately made up what became known as the Tenth Mountain Division.

M. Sgt. Clarence "Buster" Campbell of Leavenworth, Washington, winner of the military cross-country ski race at Camp Hale in 1944. Described by veteran Robert Parker as "the most grueling thing anybody in the Tenth ever did," the race required completing a 30-kilometer course while in uniform and carrying a fifteen-pound pack and an M1 rifle. Racers performed military tasks during the race including firing sixteen rounds at a target 200 yards away. At least one hit was required to qualify. Campbell's total time was 3 hours, 25 minutes. (Courtesy Buster Campbell)

Lt. Hazel E. "Ed" Link led a team of thirty-two enlisted men and three officers from Camp Hale who taught a high-angle rock and assault climbing school at Seneca Rocks, West Virginia, through the summer of 1943. Link would later manage Washington's Crystal Mountain ski area. Duke Watson, who took charge of the climbing school during the winter of 1943–44, would help found Crystal Mountain in the early 1960s and was responsible for recruiting Link for the general manager's job. Most of the top rock climbers in the United States were gathered in this school as instructors, Watson recalled.

TRIALS OF THE HOMEFRONT

Dr. Otto Trott and Hans Otto Giese, both Northwest residents of German ancestry, were impacted during these tense times. In the fall of 1941, Trott was chief resident physician at Seattle's Morningside Tuberculosis Hospital. Unmarried and active in the small community of local climbers and skiers, Trott spent nearly every weekend in the Cascades. On Sunday, December 7, while skiing at Mount Baker, he heard someone calling from the parking lot below. Thinking there might be an injured skier requiring medical help, Trott skied down quickly.

A car radio blared, but through the static the listeners made out something about Japanese planes and the Hawaiian Islands. "From the announcer's voice," Trott recalled, "we could tell it was a very serious matter." Trott and friends learned of the attack on Pearl Harbor on their return to Seattle. Many young men were enlisting in the army, and friends were having serious discussions about the future of the country.

Soon after the attack, the FBI cracked down on persons of Japanese ancestry. More than one hundred thousand were expelled from their homes along the West Coast of the United States and forcibly removed to internment camps under President Franklin D. Roosevelt's Executive Order 9066, issued on February 19, 1942. Since Germany and Japan were allies in the war, residents of German ancestry in the United States were also targeted as dangerous or at least suspicious.

Trott soon received a visit from "two most polite gentlemen" at the hospital where he worked. They said they were from the FBI and asked to speak in private. Since Trott was six months short of eligibility for US citizenship, he thought their inquiry was reasonable, and he freely shared correspondence from his German family and friends. About a week later, the FBI men returned. Still very polite, they asked if he had any weapons. Trott, whose sense of humor sometimes surfaced at the wrong time, replied, "Just a heavy machine gun under the bed." The men did not take it as a joke and actually crawled under the bed looking for a gun. When they asked where Trott's car was, he showed them without any more jokes. "You'd better lock it up," they said.

Trott was taken to the Immigration Detention Center in Seattle, where he was held for several months. His friends Dwight Watson and Erick Larson made a point of visiting him. Larson thought Trott's other friends were afraid to go see him. Apparently, the authorities believed Trott might be susceptible to extortion by the Nazis, since he still had family in Germany. Eventually a formal decision was made to intern him, though no charges were ever filed. He spent about a year in detention in Tennessee, then another seven months at an internment camp in North Dakota. Trott was finally released in the fall of 1943 and returned to Seattle, where he resumed work as a physician while reporting his daily activities to the FBI.

German American Hans Otto Giese was also targeted by the US government, despite the fact that he had lived in Seattle since the early 1920s and was a naturalized US citizen.

In the 1920s he was widely regarded as the best skier in the Northwest, and he remained a pillar of the Northwest skiing community throughout the 1930s. An attorney, Giese had helped found the Seattle unit of the Friends of New Germany in 1933. Unfortunately, the national organization was openly pro-Nazi and was supported by the Third Reich. By 1935, Nazi officials in Germany realized the organization was doing more harm than good and ordered all German citizens in the United States to leave it. In later years, Giese said he quit the group around this time.

Not long after the Friends of New Germany was dismantled, a new organization with similar goals, called the German American Bund, arose in its place. This group was dissolved after Pearl Harbor. When the United States declared war on Germany, federal officials began to arrest former Bund officials. Giese was swept up due to his earlier association with the Friends of New Germany. He was banished from Seattle and he moved his family to Denver shortly after Pearl Harbor.

When Giese returned to Seattle for denaturalization proceedings in 1943, federal prosecutors alleged that he had fraudulently become a citizen in 1930, while retaining loyalty to Germany. During the trial, however, prominent local attorneys and businessmen testified to Giese's honesty and loyalty to the United States. His defense was boosted by US Supreme Court decisions in the early 1940s that made it more difficult to take away citizenship once it had been conferred. The judge in Giese's case ultimately found that prosecutors had failed to prove that Giese had fraudulently become a citizen in 1930 and that he had not committed any overt act that could be cause to lose his citizenship. With this legal victory, Giese returned to his life in Seattle.

WAR IN ITALY AND THE TENTH MOUNTAIN DIVISION

Allied forces invaded the toe of Italy in September 1943. The campaign opened a second front in the European war, nine months before the D-Day invasion in France. The Allies advanced slowly up the boot of Italy until they were stopped in the Apennine Mountains. Twice the Fifth Army attacked Monte Belvedere, key to the defense of the road to the Po Valley, and twice they were thrown back. German forces defended Belvedere using artillery fire directed from the nearby Mancinello-Campiano divide, known to the Allies as Riva Ridge. The Fifth Army considered Riva to be unclimbable by combat troops.

In November 1944, the Tenth Infantry Light Division was designated as the Tenth Mountain Division and assigned a new commander, Gen. George P. Hays, a Medal of Honor recipient during World War I. By mid-January 1945, all three regiments of the Tenth Mountain Division had shipped out to Italy. Given their mountain training, it was hoped that

CITIZEN SKI PATROLS AND WARTIME CRASHES

Despite the loss of many members of the National Ski Patrol to the armed services, the patrol contin-ued to function in the United States wherever skiers skied. In response to a 1940 request by the War Department, volunteer wilderness patrols sprang up from California to New England. In Washington, key members of these citizen patrols were Lyle St. Louis, Ome Daiber, Will Borrow, and Dwight Watson (no relation to Duke Watson). Since the Cascade Range was considered too large to scout in its entirety, Washington volunteers focused on the region from Stevens Pass to Chinook Pass. This area was divided into ten patrol regions, each about 10 miles from north to south. Volunteers scouted these areas and prepared route maps that could be used for civil defense or search and rescue operations in both summer and winter.

In May 1943, Daiber was asked to help guide a party to recover personnel and equipment from a crashed US Navy bomber in the Olympic Mountains. He chose four volunteers, and his team guided

National Ski Patrol and mountaineering volunteers assisted military search and rescue units during World War II and beyond. This crash on Mount Pilchuck occurred in the winter of 1948. (Spring Trust for Trails)

navy personnel toward the crash site at 5,500 feet on the south ridge of Mount Washington. During the approach, he found that the navy men were poorly prepared for snow and mountain climbing, so he decided to take charge of the field operation. Since the navy had reported two live bombs aboard the bomber, Daiber left the men a safe distance away, clambered into the plane, and defused the bombs himself. Inspection of the crash site found all the crewmen dead. The patrol loaded the bodies onto toboggans and dragged them to civilization for burial.

Dwight Watson recalled other plane crashes during the war. In January 1945, a Navy PV-1 bomber crashed in the Buckindy-Snowking region of the North Cascades. Six crew members bailed out. Four men landed in the Kindy Creek drainage and were found alive within the week; after landing in a tree, Ensign Rine Kruger freed himself from his parachute and started a fire with his flare pistol to stay warm. A fifth crew member died of injuries and exposure. The pilot, Lt. Harry Tabor, landed in a different valley and was found alive five days after the crash.

In another crash, near Keechelus Ridge east of Snoqualmie Pass, Watson recalled that the pilot made his way to a cabin, scrounging for survival supplies. After tying refrigerator shelves to his feet like a pair of snowshoes, the man walked out to the highway through the drifts.

they could finally overcome the defenses of Monte Belvedere. Despite months of training on snow, however, in Italy they used skis only briefly.

On January 21–22, Lt. Don Traynor of the Eighty-Sixth Regiment led a patrol on skis deep into enemy territory on Monte Spigolino, a summit adjacent to Riva Ridge. Traynor chose the four most rugged skiers in his unit to go with him: Sgt. Steve Knowlton, Cpl. Harry Brandt, Pfc. Harvey Slater, and Pfc. Cragg Gilbert of Yakima, Washington. The patrol covered 20 miles in twenty-two hours, two days faster than the time allotted for their trip. They determined that the route over Monte Spigolino was too long and exposed to German observation to be useful for an attack on Riva Ridge. Skis, in this instance, had helped save American lives.

At the same time, men of the Eighty-Sixth were mapping five routes for an assault up the east face of Riva Ridge. Far from being impossible, the ridge was found by the mountain troops to be relatively easy for an experienced hiker. Fixed ropes were installed on two routes for the benefit of soldiers burdened with rifles and ammunition. The number of German troops atop Riva Ridge was thought to be fairly small, perhaps one hundred fifty men, but their positions provided a clear view of any attack on the ridge. General Hays had a

Lt. Don Traynor (right) and Pfc. Cragg Gilbert (left) prepare for a ski patrol on Monte Spigolino in the Apennine Mountains of Italy. (Courtesy New England Ski Museum)

simple solution: climb the ridge at night, when the defenders couldn't see. Military doctrine holds that in the mountains, assaulting troop superiority should be around ten to one. Shortly after dusk on February 18, about eight hundred men of the Eighty-Sixth Regiment began their climb. On Riva Ridge, the army expected a 90 percent casualty rate. Instead, the attack force encountered surprisingly little resistance.

The following night, units of the Eighty-Fifth and Eighty-Seventh Regiments advanced on Montes Belvedere and Gorgolesco. Hays ordered that the night attack occur without small-arms fire or artillery. The objective was to slip through and around enemy positions to gain the high ground behind them. Only hand grenades and bayonets could be used before daybreak. Artillery and air support would come afterward. By dawn, the summit of Belvedere had been taken and units were digging in along the ridge toward Monte Gorgolesco. The final objective of this drive was Monte della Torraccia, the northernmost summit of the ridge connected to Monte Belvedere.

On February 21, the attack on Monte della Torraccia was started by a battalion of the Eighty-Fifth Regiment. Over two days, the battalion was decimated. On February 24, Hays ordered the Third Battalion of the Eighty-Sixth Regiment to take over. Capt. Duke

Stringing telephone wire near Querciola, Italy. The east flank of Riva Ridge rises in the background. (Denver Public Library, Tenth Mountain Division collection)

Watson of I Company led the battalion forward onto the mountain. St. Sgt. Richard Emerson recalled the battle:

> *This was to be the first combat for these men, and it proved to be a very thorough initiation. The men were all in position waiting, and as it grew lighter, they saw the field ahead littered with the bodies of Eighty-Fifth men and some more lying in a row behind them. At 0700 Lt. Wilde blew his whistle. With one stroke all the light and heavy machine guns opened up and the second and third platoons went over the top. . . . A few seconds later the Germans pressed their triggers; Lt. Wilde was hit with the first burst from the objective. The men saw the snow kicking up around them and wondered how in hell the bullets had all missed—except those that didn't miss. They felt bewildered when the German guns rang in their ears yet couldn't be seen. From then on it was fire and movement and a lot of praying.*

On Monte della Torraccia, Pfc. William "Bill" Long found himself far from any memories of the Cascade Mountains, of Windy Pass, or of skiing with his friend Mel Gourlie. "On Torraccia," he wrote, "the standard of living hit an all-time low. The rapidly approaching whine of an already-gone-by artillery shell, the strange high-pitched zing of small-caliber stuff, the irritating buzz of flying fragments, and the dull thud of fragments hitting the ground—these sounds kept a man's head continually in that hang-dog position. When human decency and common sense have vanished like raindrops on a hot desert stone, only hate and contempt can remain."

After four hours of fighting, Capt. Duke Watson and his men reached the top of della Torraccia and called in coordinates for artillery strikes. Moments later, a 170-millimeter German howitzer shell exploded a few feet away. "I looked down and saw I'd taken a few pretty good shards in my gut," he recalled. "I knew intestinal wounds were very dangerous if not treated quickly, and so I started down." On his way down the mountain, reduced to crawling, Watson was met by his friend Ralph Bromaghin, who carried him to safety. "Ralph saved my life," Watson said. Two days later, when the division's first victory seemed at hand, a mortar shell landed 10 feet from Bromaghin as he was heating coffee on a mountain stove with Chaplain Henry Brendemihl. A chunk of that mortar hit Bromaghin in the abdomen. He collapsed and died in the chaplain's arms.

A limited second offensive extended Allied control along the hills to Monte della Spe and the town of Castel d'Aiano. After suffering heavy losses, the division was ordered to halt its advance against the better judgment of many Tenth Mountain officers, including

General Hays. Nearly six weeks later, the Fifteenth Army Group began the long-awaited push northward through Italy. April 14, 1945, the first day of the offensive, was the bloodiest single day of the war for the division, with 553 casualties. On April 20, the Tenth became the first American division to break out of the northern Apennines into the Po River valley. Encouraged by Fifth Army commander Gen. Lucian Truscott, General Hays urged the Tenth forward, far ahead of other Allied forces.

"We had more casualties because of Hays," recalled John Woodward, "but for every guy we lost, if he hadn't done what he did, there'd have been three guys in other units lost. When we'd get a breakthrough, he had a feel for when the Germans were a little disorganized. He'd start for the next objective without orders." The division continued its drive northward, cutting off the major escape route from northern Italy through Brenner Pass and trapping a large portion of the German army before they could cross into Austria.

On May 2, word was received of the German surrender in Italy. Addressing his troops at Torbole on Lake Garda, General Hays said, "When you go home no one will believe you when you start telling of the spectacular things you have done. There have been more heroic deeds and experiences crammed into these days than I have ever heard of. Many times, we stuck our neck out with exposed flanks. At one time we were 45 miles in advance with both our flanks exposed. The Lord had us by the hand." The war in Europe came to an end on May 8, 1945.

"TO THE SURVIVORS!"

On April 22, 1945, Robert Parker's platoon had just reached the south bank of the Po River. As they prepared to defend the riverbank, a machine gun began firing upstream. Looking

Crossing the Po River in a DUKW. (Denver Public Library, Tenth Mountain Division collection)

through field glasses, one of the men could see six unarmed Germans in the water. "Some-body's shooting at them!" he cried out.

Parker's platoon sergeant jumped into a Jeep and ordered a man to accompany him. "We gotta stop that!" he said as they sped away. When the men looked again, only four swimmers could be seen. Two appeared to be in trouble, but eventually the stronger of the two pulled his buddy out of the river and they disappeared.

After the war Parker attended the University of Washington. He enjoyed skiing and became president of the Husky Winter Sports Club, the largest ski club in the United States at the time, with about five hundred members. In 1952 he worked with the US Army in Austria as a civilian. One weekend, he traveled to a specialty shop in Munich to buy a pair of custom ski boots. The shop proprietor, a small man named Hans Rogg, asked about Parker's age. Parker admitted that he was thirty and asked Rogg why he was curious.

"You were in the war then," Rogg said. "Where did you serve?" When Parker said he was in the Tenth Mountain Division in Italy, the shoemaker exclaimed, "I can't believe it! We fought one another in Italy. And here I am making fine boots for you, an American GI!" The two men bonded instantly and asked each other more questions about their service. Parker asked whether Rogg had been a prisoner of war.

"*Nein*," said Rogg, "I was lucky. At the Po, we were trapped. All the bridges had been destroyed. But some of us swam across and got home over the Alps!"

"You swam the Po!" Parker exclaimed.

"Not exactly," said the cobbler. "You Americans were shooting at us. I would have drowned if my comrade hadn't been an Olympic swimmer." Now Parker shook his head in disbelief, describing that day in 1945 when he had watched Rogg's drama in the river. The two men laughed and reminisced, and the shoemaker brought out a small bottle of schnapps, pouring some into the only glass in the shop. Lifting the bottle high, Rogg pro-posed a toast. "To us survivors!" Rogg exclaimed.

"To us survivors!" replied Parker.

"Hans Rogg's schnapps," Parker later wrote, "and the shared memory of that incredible experience, warmed me thoroughly on the long drive back to Austria." The war, truly, was over.

Opposite: *Skiing above Paradise in 1948* (Spring Trust for Trails)

PREVIOUS PAGE: *Gertrude Shorrock enjoys a snowy day at Snoqualmie Pass in the 1930s.* (Othello P. Dickert family collection) TOP: *Members of the Roberts party arrive at the Ashford train station for a winter holiday on Mount Rainier in 1909.* (University of Washington Libraries, Special Collections) BOTTOM: *Paul Sceva, Jr. performs a gelandesprung on the ridge of Alta Vista below Mount Rainier in the 1930s.* (Tacoma Public Library)

TOP: *Don Fraser (right) edges out Carleton Wiegel near the finish of the 1934 Silver Skis men's race.* (Museum of History and Industry, *Seattle P-I* collection) BOTTOM: *Winners of the Women's Division in the 2017 Patrol Race: Heather Kern, Holly Davis, and Anne Marie Stonich.* (Photo by Rick Meade)

TOP: *Azurite Peak and Mount Ballard are cloaked by winter snow in this view from Tamarack Peak in the 1930s.* (Photo by Mel Gourlie) BOTTOM: *John Bissel skis near Appleton Pass in the Olympic Mountains in May 1935.* (University of Washington Libraries, Special Collections, Dwight Watson collection)

TOP: *A Forty-First Division ski trooper below Mount Rainier* (John Woodward photo, Denver Public Library, Tenth Mountain Division collection)

TOP: *Chuck Hessey and Bruce Gilbert view Chiwawa and Fortress Mountains from North Star Park above Lyman Lake in the 1950s.* (Charles and Marion Hessey collection) BOTTOM: *Dave Nicholson, Carol and Joan Marston, and Gary Rose explore the Paradise Ice Caves in the 1950s; climate change has since melted the caves.* (Spring Trust for Trails)

TOP: *An avalanche runs over the former east snowshed at Snoqualmie Pass.* (Photo by John Stimberis) BOTTOM: *Liz Daley snow-boards the Coleman Glacier on Mount Baker in the 2000s.* (Photo by Jason Hummel)

TOP: *Kathy Phibbs celebrates in a red chiffon dress and white pillbox hat near the summit of Mount St. Helens in June 1987.* (Photo by Benjamin Benschneider, courtesy *The Seattle Times*) BOTTOM: *Carl Skoog pauses at dawn near Cache Col on the Ptarmigan Traverse in 1988.*

CHAPTER 10

WILDERNESS ALPS

During World War II, Chuck Hessey was far from mountains and snow. Serving for three years on the border of India and Burma, Hessey pined for winter in the Cascade Mountains and skiing on his home hill near Chinook Pass. In January 1946, just fifty-two days after release from the service, he recruited army buddy Irwin Hall for what they dubbed their "personal veteran's readjustment program." The two men drove from Hessey's home in Yakima to Lake Chelan and stocked up with five weeks of supplies. Chelan Butte, rising 2,700 feet above the lake, was completely snow covered that winter, so they skied it from summit to toe as a warm-up run. Then they boarded the ferry and cruised 50 miles north to Stehekin, a tiny resort settlement at the head of Lake Chelan.

There, Hessey met local families including Grant and Jane McConnell, recent arrivals following Grant's discharge from the military. Hessey and McConnell

shared a love of wilderness mountains, a bond that, though they could not have known it at the time, would help shape the future of the North Cascades during the next twenty-five years.

Hessey and Hall hoped to pioneer ski runs around Cascade Pass at the head of the Stehekin River. But it was a stormy winter. Several times, they broke trail upvalley in good weather, then the next day, when they hoped to push into the high country from their cabin near Bridge Creek, it would start snowing again. Their most memorable day came in mid-February, when the men skied up the north side of McGregor Mountain and were rewarded with spectacular views of the North Cascades and a 4,000-foot run in powder snow back to the cabin.

Concluding that spring was a better time to ski in these mountains, Hessey and Hall returned to Lake Chelan in early April with two more friends, also just released from the army. This time the party traveled to Lucerne, 10 miles down the lake from Stehekin, and made their way to the 1930s copper mining town of Holden. They skied from the town to Lyman Lake and settled into the Washington Water Power Company's snow survey cabin. Intending to stay for three weeks, the group stretched it to four, skiing Chiwawa Mountain, North Star Mountain, Spider Pass, and other slopes surrounding Lyman basin. Of the mountains between Glacier Peak and Clark Mountain, Hessey wrote, "To see them was to wish to ski them, and each hungering look fed that despair in the knowledge that life is too short to do all those things we'd like to do."

A year later, Hessey returned to Lyman Lake with Marion Monter (his future wife), Harryette "Rick" Mack, Grant McConnell, and Bill Degenhardt of Seattle. Restricted by cloudy weather to slopes near the cabin for several days, they awoke to clear skies on April 11, 1947. It was, Hessey wrote, "the most beautiful morning I have ever seen in the mountains." Smitten by the North Cascades, Hessey could not resist going back, even when he could find no one to join him. In September he and friends had supplies taken by packhorse to the Lyman Lake cabin. The following spring, all his friends had to cancel their plans, but Hessey went anyway. His goal, he wrote, was "to complete a Kodachrome record of the Lyman lake area [and] to put skis for the first time on the Chickamin Glacier."

For three weeks, Hessey was the sole occupant of the Lyman Lake cabin and, on every day but one, snow fell. "Darned if I've ever seen anything like this so late in the year," he wrote in the cabin's logbook. "This is April weather, not May." His enthusiasm undimmed,

Cliff Casebolt, Irwin Hall, and Gene Louman view Bonanza Peak from Chiwawa Mountain in 1946. (Photo by Charles D. Hessey Jr., University of Washington Libraries, Special Collections, Hermann Ulrichs Collection)

Built for snow surveyors in the 1920s, the Washington Water Power Company cabin near Lyman Lake was used by hikers and skiers for decades. (University of Washington Libraries, Special Collections, Dwight Watson Collection)

Hessey wrote in his journal, "If this range in its present unexplored (winter) state were set down in the middle of Europe the people would go wild with joy. The Alps have been crisscrossed with ski trails from end to end for lo! these many years. Here we have made only a very small beginning—and so few skiers in this region realize that they have been born into a time and situation that will make them the envy of the future."

On May 17, 1948, unable to postpone his attempt on the Chickamin Glacier any longer, Hessey left Lyman Lake, crossed Cloudy Pass, and descended Agnes Creek to its west fork. As he ventured up the remote valley beneath the soaring walls of Agnes Peak, he sensed that "this is the very heart of the range." The morning of May 21 was fine and warm, and he started toward the glacier in high spirits. To his dismay, he discovered that the log he'd previously scouted for crossing the river was awash in a growing flood. It was the beginning of the historic floods of 1948 that would displace thousands of families in eastern Washington and cause millions of dollars of damage. Hessey abandoned his attempt to ski the Chickamin Glacier and hiked out safely to Stehekin, ending an adventure in the North Cascades that would by no means be his last.

TROUBLE IN PARADISE

During the war, both Paradise on Mount Rainier and Timberline on Mount Hood were closed in winter. Snoqualmie Pass remained the only ski area in Washington with tows operating. After the war, there was a frenzy of enthusiasm by skiing veterans and other winter sports lovers to "go back." Wartime restrictions were lifted, and a big snow year in 1945–46 sent skiers flocking to the mountains. Mount Rainier was closed during the first half of the season, and Deer Park and the Milwaukee Ski Bowl remained closed all winter, causing overcrowding at other areas. By 1946 the National Park Service was ready to authorize construction of a T-bar at Paradise, but the park concessionaire was unwilling to risk the investment, since its winter operations had never turned a profit. "The Company will not spend another dollar in winter operations," said the Park Company manager.

After operating intermittently during the first two winters after the war, the Park Company provided daily service at Paradise throughout the winters of 1948 and 1949. Again, they lost money on the winter seasons. When the Park Company's contract was due to expire at the end of 1949, no other vendors were interested in taking over operations. The contract was extended, but the Park Service no longer required the Park Company to furnish winter accommodations at Paradise. Company management could not have been more pleased—Paradise ceased to be a winter resort.

With no accommodations available at Paradise, the Park Service stopped clearing the road in the winter of 1950 and for several winters after. Instead, the Park Service shifted the focus of skiing in the park to Cayuse Pass, where plowing of the road was provided by the state highway department. For several years, a small ski area had been operating there with three rope tows but no overnight accommodations.

Other Northwest ski areas rebounded quickly after the war. The Milwaukee Ski Bowl at Hyak installed a barge-like "ski-boggan" lift during the winter of 1947. A year later, Stevens Pass added Washington's first T-bar. Ski Acres (known today as Summit Central), between Snoqualmie Summit and Hyak, opened for the winter of 1950 with Washington's first chairlift. On Mount Hood in Oregon, the Sky Hook was installed, a steel-tower contraption on which forty-passenger gasoline-powered cars ran back and forth on cables from Government Camp to Timberline.

While Paradise remained closed in winter during the early 1950s, plans were laid to bring skiing back to Mount Rainier along with greatly increased development. In the fall of

Skiers take in the view of Mount Rainier from Naches Peak near the Cayuse Pass ski area in the 1940s. (Spring Trust for Trails)

1953, Governor Arthur Langlie proposed a major development program on Mount Rainier, with overnight facilities, a year-round road, and an aerial tramway extending from Paradise Valley to Camp Muir at about 10,100 feet. A meeting held by the governor in December was attended by representatives of chambers of commerce, hotels, ski organizations, railroads, and airlines. The only dissenting voice was that of Leo Gallagher of Tacoma, a member of The Mountaineers who attended the meeting as an individual. According to the *Tacoma News Tribune*, "Gallagher cautioned that if the Park Service should give an inch by permitting an aerial tram in Mt Rainier National Park, the money grabbers and commercial interests could open the aperture up a mile wide by coming in with other commercial features."

A motion to approve the tramway and request a survey by the Park Service passed overwhelmingly during the meeting. As Gallagher feared, the proposal grew over time to include a deluxe lodge, a swimming pool, and a golf course in addition to the tramway at Paradise. The Mountaineers board of directors, alerted to the development plans, passed a resolution in January 1954 to seek a suitable area for ski development outside Mount Rainier National Park. Interest was growing at the time in a potential site near Corral Pass, above the Silver Springs Lodge on the Chinook Pass highway.

The club formally declared opposition to the Rainier tramway a few months later. Hearings held in Seattle in August 1954 generated strong opposition to the plan. Bill Degenhardt, now president of The Mountaineers, conducted the meeting with what was described as "masterful restraint." The Mountaineers called upon its membership to oppose the tramway. Two thousand letters were generated against the development. Letters in opposition outnumbered letters in support by ten to one. In December 1954, Secretary of the Interior Douglas McKay announced that the department would give no further consideration to proposals for constructing a tramway on Mount Rainier.

Art Winder, Mountaineers conservation chairman during the tramway controversy, later observed that this event marked a decisive turning point in Northwest conservation, forging a closer unity and cohesiveness among conservation groups. An indirect result of the hearings was to highlight the need for expanded ski facilities in the region. Due to public demand, the road to Paradise on Mount Rainier was kept open again during 1954–55, the first winter season since 1948–49. Winter travel to the area increased, but the majority of visitors to Paradise were no longer skiers.

THE LIFT SKIING BOOM

The closure of Paradise in the early 1950s forced skiers to look elsewhere. Snoqualmie Pass was the busiest area in Washington, and crowding increased with the closure of the Milwaukee Ski Bowl after its lodge burned down in 1949. Ski patrol leader James Langdon recalled skiing at Snoqualmie:

> When the day's skiing started, the scene usually presented utter chaos. Lift lines were interminable. Lost kids were squalling, novices going up the rope were falling and being run over by the following skiers who, after waiting so long in line, refused to let go of the rope and either ran over the unfortunate who was struggling to get

Grabbing a rope tow in the 1960s (Spring Trust for Trails)

up or contributed another body to what generally became a great pile of enmeshed arms, legs, skis, poles, etc. We often felt that there were more injuries occurring getting on, riding and getting off the rope tow than there were on the hill.

Amid the crowding and general chaos, some skiers reckoned they could sneak on the lifts without tickets. A story published in a Pacific Northwest Ski Areas Association news release, and later picked up by *Reader's Digest*, described how two lift attendants set out to discourage this. One dug up an old pair of discarded skis and fastened them to his feet, then returned to elbow his way to the front of the lift line. "Where do you think you're going?" asked the attendant. "Do you have a lift ticket?" The other snapped, "I don't need a ticket to ride this tow." The attendant on duty then wielded a double-edged axe, chopped off the lift crasher's skis a few inches in front of his toes, then looked up at the amazed skiers in line who had witnessed the whole affair. "Anyone else out there doesn't have a lift ticket?" Lift chiseling fell off dramatically, for a while at least.

In 1951 a third all-season highway, US 12, was completed across the Washington Cascades via 4,470-foot White Pass. Chuck Hessey and friends were the first skiers to explore

Hogback Mountain above the new pass highway, before a ski area was established. The ski area opened at the pass with a rope tow and warming hut during the 1952–53 winter. Distant from the large cities on Puget Sound, White Pass drew skiers mainly from the Yakima Valley and southwest Washington. A chairlift was installed at White Pass for the winter of 1957, and a second chair was added two years later. White Pass became the first Washington ski area to operate seven days a week.

In March 1953, near the end of the ski area's first season, Hessey and his wife, Marion, invited Dorothy Egg and their young friend Tom Lyon on a weeklong ski trip from White Pass to the Goat Rocks and back. Climbing over Hogback, the party spent two days skiing to McCall Basin, where they camped for three nights. A storm dropped about eight inches of new snow after they arrived in the basin, but the weather cleared the following day. "I have not experienced many winter days to equal that one in the ensuing fifty years," Lyon recalled. "We went up into the big open glacier basin that leads to the saddle on the Cascade crest just north of Old Snowy. The sun was bright, the sky was blue, the air cold and the powder perfect." They broke a trail to the saddle and skied the basin repeatedly. "Two days later," Lyon continued, "as we returned over Hogback, we had another cold sunny day. In all the times I have been to Hogback since, I have never seen the trees more completely plastered with snow."

After the war, small ski areas sprang up throughout the Northwest. Many didn't last long. One of the survivors was Loup Loup, near State Highway 20, started by Ralph Parks and Tom Meyer of Okanogan. Parks, a veteran of the Tenth Mountain Division, began looking for a ski hill shortly after he got out of the army. "I must have skied over most of the mountains from Okanogan to Twisp before this spot was picked," Parks said. Launched in 1946, the ski hill was moved in 1958 to the northeastern slope of Little Buck Mountain for better snow conditions. They began with a rope tow that took skiers about a third of the way up the hill. More rope tows and a Poma lift followed, and today the hill is served by a quad chairlift. A section of the old Poma still offers a taste of the 1950s on the beginner hill.

Satus Pass, located at 3,107 feet along US Highway 97 between Goldendale and Toppenish in southern Washington, had a small ski area a couple miles north of Brooks Memorial State Park. Established in 1952 by enthusiasts from Goldendale and the Yakima Valley, the ski area consisted of three rope tows powered by a flat-head Ford V-8 engine. The Goldendale Jaycees operated the area in the mid-1960s, with a lodge, T-bar, night lighting, and parking for one hundred cars. By the mid-1970s, the ski area was struggling financially due to unreliable snowfall. The lodge burned down in 1976, and the area never reopened.

Skiers load the upper chairlift at Mount Pilchuck in the 1960s. (Western Ski Promotions collection)

In the early 1950s, logging operations built a road to Cedar Flats on the north side of Mount Pilchuck, about 35 miles northeast of Everett. The Mount Pilchuck ski area was launched with a single rope tow in 1956. Over the next decade, the area added a day lodge, more rope tows, and two chairlifts, one above the lodge and the other below. Pilchuck had a reputation as a tough ski hill—steep, with rugged contours and multiple fall lines. There was no snow grooming. With a base around 3,100 feet located 30 miles west of the Cascade crest, the area often had rain when pass ski areas were getting snow—but Pilchuck could get huge snowfalls. In 1963–64, the year the upper chair opened, there was 52 feet of snow at the top of the lift and more than 14 feet at the lodge. For three weeks, the ski area was too buried in snow to operate.

The opposite occurred during the winters of 1977 and 1978, the last seasons of operation for the ski area. Operators of the ski area argued that Mount Pilchuck needed to expand to be economically viable. The Forest Service, however, felt that expansion was unjustified because the area, being at a low elevation, was inherently poor for skiing. Eventually the lifts were removed and the forest took over. Today a visitor to the Mount Pilchuck trailhead struggles to imagine open ski slopes where thick trees now stand.

In 1960 the old Milwaukee Ski Bowl reopened as Hyak, with two Poma lifts. It became the second ski area in Washington, after White Pass, to operate seven days a week.

THE QUEST FOR CRYSTAL

Interest in a ski resort northeast of Mount Rainier, outside the national park, emerged shortly after World War II. In 1950, Mary Lea Griggs (a cousin of Chauncey Griggs, who had developed the first rope tow at Paradise in the 1930s) proposed a ski area on Castle Mountain near Corral Pass, above the Silver Springs Lodge. The proposal was approved by the US Forest Service, but the project was derailed by the Korean War from 1950 to 1953. After the war, the idea was revived by a group that included Don Amick, a former Olympic skier; Joe Gandy, later president of the Seattle World's Fair; and several other prominent skiers and businessmen. Surveys of the Corral Pass area over the next two years found problems with the site. The area, dubbed the "Sun Bowl of the Cascades," was squarely in the weather shadow of Mount Rainier and received little snow. Also, the site lacked suitable terrain for a base area, so its boosters proposed a parking lot near State Highway 410 and a three-mile-long gondola to reach timberline. Duke Watson, a member of the group studying the site, observed, "It just didn't pencil out."

The group began looking south of Corral Pass, around the headwaters of Silver Creek. Watson recalled a scouting trip with Walt Little and two others to Silver Three, a peak above Goat Lake that they'd spotted from Corral Pass. "We were sitting up there on this beautiful spring day and we looked over and said, 'What is that?'" They were looking at the summits known as Silver King and Silver Queen that rise above today's Crystal Mountain ski area. They got out the maps and concluded that it was the place they should be scouting.

A few weeks later, they made an overnight trip into the area to check it out and immediately switched the focus of their study to upper Silver Creek. During the winters from

Chuck and Marion Hessey skiing above the Gold Hill cabin near
Crystal Mountain (Photo by Stella Degenhardt)

1956 through 1958, Little led five trips a year up Silver Creek for snow surveys. Warren Spickard, a medical doctor and avid skier, also led five trips. The surveys were scheduled every other week, providing the study team with five months of snow data each year. "By the time I'd run fifteen trips up there," Little recalled, "I'd had enough ski mountaineering to last me the rest of my life."

Unknown to the Seattle-Tacoma group, Silver Creek had been enjoyed by Yakima skiers for decades. Chuck and Marion Hessey were members of a loosely organized club that had skied the area since the 1930s. The club used a cabin on Morse Creek below Gold Hill, just over the Cascade crest from Silver Creek. In winter they hauled a portable rope tow up to the cabin, and sometimes they set up lights for night skiing.

Before the road was improved up Silver Creek and plowed in winter, the shortest ski route to Crystal Mountain from the west was via the Crystal Lake trail above State Highway 410. Duke Watson recalled a scouting trip to the upper basin during which they met the Hesseys on skis. "Who has discovered my secret area?" inquired Chuck. After introductions, Chuck said, "Darn it, the word's going to get out. We've always had this totally to ourselves." He made peace with the inevitable, and in 1959, at the request of the Crystal Mountain board of directors, he completed a fifteen-minute film called *Crystal Mountain and You* that could be shown to potential investors. "Today it is wilderness skiing," wrote Hessey for the film's script. "Tomorrow it will be one of the most completely developed areas in America." In 2008, Marion Hessey's estate donated the film to The Mountaineers in Seattle. In 2012, clips from the film were used in Crystal's fiftieth-anniversary video.

In the fall of 1958, the board of Crystal Mountain issued a stock offering to finance initial construction of the ski area. Investors who purchased at least twenty shares of stock (at fifty dollars a share) would receive an annual dividend of one lift ticket per share, at not more than 10 percent of the ticket's face value. More than eight hundred families in thirty-six communities around the state participated in the stock offering. Board president Joe Gandy described the venture as "almost a skiers' cooperative." The ski area opened in the fall of 1962 with two chairlifts, a T-bar, and seven rope tows. Despite a very lean snow year, the resort earned 70 percent of its estimate for the season. A third chairlift, in Green Valley, was constructed during the summer of 1963.

The can-do spirit of the founders was demonstrated by Duke Watson and a few friends during the summer of 1964. With little more than a chain saw (and tremendous persuasive power to recruit help), Watson cleared Northway, an expert run descending from 6,776-foot Northway Peak for a mile and a half and nearly 3,000 vertical feet to the road next to Silver Creek. During the early years of the resort, Northway was the premier long powder run at Crystal Mountain, with shuttle bus service from the bottom of the run back to the base lodge at about 4,400 feet elevation. A long-awaited beginner-intermediate chair called Quicksilver was installed in 1965; the highest chairlift tops out at more than 6,960 feet.

"NOBODY WANTS TO WALK ANYWHERE ANYMORE"

While Crystal Mountain was the largest, it was just one of several new ski areas developed in the 1950s and 1960s. A 1964 *Seattle Magazine* article noted that the downhill skiing boom in the Washington Cascades started around 1956. Since the early 1950s, attendance at ski areas within a day's round-trip of Seattle had increased five times over. In 1964 the annual growth rate was nearly 30 percent, and the number of regular skiers in the greater Seattle area was estimated at 170,000. As many as 150 ski school busses were running to Snoqualmie Pass each Saturday during the winter.

By the mid-1960s, there were seven small community ski areas in Okanogan, Douglas, and Chelan Counties of north-central Washington. A larger-scale development at Mission Ridge, 14 miles from Wenatchee, was launched in 1959. Mission Ridge was spearheaded by Wilmer and Walt Hampton, Leavenworth skier Magnus Bakke, and others. After a $1 million stock drive, the area opened in December 1966 with two chairlifts and five principal

Skiers at Mission Ridge in the 1960s (Western Ski Promotions collection)

runs. Walt Hampton, a Tenth Mountain Division veteran and four-event ski competitor before the war, was the area's first manager.

A year after Mission Ridge opened, a major new area at Snoqualmie Pass made its debut. Conceived by Bob Mickelson and Jim Griffin, Alpental was located on the northeast flank of Denny Mountain, with a top elevation 1,600 feet higher than any other ski area near the pass. Mickelson recognized that although the existing areas at Snoqualmie Pass were smaller and lower in elevation than Stevens Pass, Crystal Mountain, and White Pass, they had more skier-days than the other three areas combined. From a business standpoint, Alpental seemed like a sure bet. The area opened for the 1967–68 season with three double chairlifts and five rope tows.

· Early plans called for a tramway from the base lodge to Cave Ridge, between Guye Peak and Snoqualmie Mountain, with a chairlift continuing to the top of Snoqualmie. Those plans were never completed, however, and in 1976 Snoqualmie Mountain was included in the new Alpine Lakes Wilderness. Although Alpental was ultimately successful, it was not the bonanza that Mickelson and Griffin had envisioned. Skiers from the other three Snoqualmie Pass areas didn't switch to Alpental in large numbers, because the latter's beginner and intermediate terrain was limited. Advanced skiers from Stevens Pass, Crystal Mountain, and White Pass didn't switch in great numbers either: most remained willing to drive farther for the drier snow and fewer rainy days at the other areas.

In the mid-1960s, the US Forest Service solicited bids to develop a new ski area on the southeast flank of Mount Hood, about two and a half miles east of Timberline Lodge. Franklin Drake, head of a Portland construction company, visited the area and was impressed by "the variety of the terrain, the beauty of the alpine meadows providing natural open spaces to the tall stands of timber, and the wide open un-timbered spaces above the treeline." In April 1966 the Forest Service awarded a thirty-year permit to Mount Hood Meadows Ltd. to develop the resort. Construction began in 1967, using a helicopter to install towers for two chairlifts. The ski area opened for the 1967–68 season. The inaugural run to open the slopes to the public was made by Gretchen Kunigk Fraser, 1938 women's champion in the Silver Skis race on Mount Rainier and the Golden Rose race on Mount Hood, and America's first gold medalist in alpine skiing in 1948.

In 1968 Wendell Carlson and Art Granstrom of Everett began developing Yodelin, a residential ski area east of Stevens Pass. Their plans called for four chairlifts, a lodge, and

Following completion of the Heart o' the Hills road in 1957, skiing in Olympic National Park shifted from Deer Park to Hurricane Ridge, where three rope tows were installed. (Spring Trust for Trails)

restaurants, plus residential lots and condominium units. The area opened in December 1969 with a double chairlift, rope tow, and Tyrolean-styled lodge. Future plans called for a cable car on nearby Lichtenberg Mountain and four chairlifts on Barrier Ridge. However, in January 1971 an avalanche on the southeastern flank of Skyline Ridge crushed two cabins, killing two adults and two children; more than half a dozen lawsuits followed. The ski area installed a second chairlift in 1972 and continued operating into 1973, but closed soon thereafter. The two chairlifts were later sold to Stevens Pass and Crystal Mountain.

The closure of Paradise in the early 1950s and the emergence of other ski areas accelerated a trend that had begun when Jim Parker and Chauncey Griggs built their first rope tow in 1937. Ski touring—and climbing mountains to ski down them—declined dramatically. Ski clubs embraced the up-ski revolution. Rope tows and chairlifts became the entirety of most skiers' experiences. Clubs continued to provide ski lessons and lodging, but many skiers didn't bother with clubs at all and just commuted each weekend to their favorite ski area. Ski manufacturers designed their products for lift skiing, not touring, as Michael Borghoff observed in *Summit* magazine in 1959:

> This business of downhill skiing, my friend
> Is a bit more involved than it looks—
> You need buckles and long-thongs and cables
> And gadgets and gizmos and hooks.
>
> Yes, and pneumatic ankle supporters
> Are available in better ski shops,
> As well as torsional tension click bindings
> For unexpected embarrassing flops.
>
> And the latest designs in boot making
> Give the fashionable skier great news!
> Two boots (one inside of the other),
> Make them as heavy as a diver's lead shoes.

As early as 1951, Roger Freeman of The Mountaineers observed that "climbing to ski has lost favor in the past ten to fifteen years." He continued, "It is amazing to discover that very few skiers know that there is such a thing as climbing uphill with skis on your feet." By the 1960s, pioneer skier Hans Otto Giese lamented, "People are too lazy now. They'd rather

sit on a chair, get hauled up, ski down and then take the next chair up—just like a yo-yo."
Veteran ski jumper Olav Ulland observed, "Nobody wants to walk anywhere anymore."

MOUNTAINEERING ON SKIS
Walt Little was the architect of The Mountaineers' first ski mountaineering course,
launched in 1941. The course prepared skiers to tackle the highest and remotest peaks

Chuck Welsh skiing in Austria in the early 1950s (Courtesy Chuck Welsh)

Erline Reber, first woman to ski from the summit of Mount Rainier (Courtesy Yakima Herald)

in the Northwest, with instruction in routefinding, snow camping, glacier skiing, avalanche safety, and more. Little's course ran through most of the war years, and around twenty club members had graduated by the end of 1944. They included future club president Bill Degenhardt and a young mountaineer named Chuck Welsh.

Welsh served in the Army Air Corps during the war and later applied lessons from the ski mountaineering course to make the first complete ski descent of Mount Rainier. In 1948 he joined with Kermit Bengtson, Dave Roberts, and Cliff Schmidtke to climb Rainier by the Emmons Glacier route. Getting permission from the Park Service for a ski descent took persistence. "They had some theory about ski mountaineering in the winter," Welsh recalled, "and they weren't going to let anyone even try it. Finally, they made up some excuse that it would be okay for us to do it but we had to give them a full report."

Reaching the summit on the afternoon of July 18, Welsh and friends strapped into their skis at the crater rim. They began their descent two to a rope, with each man carrying a ski pole in one hand and an ice axe in the other. Over icy and exposed sections, they moved one at a time, with the stationary man giving a running ice-axe pick belay. Belayed skiing was something Welsh had practiced in The Mountaineers ski mountaineering course. "There was nothing spectacular about it," he said. "You just put an ice axe in. The trick is to let the rope out fast enough so you don't pull the guy ahead of you down." When the snow softened lower on the mountain, they moved together and descended much more quickly. Welsh completed his report to the Park Service, saying that as long as summit ski parties were of proven experience and capability, they'd probably make less trouble for the park than climbing parties on foot.

Seven years passed before Rainier was skied again from its summit, this time by Bob McCall and Marcel Schuster of Yakima. Schuster had served in the German mountain troops during the war and worked as a mountain guide in Europe afterward. McCall was a Tenth Mountain Division veteran. The pair got a special permit from the Park Service to take skis above Steamboat Prow. During their 1955 descent, roped together, Schuster skied at the rear holding two ice axes, while McCall led the way using ski poles. McCall repeated the descent in 1961 with Erline Anderson Schuster (later Reber), the first woman to ski from the summit of Mount Rainier. Erline also skied Mount Adams with McCall, and friends credited her with being the first woman to ski from the summit of Mount St. Helens. She completed her skiing and mountaineering adventures despite being born without fingers on her right hand.

A second route on Mount Rainier was skied in 1961 by a party making a film called *Out to Ski*. On June 18, John Ahern and Roger Brown of Summit Films accompanied visiting skiers Bill Briggs, Gordon Butterfield, Joe Marillac, and Roger Paris, together with Mount Rainier guides Jim and Lou Whittaker, to ski the Ingraham Glacier route from the summit to Camp Muir.

BOARDS WITHOUT HORDES

As lift skiing grew in popularity during the 1950s and early 1960s, changes were occurring in the remote Northwest mountains, out of the sight and awareness of most skiers. Logging and mining extended roads up former wilderness valleys. Helicopters transported prospectors to potential mining claims, and plans were laid for a cross-state highway through the North Cascades. For a small number of wilderness skiers and mountaineers, the new roads created tantalizing opportunities. In 1948 mining interests extended the North Fork Cascade River road to Gilbert Creek, three miles below Cascade Pass. Within a few years, adventurous skiers were using this access route to explore the glaciers of Eldorado Peak and the expansive slopes of Boston Basin and Sahale Arm.

Joe and Joan Firey, with their friends John and Irene Meulemans, skied the south side of Eldorado Peak in the late 1950s. Their approach up Eldorado Creek was shorter and less exposed to avalanches than the route from Sibley Pass used in the 1930s by Dwight Watson and friends. The Fireys and Meulemans were part of a mixed group of skiers associated with The Mountaineers of Seattle and Tacoma. The group included Bill Degenhardt and his wife, Stella; Gary Rose and Cal Magnusson, longtime employees of REI Co-op in Seattle; photographers Ira Spring and Keith Gunnar; as well as Dave Nicholson, Marilyn Loranger, and several others.

After logging roads were extended up Shuksan and Sulphur Creeks in the late 1950s, the approach to the south sides of both Mount Baker and Mount Shuksan became more attractive. The Fireys and their friends skied the south side of Mount Shuksan by the mid-1960s, if

A DINTY MOORE WHODUNIT

Chuck and Marion Hessey returned to the Lyman Lake cabin many times and in 1956 produced a half-hour color film of the area called *Skiing Cascade Wilderness*. The movie was later broadcast by Seattle's KOMO-TV station on its weekly *Exploration Northwest* program. The Hesseys were accompanied on this trip by their young friends Tom Lyon and Phil Dahl. Since the group packed in a lot of movie gear, they didn't carry much food. Chuck arranged for a food drop by a Civil Air Patrol plane after their arrival. The flight was delayed by weather, however, and their food dwindled to just a single bag of rice. Looking around the cabin, they found a few cans of Dinty Moore stew and some dog food. They cooked up the rice and added the contents of one of the Dinty Moore cans to complete their dinner.

Tom recalled that the meal was "kind of crunchy." Chuck said it was just partially cooked rice, but Tom was not so sure. He asked to look at the stew can again. In the dark cabin, buried in snow and lit by a lantern or two, it was hard to see much of anything. Tom asked, "Where are the potatoes and carrots that are supposed to be in this stew? If I didn't know better, I'd swear this was dog food." After inspection of the opened and unopened cans, they found that the serial number on the bottom of an unopened dog food can matched the one on the "stew" they had cooked up. Fortunately their airdrop arrived the following day.

More than forty years later, Gary Rose of The Mountaineers recalled a week spent at the Lyman Lake cabin when his group was cooped up by bad weather. "We were in this dark little hutch with nothing to do all week," he told me. "The snow survey crew the previous week had a dog with them and they had cached some food, including some dog food. So we peeled off the label of one of the cans of stew and pasted it on the dog food can and put it back in the cache."

While it was rare for skiers from the east and west sides of the Cascades to plan trips together in the early postwar years, the ski touring community was small enough that they often knew each other. Chuck Hessey knew Rose's group had used the cabin before his party's stay there, and he figured out whodunit. "I worked at REI in Seattle for a number of years," Rose said, "and every time Chuck came in, I'd run and hide. He'd always look me up, you know, and ask for me. We'd laugh about that."

not earlier. Thanks to favorable road access, Shuksan's Sulphide Glacier eventually became a popular spring ski tour. Across the Baker River valley, the Fireys and Meulemans spied what they hoped would be a similarly attractive trip: the western slopes of Mount Blum and Hagan Mountain. In June 1966 they approached the area from the Baker River.

Born in Czechoslovakia, Irene (Witlerova) Meulemans had done some skiing while living in New Zealand. That experience did not prepare her for skiing in the North Cascades. "When I got here I thought, 'Gosh! We are crossing the creeks! And we are climbing the trees—on our skis!' If you went with Cal Magnusson that's what you did. That was really exciting." The approach to Mount Blum started with a river ford and a steep forest, then got worse. "We carried skis in devil's club and everything," recalled Irene. "Such a miserable way up. And halfway up it started to rain. So we sat there and we said, 'What do we do now?' We decided it's easier to go up than go all the way down that day. It was one of those times when the next day there wasn't a cloud in the sky." They skied Mount Blum and climbed one of the peaks of Hagan Mountain but returned to the valley with a firm conviction: "Never again," Irene said. "When you've got your skis on your pack, it doesn't feel very good anymore," added Joe Firey.

SKY-HIGH SKI TRIP

During the Cold War years of the 1950s, more than sixty countries agreed to participate in a worldwide science project known as the International Geophysical Year (IGY). The IGY was scheduled to run from the summer of 1957 through the end of 1958, involving studies in eleven earth sciences including oceanography, seismology, and precision mapping. Meteorology was on the agenda as well, and in Washington State this led to the establishment of glacier monitoring stations in the Cascade Mountains on the South Cascade Glacier and in the Olympic Mountains on the Blue Glacier of Mount Olympus. The IGY is considered to be the foundation of today's climate science. Much of the historical data collection that we rely on today, including the critical carbon dioxide measurements by Charles David Keeling, began during the IGY project.

Glaciologist Ed LaChapelle, a skier and member of the Tacoma Mountaineers, led the study team on Mount Olympus. Early studies on Olympus were under way by 1955. A small team was supplied during the summer using airdrops by pilot Bill Fairchild and his Angeles Flying Service. But the eighteen-month IGY project would require building a larger shelter at the site and supplying it in both summer and winter. Recognizing the difficulty of supplying the station by airdrop, and the desirability of rotating out the staff, LaChapelle suggested to Fairchild that he become a true glacier pilot, able to land and take off at 6,800 feet on the Blue Glacier's Snow Dome. Fairchild agreed to rebuild a little two-seater Aeronca Champion for the project if LaChapelle would supply a pair of expensive retractable skis for it.

LaChapelle bought the skis, and early in the summer of 1957 Fairchild flew him in the Aeronca to make the first glacier landing ever recorded in Washington State. To take off from the glacier, Fairchild flew off the northern edge of the Snow Dome, a slope that soon earned the nickname Fairchild's Leap. "Bill discovered he could coast down the steep slope like a ski jump, barely requiring any assistance from the engine," LaChapelle recalled. "He delighted in scaring the wits out of any passenger who had experience as a pilot. He would roar up to the edge with the engine wide open as for a normal takeoff, then at the last moment cut the ignition and toboggan down the steep slope and into the air, thereby achieving what to the conventional pilot was an aeronautical impossibility, a dead-stick takeoff."

Photographer Ira Spring visited the Blue Glacier twice during the IGY project, first in summer and then during the winter of 1958. His images of the scientists at work on foot and by ski were published in pictorial features in the *Seattle Times*. A few months after the IGY formally ended (though studies continued on the Blue Glacier for years), Spring

Pilot Bill Fairchild inspects his airplane on the Blue Glacier of Mount Olympus in 1957. (Spring Trust for Trails)

A skier unloads from Bill Fairchild's airplane on Glacier Peak's Honeycomb Glacier in 1959. (Spring Trust for Trails)

enlisted Fairchild for a most unusual ski outing. His idea was a ski-plane-supported trip to Glacier Peak, the remotest volcano in the Cascade Range. Flying to a glacier high camp might be commonplace in Alaska or far corners of Canada, but it was a novel idea in the Washington Cascades.

The trip was scheduled for May 1959. Joining Spring were nine Mountaineers friends, including John and Irene Meulemans, Gary Rose, Dave Nicholson, Keith Gunnar, and Stella Degenhardt, among others. The plan was to fly from the Darrington airstrip to the Honeycomb Glacier, about 30 miles away. There Fairchild would land the Aeronca at 7,800 feet on the glacier, unload his single passenger, and fly back to Darrington. Ten flights would be required to shuttle the entire party to the mountain.

With clearing weather on the morning of May 11, the party hurried to the Darrington airstrip after shuttling cars to the Kennedy Hot Springs trailhead. "Once every fifty-five minutes," wrote Degenhardt, "the plane purred into view, landed gently, and rolled toward us. Men ran to pour more gas into the tank and push a pack, skis, and passenger into the rear seat, then stood back waving as the plane took off again."

At 7:30 p.m., as shadows lengthened across the snow, the Aeronca deposited its last passenger on the glacier. "We speculated on whether or not Bill could make it back to the airstrip before dark," recalled Degenhardt, "and decided he probably couldn't." But he returned safely nonetheless. With good weather but no guarantee that it would last, the party set out for the summit of Glacier Peak the next morning. A steady ascent of the Suiattle and Cool Glaciers eventually brought them to the summit around 2:00 p.m. They could see from Puget Sound to Lake Wenatchee and from the Canadian border to Mount Adams, Degenhardt recalled. The descent from the summit was ecstatic. "Miles of downhill skiing," said Degenhardt, "where you only had to 'think' a turn. . . . An occasional sitzmark indicated somebody's mind was wandering."

Most of the party spent the following day exploring the area around camp while Spring took photos. After a songfest that night, with all ten skiers squeezed into a four-person tent, they prepared to start for home the following day. Degenhardt observed that when they left their campsite, some of the men's packs weighed more than seventy pounds. Over two long days, the party made their way to Kennedy Hot Springs, encountering steep forested slopes, open streams, rotten snow in gullies, logs to cross, "and every now and then, a short stretch of decent, skiable terrain."

At the hot springs the three women luxuriated in the pool until the men complained they'd been in for an hour and started lobbing snowballs. While undressing in the three-sided shelter had been plenty unpleasant, Stella noted, getting out of the water into 25-degree air was horrible. "Even our blood seemed to stiffen. We had one small hand towel between us. It was not adequate." On the sixth day, they continued out to the White Chuck River road. Where the snow ended, Rose, Nicholson, and Gunnar discarded their old wooden skis. A funeral pyre was proposed but rejected due to the potential fire hazard.

THE BATTLE FOR AMERICA'S ALPS

Writers had long extolled the beauty of the North Cascades. University of Chicago political science professor Grant McConnell, who lived at Stehekin at the far end of Lake Chelan with his wife, Jane, after the war, described viewing the range from a small plane: "It is an awesome sight. As far as can be seen, there is no end to the succession of ice-hung peaks. Those close by are more menacing, but they are so only because they are close; those far off are as sharp, as icy and as forbidding. . . . This is the sea of peaks which so many travelers spontaneously have discovered on first looking out upon it from a height, a sea lashed by some cosmic storm, a sea heaving its surface into a multitude of curling, twisted, white-crested points."

Glacier Peak itself was at the center of a long-running controversy. In the 1930s the Forest Service and Park Service engaged in a debate over which agency could best protect wilderness. In 1935 Bob Marshall of the Forest Service and his boss, Ferdinand Silcox, proposed a 794,000-acre Glacier Peak Wilderness Area. Two years later, Interior Secretary Harold Ickes initiated a study of a potential Ice Peaks National Park that would encompass the entire Cascade Range in Washington, including its five volcanic peaks. Covering 5,000 square miles, Ice Peaks was touted to "outrank in its scenic, recreational, and wildlife values any existing national park and any other possibility for such a park within the United States."

The Forest Service plan was on its way to being adopted in 1939 when both Marshall and Silcox died. In their memory, the Forest Service established a Glacier Peak Limited Area, but its size was reduced by 60 percent by the Northwest regional forester. As World War II loomed, the Ice Peaks National Park idea faded away entirely. After the war, the North Cascades began to feel pressure that was increasing throughout America's wildlands, as the Forest Service sought to meet the demands of a growing population and the postwar housing boom.

In 1955 McConnell became aware of a timber sale offered by the Forest Service in the Stehekin valley. He recognized an emerging pattern: "Logging begins near the head of the wilderness valley," he wrote, "with a road leading to the operations; therefore, whole valley precluded from wilderness status. Log the remainder at leisure. Smart, real smart." An encounter at Stehekin between the McConnells and Mountaineers conservationists Polly Dyer and Phil and Laura Zalesky began a debate about the best strategy to protect the North Cascades. McConnell urged the creation of a single-issue group devoted to the task. In 1957 about fifty men and women from both sides of the Cascades formed the North Cascades Conservation Council (NCCC). Phil Zalesky was elected president, with Patrick Goldsworthy as vice president. McConnell was one of the directors, and Chuck and Marion Hessey were founding members.

In 1958 David Brower of the Sierra Club worked with McConnell and the Hesseys to produce *Wilderness Alps of Stehekin*, a half-hour color film that made the case for protecting the North Cascades. It included winter scenes by Chuck Hessey of skiing in the Lyman Lake area. The Hesseys spent weeks crossing the North Cascades from one side to the other, producing a forty-five-minute film, *From East to West in the North Cascades Wilderness*, that celebrated the range and argued for its protection.

Skiers climb the slopes of Sahale Mountain in the North Cascades, circa 1958. (Spring Trust for Trails)

In 1959 the Forest Service proposed a 422,925-acre wilderness surrounding Glacier Peak that excluded most of the low-elevation forested valleys. Critics decried the proposed area as a "misshapen starfish," as seen on a map. In response, nearly a thousand letters were submitted to the Forest Service, and conservationists appealed directly to the secretary of the Department of Agriculture to expand the area. On September 10, 1960, Agriculture Secretary Ezra T. Benson designated a 458,505-acre wilderness that restored some lands omitted in the proposal. The Glacier Peak Wilderness protected just a portion of the mountains south of the Skagit River and none of the country north or east of it. Under the law of the time, nothing prevented the Forest Service from later rescinding the wilderness designation it had bestowed.

NCCC decided to push for a national park to protect more of the North Cascades. In 1963 the White House created the North Cascades Study Team with representatives from both the Forest Service and Park Service to draft a proposal for managing the North Cascades. The Forest Service then released a plan calling for intensive development of what they called the Eldorado Peaks Recreation Area. Focused on the mountains north and east of Cascade Pass, the development would include three potential ski areas, more than a hundred additional campgrounds, three visitor centers, six resorts, fifteen overlooks, four new organizational camps and lodges, and a road from Harts Pass down Canyon Creek to the North Cascades highway, then under construction. Timber harvesting and mining would be permitted.

Dangling the lure of new ski areas seemed a promising strategy for the Forest Service. With the explosive growth of skiing during the 1950s and 1960s, the promise of new resorts had the potential to split a large group of recreationists away from support for park or wilderness designation. Bill Lenihan of the Pacific Northwest Ski Association (PNSA) encouraged skiers to support Forest Service ski area proposals by writing letters and attending hearings. Ben Hinkle, president of the Multiple Use for Cascades Club, distributed postcards that could be easily signed and mailed to the Forest Service with this printed message:

> *Dear Sir:*
> *I am a skier and I oppose Senate Bill 1321. If the North Cascades is established as a national park and more wilderness areas are dedicated, many potential good ski areas will be lost. Please help defeat SB 1321.*

It was later revealed that Hinkle had a financial interest in a mine in the North Cascades.

As a founding member of the Crystal Mountain board of directors, Duke Watson was a strong supporter of organized skiing. But he expressed his support for the park in a 1963 letter to *Northwest Skier* magazine:

> *Along with lift skiing, a number of us have also found time for touring in the high Cascades. As a result of more than sixty trips throughout this area during recent years, we have become acquainted with many ski fields both within and outside of the proposed park. From this experience I can state with conviction that there are alluring prospects for lift development almost too numerous to count outside the boundaries, including every type of terrain that is found within. The well-meaning officials of the USSA [US Ski Association] and PNSA should put on climbing skins and take a look for themselves!*

In September 1964, the US Congress passed the Wilderness Act, which provided permanent protection for wilderness areas surrounding Glacier Peak, Mount Adams, and the Goat Rocks in Washington. Passage of the act made the campaign for a national park tougher, since opponents pointed out that large portions of the region were already safely set aside in the Glacier Peak Wilderness.

After the North Cascades Study Team released its report in January 1966, Washington senators Henry M. Jackson and Warren G. Magnuson modified the recommendations to obtain the endorsement of President Lyndon B. Johnson's administration. The resulting bill proposed a two-unit North Cascades National Park (north and south of State Highway 20), a Ross Lake National Recreation Area, additions to the Glacier Peak Wilderness, and conversion of the 1930s North Cascades Primitive Area east of Ross Lake into a new Pasayten Wilderness.

At hearings held in Seattle in April 1968, more than eight hundred people requested to testify. Supporters of the park outnumbered opponents by three to one. Representative Wayne Aspinall of Colorado, who had gained a reputation as the most stubborn foe of the Wilderness Act, remarked that he had never seen anything like it. Who were all these people? he wondered. "Are they hippies or part of a Seattle drive to get out into the country?"

Amazed and gratified, Grant McConnell wrote, "By all that's holy, it's a movement now. More going on than any one person can know. The myth of local unanimity against conservation is exploded. And the North Cascades are a national cause." In the final negotiations, Washington governor Dan Evans provided crucial support for the Senate bill. After more congressional wrangling, both the House and the Senate passed the bill, and President Johnson signed the North Cascades Act on October 2, 1968.

An outdoorsman since his youth, Chuck Hessey had explored the North Cascades as thoroughly as anyone. After the war, he became one of the region's most passionate advocates. In his 1958 film *From East to West in the North Cascades Wilderness*, Hessey expressed his wish for the mountains that he loved: "It is now our prayer that some of the glory of God's mountain world can be saved for viewing in solitude and for contemplating in the midst of silence. The trails we have known, others will need to travel, even more than we. If we save enough for them, we can go on, not without honor."

With protection of America's wilderness alps, that honor was secured.

Opposite: *Sally Vynne, a Hyak cross-country ski instructor, adjusts her ski binding, circa 1975.* (Spring Trust for Trails)

CHAPTER 11

COUNTERCULTURE

During the campaign for North Cascades National Park, The Mountaineers collaborated with authors Marge and Ted Mueller and photographers Bob and Ira Spring to publish a guidebook for skiers titled *Northwest Ski Trails*. The book was released in December 1968, two months after the North Cascades Act became law. Mindful of attempts to divide skiers and conservationists during the North Cascades campaign, the book showcased both lift skiing areas and backcountry tours from Oregon to British Columbia. In the foreword, Harvey Manning wrote, "The purpose of this book is to introduce touring to skiers who may have wondered about the snow country over the ridge from the chairlift, in the quiet valley beyond, but haven't known how to get there."

The publishers knew there weren't many ski tourers at that time, but they hoped to entice downhill skiers to try the sport. It didn't work. Backcountry skiing in alpine terrain wouldn't grow significantly for another twenty to thirty years. However, Nordic cross-country skiing using simple three-pin bindings, flexible shoes, and lightweight narrow skis was growing rapidly. Light cross-country equipment wasn't suitable for ungroomed steep slopes, but it was fine for gentle terrain. The sport was also inexpensive, both because the gear was cheaper and because no lift ticket was required. Nordic skiing was suited to the counterculture era of the 1960s (and beyond), when a new generation explored alternatives to lifestyles established after World War II.

WHAT'S OLD IS NEW AGAIN: CROSS-COUNTRY SKIING

In 1964 Nordic skiing coach John Caldwell, a former Olympic skier, wrote *The Cross-Country Ski Book*, a guide to Nordic ski touring. He described cross-country skiing as both the "newest" big winter sport in the United States and also the oldest organized snow sport in North America. The sport had been part of the first Winter Olympic Games in 1924, twelve years before alpine skiing events were introduced to the games. "The first phase of man's inventions has often been the simplest and most beautiful," Caldwell wrote. "I believe this holds true in skiing, for what could be more natural than to use it in its primary form as a means of going from place to place?"

Two years later, Michael Brady published *Nordic Touring and Cross-Country Skiing*. In the book's fourth edition, he wrote: "The grace and speed of the cross-country racer, the distance-covering, steady stride of polar explorers, and the easy pace of weekend touring groups all share a common skiing technique now known as cross-country, the most ancient, most recently re-discovered winter sport." The time had come for a renaissance for the sport and the Northwest was ready.

In 1967 Klindt Vielbig organized the first Nordic ski school on Oregon's Mount Hood. His Cloud Cap Chalet was the first store in Oregon to sell cross-country ski equipment, and he later wrote a guidebook to the state's cross-country ski routes. Seattle's REI Co-op was selling a full line of Nordic ski equipment by the winter of 1969.

In 1970 the Oregon Nordic Club revived a memorial race over McKenzie Pass in memory of John Templeton Craig—a legendary postmaster who died in 1877 while delivering mail from the Willamette Valley to eastern Oregon, a job he'd performed on skis for twenty-five years. Oregon historians and skiers established the memorial race in the early 1930s, but after downhill skiing became popular in the 1950s the race had been abandoned. During the 1970 event, won by Seattle's Gunnar Unneland, each of the thirty-six competitors carried a small pouch reminiscent of Craig's and filled with genuine mail to be delivered. By the 2010s, the event was no longer a race, but it continued as a memorial ski.

Cross-country skiing in the Methow Valley, circa 1980 (Spring Trust for Trails)

In 1973 Wenatchee skiers organized the first annual Mission Peak Citizens Classic, a 21-mile race from Mission Ridge to 4,094-foot Blewett Pass with a "mass shotgun-style Western start." Later called the Hog Loppet (*loppet* is a Swedish term for a backcountry ski trek), the event was promoted as a noncompetitive outing, although many skiers raced it for fun. The Hog Loppet ran for decades but was moved to Lake Wenatchee (and renamed) in 2015 after a series of bad snow years canceled the event at Blewett Pass.

Organized cross-country skiing came to Snoqualmie Pass with the Gold Creek Citizen's Race sponsored by REI in February 1974, when 160 racers competed over a five-mile course across the highway from the Hyak ski area. A year later, the first official cross-country ski trail system in Washington was opened by the Forest Service at Hyak with about 40 miles of marked trails, including the Twin Lakes Trail, the Rockdale Loop, and the Mount

Catherine Loop. The Hyak cross-country center, headed by Pat Deneen, offered rentals and instruction exclusively for cross-country skiers, a first in the state.

Writing in the *Mountaineer Annual* in 1974, Dave Chantler of REI noted that in the previous decade, the number of cross-country skiers in the United States had grown from just a handful to nearly one million. REI's business surged in the early 1970s, and it was selling three thousand pairs of Nordic skis annually by 1975.

EAST MEETS WEST

Long before roads were planned through the Cascade Mountains at Stevens, Snoqualmie, and White Passes, a highway across the North Cascades was the dream of miners and stockmen. A 1945 reconnaissance determined that a route up the Skagit River gorge past the Seattle City Light dams was practical. Beyond Ross Dam, the proposed highway would follow Ruby and Granite Creeks to 4,875-foot Rainy Pass, then cross 5,477-foot Washington Pass before descending Early Winters Creek to the Methow Valley. Construction of the road began in 1959.

During the North Cascades park campaign, conservationists lobbied to run the highway from Ruby Creek along Canyon Creek to connect with the old mining roads up Slate Creek and over Harts Pass. This would have preserved 30 miles of pristine forested valleys over Rainy and Washington Passes. Conservationists lost that battle. Following a Mountaineers summer outing in 1963, Mary Fries wrote, "Regret at leaving Washington Pass was intensified by the thought of this scenic spot soon being invaded by bulldozers for construction of the new road."

A rough pioneer road was completed during the summer of 1968. On September 29, three days before President Johnson signed the North Cascades Act, hundreds of four-wheel-drive vehicles formed a caravan to make the crossing and celebrate at the summit of Rainy Pass. When the North Cascades highway—State Highway 20—finally opened on October 2, 1972, it was no longer regarded as a trade route for miners, ranchers, and lumbermen. Most of the North Cascades were by this time under some sort of protected recreational status. Backcountry skiers such as REI employees Dave Chantler and Gary Rose began exploring slopes around the North Cascades highway as soon as it was plowed in the spring of 1973.

Completion of the highway spurred major changes in the Methow Valley, which had a long history of skiing on a small, community scale. During the 1930s, the valley high school had a ski program, and there was a small ski jumping hill. Loup Loup ski area, located 15 miles east of Twisp on State Highway 20, had offered downhill skiing since the 1940s. In

Dave Chantler explores ski terrain near Rainy Pass in May 1973 following the first spring opening of the North Cascades Highway. (Photo by Gary Rose)

the mid-1960s, Jack Barron took over management of the Sunny M, a combination cattle and dude ranch near Winthrop. Barron quietly acquired 4,000 acres of adjacent property. Sun Mountain Lodge, the successor to the Sunny M, opened in 1968 with a main lodge, restaurant, swimming pool, tennis courts, and more, located atop a hill with sweeping views over the valley.

Anticipating a flood of tourists over the new highway, residents of Winthrop hatched a plan to reinvent the town as an old-fashioned Western town with boardwalks, weather-beaten storefronts, and frontier ambience. The makeover was a success, and during the 1973 tourist season, town businesses struggled to keep up with visitor demand. After Sun Mountain was established, Barron contacted Jim Whittaker at REI for advice on developing skiing in the Methow Valley. Whittaker recommended that Dave Chantler, the cross-country ski buyer at REI, take a look. After visiting, Chantler organized a ski bus to Sun Mountain Lodge the following winter.

Around 1970, Don Portman was an elementary schoolteacher in Seattle who enjoyed downhill skiing. He saw an REI ad for free cross-country ski lessons and signed up with his wife, Sally, for a lesson at Snoqualmie Pass with Chantler himself. The Portmans enjoyed cross-country, so they bought wood skis from REI and pursued the sport with enthusiasm. The Portmans bought land in the Methow Valley and started to think about how they could live there year-round. Chantler suggested to Jack Barron that he hire Don to become the director of skiing at Sun Mountain Lodge.

Portman came on board during the snow drought winter of 1976–77. During that year, the North Cascades highway remained open through the winter, so Don took Sun Mountain Lodge guests to Washington Pass for cross-country skiing. Don developed primitive cross-country trail grooming in the Methow Valley, his days revolving around late-night or early-morning grooming sessions until the snowmobile would inevitably "blow up." He'd spend the rest of his day rebuilding the machine for the next session.

In the Mazama area in the 1970s, Dick and Sue Roberts established North Cascades Basecamp and began connecting trails in collaboration with Jack Wilson, who had a guest ranch in the area. Enoch Kraft began grooming trails in the Rendezvous area, northeast of the valley, and Steve Farmer and Dale Caulfield installed a series of huts along this trail system. As cross-country skiing grew in scale in the late '70s, local residents organized the Methow Valley Ski Touring Association (now called Methow Trails) to link separate trails into a unified system, now the largest cross-country trail network in North America. Jay Lucas was a key contributor in the 1990s and 2000s, providing the vision and groundwork for what the system would eventually become.

CROSS-COUNTRY DOWNHILL

Jack Hughes landed a job as a Yellowstone National Park ranger in the fall of 1958, following army service in Korea and college in Colorado. He took up skiing in Yellowstone and did a lot of ski touring during his seven winters in the park. In the fall of 1965, Hughes transferred to Olympic National Park in Washington. The Hurricane Ridge ski area was busy in those days, but there was little cross-country skiing. Encountering another cross-country skier was like meeting a fellow pilgrim. Most of Hughes's patrol work was along the ridge between Hurricane Hill and Obstruction Point, but he did many patrols to Seven Lakes Basin and other park locations. He recalled a February crossing of the Olympics from the Elwha River to the Dosewallips over Hayden Pass, a ski trip of around 40 miles.

In the early 1960s, alpine touring skier Eric Burr was using Head metal skis, cable bindings, and leather ski mountaineering boots. He made an early ski crossing of the Sierra

Nevada with this gear in 1965. Three years later, Burr landed his dream job as a snow ranger under Jack Hughes at Hurricane Ridge. To make it easier to keep up with Hughes, Burr converted to Nordic ski gear during his stint in Olympic National Park and learned about waxing from his boss. Burr experimented with Nordic ski techniques including the telemark, the open christie, and the "Gunnar," a maneuver that links one telemark turn to another without changing the lead ski.

Jack Hughes patrols the backcountry at Hurricane Ridge in Olympic National Park, circa 1970. (Olympic National Park Archives)

The telemark, a free-heel turn in which the ski on the outside of the turn is advanced while the inside leg is bent as in a curtsy, was a traditional technique of old-time Nordic skiers (see the "Early Skiing Techniques" sidebar in chapter 3). The turn fell out of favor in the early 1900s with the rise the Arlberg (or "christie") technique. In stem and parallel christies, the feet remain more or less side by side throughout the turn. Christies are helped considerably by bindings that hold the heel of the boot firmly on the ski. This enhances downhill control but makes walking and climbing on skis a chore.

For roughly fifty years, the telemark turn was ostracized by leading proponents of "modern" skiing. But a few skiers imagined it making a comeback. Writing in 1949, Swiss author Christian Rubi observed, "Long a tradition with the Swiss Ski School, this graceful turn has all but disappeared and is only used on rare occasions. However, we would not be too surprised if the telemark were to reappear someday as an 'entirely new and revolutionary method of skiing.'"

Steve Barnett skis the Mount Baker ski area backcountry, circa 1982. (Photo by David Barnes)

Steve Barnett grew up in Chicago and learned to ski on trips to the Rockies in the late 1950s. While ski bumming in Colorado around 1968, he met some ski tourers and decided to try it. After experimenting with heavier gear, Barnett got a pair of wooden Bonna Fjellskis mounted with Silvretta Saas Fee cable bindings. He used climbing boots to ski on them. He didn't trust the cable bindings, doubting that the cable release would work in a fall. Since there was no side release designed into the binding and only an unreliable forward release, Barnett skied free-heel parallel turns most of the time. The cables on the Silvretta bindings were constantly breaking due to metal fatigue. "Silvretta junk was unreliable in a reliable way," he recalled. "You carry a spare cable or two and you're gonna be okay."

After moving to Seattle, Barnett experimented with Nordic skis and boots with three-pin bindings for backcountry skiing. "I had identified routes in the Pasayten Wilderness that I thought you could do in winter and avoid most avalanche danger," he said, "and I wanted to do them, and I didn't think my Silvretta outfit was really up for that kind of thing . . . the distance and the reliability." During a trip to Galena Summit in Idaho around 1976, Barnett practiced telemark skiing and concluded that "it was working better than the Silvrettas ever worked, just in terms of pure downhill skiing, let alone in every other way. And I thought, 'There's no information whatever, and this could open up a lot of terrain, and activity, to people,' so I wrote the book to introduce it, and it more or less did."

Barnett's 1978 book *Cross-Country Downhill* addressed free-heel skiing in mountainous terrain, building on the experience of skiers like Eric Burr and Jack Hughes. The book boosted Nordic downhill skiing for a new generation, and telemarking would be the most popular form of backcountry skiing in the Pacific Northwest for the next couple decades.

SKI WARS IN THE METHOW VALLEY

In the late 1960s, Jack Wilson started thinking about adding downhill skiing to his Early Winters guest ranch near Mazama. He shared his idea with Doug Devin, a neighbor who worked in the ski industry. Wilson originally thought of installing a rope tow on a small hill behind his cabins, but Devin suggested looking at Sandy Butte, a 6,076-foot mountain behind the ranch that offered 4,000 vertical feet of potential ski terrain.

When North Cascades National Park was established in 1968, more than a dozen potential winter recreation sites had been identified by the North Cascades Study Team. Three sites were included in the new park, preventing their development. After the park was created, the Forest Service was directed to study the remaining sites. Sandy Butte was identified in 1970 as the only site with the potential to become a major ski area. Along the North Cascades highway, a proposed tram from Thunder Arm to Ruby Mountain was still

The proposed Early Winters Resort, with golf course, village, and ski hill, as rendered by artist Ron Bomba. (Courtesy Ron Bomba)

under consideration in the mid-1970s. The tram was conceived as a scenic viewpoint, but Park Service managers were concerned that if it were built, skiers would pressure the agency to develop a ski area there. Ultimately the tram idea was abandoned.

Farther south in the Cascades, other ski areas were being considered. Between Snoqualmie and Stevens Passes, proposals were floated for ski lifts on Mount Hinman, Mount Cashmere, Snowgrass Mountain, and several other locations. But many of these sites were no longer an option after they were included in the Alpine Lakes Wilderness, established in 1976.

After the North Cascades highway opened in 1972, word got out about a potential new ski area in the Methow Valley. The Aspen Skiing Company purchased options on 1,200 acres of land at the base of Sandy Butte in 1974. Through the 1970s and beyond, the proposed Early Winters development held the promise—or threat, depending on one's point of view—of the only major new ski resort in Washington. This prompted a land rush throughout the upper valley, mostly by people with connections to Aspen.

In response to the potential development, a mix of longtime residents and valley newcomers formed the Methow Valley Citizens Council. The influx of new young residents in the valley generated backlash, including this ad in the valley newspaper: "Tell all your Seattle hunters, if they don't get stampeded by a deer, not to go home empty handed. Take a hippie. They are kind of hard to clean, but with an apple in their mouth they make good decorations on the fender of the car." The controversy became a standoff in the late 1970s, as the Forest Service reviewed its plans for roadless areas throughout the nation. In the meantime, the Aspen Skiing Company pulled out of the Methow Valley to develop Black-comb Mountain ski area in British Columbia.

The Washington Wilderness Bill of 1984 excluded Sandy Butte from wilderness des-ignation, enabling Doug Devin and his company, Methow Recreation Inc., to pursue a permit to develop Sandy Butte. The local "ski war" reached the US Supreme Court in 1989, when portions of the project's environmental impact statement were found inadequate. Environmental concerns and management problems ultimately ended the idea of a major ski resort complex in the upper Methow Valley. Today the Freestone Inn at Wilson Ranch remains the most visible legacy of the long Early Winters ski area campaign.

One of those who came to the Methow Valley during this period was Eric Sanford, an Aspen transplant who billed himself as "Mr. Fun." A former Yosemite climber, skier, and entrepreneur with boundless energy, Sanford moved to the valley in the late 1970s. He founded Liberty Bell Alpine Tours to offer kayak lessons, rafting trips, backpacking trips, and mountaineering and ski tours. During the winter of 1983, he introduced helicopter ski-ing to the area. Sanford's guides included Eric Burr, Jay Lucas, and Don Portman, longtime skiing residents in the valley. The company had a large potential tenure accessible from their Mazama base, bounded by the Pasayten Wilderness to the north, North Cascades National Park to the west, and the Lake Chelan–Sawtooth Wilderness to the south.

Sanford moved on after 1987 due to financial troubles, and the heli-skiing permit was taken over by Randy and Kathy Sackett. Their company, North Cascade Heli-Skiing, con-tinues today under the ownership of Ken Brooks and Paul Butler. In 1997 the outfit erected a yurt near Windy Pass on the edge of the Pasayten Wilderness, a snowball's throw from the cabin (still standing) that Mel Gourlie's family built in the 1930s.

The Methow Valley became a hotbed for telemark skiing throughout the 1980s, with ski camps run by Eric Sanford and others. Steve Barnett moved to Mazama around 1980 and helped organize these camps. During a spring camp in 1981, he and Sanford staged an unusual competition called the Berzerkebeinerrennet, a reaction against specialized slalom competitions for telemark skiers. The event, conceived by Barnett's friend Todd Eastman, was designed as a proper mountain trip in miniature, with climbs, traverses, flat terrain, and downhill runs. These ideas didn't gain much acceptance at the time, but they reemerged twenty years later in "randonnée rallies," now commonly known as ski mountaineering races.

THE BLIZZARD OF ASH

In late March 1980, Mount St. Helens in southwest Washington began rumbling with a series of earthquakes. On the 27th, a steam explosion opened a new crater at the top of the volcano and sent an ash plume 7,000 feet into the air. By the 30th, earthquakes beneath the mountain were so frequent that the recording paper on quake monitors had become a solid black blur. Despite a closure by the US Forest Service, curiosity seekers were drawn to the mountain, and during the first two weeks in April, at least three climbing parties reached the crater rim. Hoping to make some money, one climber filmed his buddy drinking a beer (several brands, in fact) with the steaming crater as a backdrop. The footage never made it to the TV screen. Washington governor Dixie Lee Ray declared a "red zone" around the volcano, with trespassers subject to a $500 fine or six months in jail.

In spite of the risk, public pressure convinced officials to allow fifty carloads of property owners to enter the danger zone on May 17 to gather their belongings. Another trip was scheduled for 10:00 a.m. the following day, but at 8:32 a.m., a magnitude 5.1 earthquake caused the bulging north flank of Mount St. Helens to collapse. This triggered the largest landslide in recorded history, sending a 600-foot-high wave of debris-filled water across Spirit Lake at 100 to 150 miles per hour. The wave was deflected by a ridge north of the lake and thrown back toward the mountain with a torrent of downed trees, raising the level of the lake about 200 feet. Within ten minutes, the column of steam and ash from the eruption reached an altitude of 12 miles. Fifty-seven people were killed during the blast.

On the morning of the eruption, Jens Kieler, Rich Lowell, and John Mueller were at a high camp below the Kautz Icefall on Mount Rainier hoping

Mount St. Helens erupting on May 18, 1980 (US Geological Survey)

to make a ski descent of the mountain. Lowell had just finished a photographic study of Mount St. Helens, using up his remaining film, when the mountain suddenly exploded. Initially it looked as though thunderheads were forming in the sky. Then lightning flashed and a huge column of ash rose from the volcano. "The lightning was flashing around like the spokes of a wheel might flash through a strobe," recalled Kieler. Before long, a fog of gray ash blackened the snowfields of Mount Rainier. About two hours after the eruption, the three men skied down to Paradise, tracing white tracks in the black snow. "It was like skiing on sandpaper," recalled Kieler. Oddly, the noise of the blast, heard all over the Northwest, had not been audible to the three skiers. "We never even heard the initial 'big bang,'" Kieler said. The eruption blew more than 1,300 feet off the top of the formerly 9,677-foot peak.

It wasn't long before curiosity-seeking climbers returned to what was left of Mount St. Helens. During a flight over the mountain, Oregon photographer Ancil Nance took a picture of a friend standing on the crater rim in July. Climbers told stories of a summit register,

DRESSED TO THRILL

On June 5, 1987, the *Seattle Times* published a front-page photo of a skier standing atop Mount St. Helens in a red chiffon dress and white pillbox hat. Kathy Phibbs was outfitted in shorts and a sleeveless top accessorized with mirror sunglasses and Swix cross-country ski earmuffs. Accompanied by four friends, Phibbs and the group did a cancan dance in their thick-soled boots for the benefit of photographers. The newspaper declared the climb of Mount St. Helens "one of the state's newest and most intoxicating tourist attractions," "a blast" with "less mountain now, but more fun."

In the years that followed, the last weekend in May before permits were required (often Mother's Day weekend) became one of the most popular times to climb the mountain. (Today, permits are required year-round, but the number issued per day decreases after mid-May.) A tradition emerged for climbers to make the ascent in women's clothing—the more outlandish the better. Writer Cassandra Overby described the attire as "elegant ball gowns, glittery tutus and suggestive fishnet stockings." And she was describing the men.

Phibbs died in a climbing accident in 1991. Friend Kristen Laine described the tradition Phibbs had started: "When we pack the box of party dresses for a skiing trip, we are out to capture a playfulness we think we have lost, even if we never allowed our younger selves such latitude. We pull on a polka-dot tutu and—man or woman—some mischievous spirit enters us. We banter with strangers on the mountain, we grin wider and longer than we might otherwise, and when it comes time to ski down, we carve our turns with more abandon and joy than we would have if we hadn't become 'the girls and boys in our summer dresses.'"

Rich Lowell (left) and John Mueller descend Mount Rainier on the morning that Mount St Helens erupted in 1980. (Photo by Jens Kieler)

hidden in a stone cairn on the crater rim, that contained first names only. In 1981 an outlaw group from Olympia, calling themselves the Gonzo Climbers, dressed all in white, in women's clothing from Goodwill, to blend in with the summit snows. Finding the snow darkened by volcanic ash, they rolled in the ash to better camouflage themselves, then dashed to the summit. Skiers were known to climb to the summit carrying white bedsheets as "cloaking devices" to hide underneath when aircraft flew by.

In February 1987, a judge in Skamania County struck down the 1980 governor's order establishing the "red zone" around Mount St. Helens. The judge said in his ruling that "there is no standard for common sense determination of when the emergency was over." The Forest Service announced a new policy to reopen the mountain to climbers: from November 1 to May 15, climbers would simply register before and after their climb; from May 16 through October 31, a limited number of permits would be issued each day, with most assigned by advance reservations. The mountain formally reopened on May 4, 1987. Over the weekend of May 9–10 (Mother's Day), about sixteen hundred people climbed the mountain. The Forest Service issued more than twenty thousand permits that year, making Mount St. Helens one of the most climbed peaks in the world.

Opposite: *The North Cascades*

CHAPTER 12

SKIING THE SKYLINE

Early skiing in the Northwest developed in mountains close to timberline. A few pioneers explored glaciers and higher summits, but they returned to lower country as soon as possible. The attempt by Ben Thompson and friends to ski around Mount Baker in 1932, camping for several nights high on the glaciers, was decades ahead of its time. It didn't inspire imitators for many years. But some adventurous long trips were in fact made, particularly in Oregon, where much of the Cascade crest is near or below the tree line.

In 1917 Dean Van Zant, Clem Blakney, and Chester Treichel skied from Mount Hood nearly to Mount Jefferson, a trek of about 60 miles. Carrying sixty-pound packs with snowshoes as backup for their skis, they hoped to climb Jefferson near the end of their trip but abandoned that plan due to a snowstorm. Instead the men skied and snowshoed out to Breitenbush Hot Springs and the town of Detroit.

In northeast Oregon, Pete Eyraud completed a 60-mile ski trip in 1936 along the Blue Mountains Skyline Trail, between Tollgate, Oregon, and Dayton, Washington. He spent most nights in Forest Service lookouts, but Eyraud passed his fourth night shivering without blankets or fire in a lean-to that he found buried in the snow.

By the mid-1930s, the Oregon Skyline Trail (now the Pacific Crest Trail) between Mount Hood and Mount Jefferson was being developed, and parties from the Forest Service's Mount Hood office skied it several times. In 1948 Jack Meissner skied the trail from Mount Hood all the way to Crater Lake, a distance of about 300 miles. Completed during one of the coldest and snowiest winters in years, the trek required thirty-three travel days, and Meissner broke trail by himself for most of them.

The growth of lift-serviced skiing after World War II produced a baby-boom generation of downhill skiers with little exposure to or interest in high-mountain ski touring. It would fall to the counterculture of mostly Nordic backcountry skiers of the 1970s and 1980s to begin exploring the potential for long high-level ski routes in Washington's Cascades and Olympics.

THE PTARMIGAN TRAVERSE

The classic alpine trek in the North Cascades is the Ptarmigan Traverse, first explored on foot during the summer of 1938 by four members of Seattle's Ptarmigan Climbing Club. Continuously above tree line, the route threads its way across alp slopes, glaciers, and high passes for about 15 miles between Cascade Pass and Dome Peak, offering mountaineers more than a dozen peaks to climb and an array of scenic high campsites to choose from. It would be another four decades for the Ptarmigan Traverse to be skied for the first time.

In January 1977, Nordic skier Steve Barnett invited his friend Bill Nicolai to try telemark skiing near Excelsior Pass above the Mount Baker highway (State Highway 542). Nicolai was founder of Early Winters, which in 1976 had introduced the first line of waterproof-breathable outdoor gear, including gaiters, parkas, and tents, using a new fabric called Gore-Tex. He designed a two-person single-wall lightweight tent using this material that seemed tailor-made for spring ski trips. Nicolai had backpacked the Ptarmigan Traverse in summer and suggested that it would be a perfect trip to do on skis. He and Barnett attempted the route in May 1977 after a series of spring storms. As they contemplated the steep traverse from Cascade Pass to the Cache Glacier below the walls of Mixup Peak, they watched avalanches repeatedly sweep the slope and wisely aborted their trip.

A year later, Barnett returned with skiers Dave Kahn and Mark Hutson. They made it beyond Mixup Peak but were pinned down by drizzle and fog near the South Cascade

Mark Hutson (left) and Gary Brill ski toward Yang Yang Lakes in 1982.

Glacier. "To make a long story short," Barnett wrote, "we ended up sitting out many days in the middle of the traverse, running out of food, and then navigating through the fog with map, compass, and altimeter to the one bailout route available on the whole traverse," the rudimentary trail used by University of Washington glaciologists doing research on the South Cascade Glacier. "The ten rainy miles out on this trail are not remembered with a warm glow," he concluded.

In 1981 Dan Stage and Brian Sullivan skied the Ptarmigan Traverse for the first time. The two skiers had attended a lecture by Barnett at the University of Washington during which he described his attempts to ski the traverse. In June, not long after the lecture, Stage and Sullivan set out on their trip. During two days of fine weather, they skied to Kool Aid Lake and continued to the shoulder above Yang Yang Lakes, climbing Spider and Le Conte Mountains along the way. On their third day, they continued to White Rock Lakes and enjoyed a side trip without backpacks, skiing partway down the South Cascade Glacier. The weather deteriorated, however, and the pair spent a rainy day pinned down at the lakes. Sullivan recalled that each man had a tiny single-wall tent (a "squeeze tube") that was wholly unsatisfactory when cooped up in the rain. Vowing to escape on their fifth day, they broke camp, skied over the Cascade crest next to Spire Point, and descended into Bachelor and Downey Creeks—a route they hadn't followed before. The overgrown wet trail turned into a grueling, hypothermic ordeal, and they arrived at the Suiattle River road long after dark, soaked to the bone.

Two parties skied the route in 1982. In early June, I joined Mark Hutson, Gary Brill, and Kerry Ritland to make the second ski crossing of the route. It was my first real ski traverse, my first time along the Ptarmigan, and something inside me resonated with the experience. I was captivated by the sense of flowing through an untouched wilderness on skis. I remember scrambling up three different summits on our second day, then skiing with Mark down the South Cascade Glacier as sunset bathed our tracks in golden light. There were no tracks, no fire rings, no trampled meadows, nothing to dispel the illusion that we were the first people ever to set foot or ski in this country.

In late June, Barnett completed the traverse with Harry Hendon and Spencer Stoddard. They made a ski ascent of Dome Peak, fulfilling Chuck Hessey's dream of laying ski tracks on this magnificent fortress of glaciers. It was a worthy cap to Barnett's efforts on the Ptarmigan Traverse. In 1987 he published *The Best Ski Touring in America*, a selection of thirty-one trips from Mount Mansfield in Vermont to Mount Olympus in Washington and from the Grand Canyon in Arizona to the Ruth Amphitheater in Alaska. The book was the summation of a decade of ski exploration, during which Barnett crisscrossed North America, writing magazine articles and teaching ski clinics, as a sort of pied piper on Nordic skis.

INTO THE WILD

The year 1982 brought a record dry spring to Seattle, twenty-nine consecutive days without rain. This provided an unusual opportunity for skiers to explore high-level multiday ski trips in the North Cascades. A few weeks before his successful crossing of the Ptarmigan Traverse, Steve Barnett skied a seven-day trip he called the Eureka Creek Loop in the Pasayten Wilderness with John Almquist, Greg Knott, and Doug Veenhof. It was the dream of doing Pasayten trips like this that had inspired Barnett to switch from alpine ski touring to Nordic downhill skiing five years earlier.

In mid-June, not long after he skied the Ptarmigan Traverse with me, Gary Brill recruited Joe Catellani and Brian Sullivan to traverse the Dakobed Range, a string of high glaciated peaks extending from Glacier Peak to Boulder Pass above the Napeequa Valley. Brill's photos from the trip show his partners skiing the glaciers in shorts and T-shirts. The trio was out for five days.

These trips were inspired by not only improvements in ski equipment but also a trove of new information. In 1973 The Mountaineers published the first volume of the *Cascade*

Alpine Guide, an encyclopedic reference to climbing and high routes in the Washington Cascades. The book was compiled by Fred Beckey, who at fifty was already a legend in Northwest mountaineering. The first volume covered the southern Cascades from the Columbia River to Stevens Pass. Subsequent volumes were published in 1977 (extending the coverage north to Rainy Pass, including the Glacier Peak Wilderness and the south unit of North Cascades National Park) and 1981 (extending the series to the Canadian border, including the north unit of the park and the Pasayten Wilderness).

Two features made these guidebooks irresistible to a new generation of ski mountaineers: Beckey's descriptions of North Cascades high routes, exemplified by his thousand-plus-word account of the Ptarmigan Traverse, coupled with breathtaking images by mountaineer-photographers such as Austin Post, Tom Miller, Dwight Watson, Bob and Ira Spring, and Philip Leatherman. Young climbers and skiers pored over the guidebooks, dreaming of clear skies, tall summits, and shimmering glaciers. Readers also noted warnings of "impenetrable jungles of rain forest in such valleys as the Sultan, Sauk, Suiattle and Cascade Rivers."

Gordy Skoog crosses Granite Creek with skis in 1986.

The most popular North Cascades high routes have at least a rudimentary trail leading to timberline at each end. Carrying skis makes traveling an overgrown trail more difficult, but even a faint trail is nearly always better than no trail at all. The biggest concern for a mountain traveler is being forced by bad weather to flee the high country in the middle of a route, as Barnett's party did on the Ptarmigan Traverse in 1978. In addition to rushing streams, fallen trees, and mossy cliffs, one of the greatest problems facing the subalpine mountaineer—and the skier even more so—is dense brush.

Devil's club is the most notorious North Cascades shrub, innocuous looking until you inspect it closely. Skier and climber Michael Borghoff described his first encounter with the plant in *Summit* magazine: "Along the trunk and narrow branches were thousands of tiny, needly barbs, thickly clustered; they looked—well, they looked just like the spikes of a medieval club. A devil's club. It bowed to me in mocking salutation. A botanical Mephisto."

Slide alder is an even greater foe than devil's club, especially to the ski-toting mountaineer. Dense slide alder can slow a hiker's progress to much less than a mile an hour, and in wet weather every move through the brush can bring down more moisture than falls from the sky. Borghoff put it this way:

> *Slide alder is a perfectly respectable deciduous tree, only instead of growing upward like it should, it has assumed the curse of the serpent and slithers along the ground; it grows outward horizontally from the slope, making each upward step a monumental effort against crisscrossed twining branches. Add devil's club to it, and you have an immense problem.*
>
> *You fight; you grab, stumble, slip, slither backward, and land like an upended beetle on your pack. The brush pushes you down. Mud oozes up. Your ice axe is caught. You are on top [of] a mess of devil's club. It starts to rain. Your feet hurt. You are bushwacking in the Cascades.*

Though the North Cascades are of modest elevation compared to the Alps or Alaska Range, the combination of rugged topography, dense undergrowth, and fickle weather can make them just as formidable. Writing in the *Mountaineer Annual*, Alex Bertulis described a 1977 visit by a team of Soviet climbers following a trip to Alaska. After storming up classic and new routes in North Cascades National Park, the party found themselves at the mercy of high winds and horizontal rain on Sourdough Ridge. "In diminishing daylight," wrote Bertulis, "Ivanov, looking wet and miserable exclaimed in his limited English: 'McKinley: no problem. North Cascades: problem!'"

Mount Fury viewed from the Challenger Glacier in 1985 (Photo by Carl Skoog)

BRANCHING OUT

In 1983, a year after I'd skied the Ptarmigan Traverse, Gary Brill suggested another trip, this time from Diablo on the North Cascades highway to the Cascade River. The journey would connect two icefields: the Colonial Glacier–Neve Glacier region near Snowfield Peak and the McAllister Glacier and Inspiration Glacier system on Eldorado Peak. During the final days of winter, we were joined by Mark Hutson and Brian Sullivan, both experienced telemark skiers. Gary and I were unusual in the small community of backcountry skiers at that time because we skied on alpine touring equipment rather than Nordic gear. My equipment consisted of 65-millimeter-wide alpine skis, Ramer bindings, and plastic climbing boots, which were cheaper than the alpine ski-touring boots of the day (plus they walked better).

Over three days we climbed Snowfield and Isolation Peaks and skied around the head-waters of McAllister Creek to a campsite near Early Morning Spire. A snowstorm confined us to our tents for a day, and on the fifth day we climbed and skied Eldorado Peak before descending to the Cascade River Road. There was no commonly used name for this route at the time, so I started calling it the Isolation Traverse. The name stuck. The Isolation Traverse offered tantalizing views of the high glacier country between Eldorado and Primus

THE PICKETS

The Picket Range is a supremely rugged area between Mount Baker and Ross Lake, between the North Cascades highway and the US-Canada border. In the 1980s, there was no internet, no cell phone network, no cheap pocket-sized satellite communication. The easiest way to get an up-to-date weather forecast was to carry a NOAA weather radio and hope for reception. Mountaineers would plan a trip and wait in town for a good weather forecast, continuously rearranging vacation schedules and banking extra work hours. As soon as the weather looked promising, they'd bolt for the mountains, squeezing as many peaks into the trip as possible before time and weather ran out.

In 1985, hoping to extend the network of Cascades high routes farther north, I recruited Jens Kieler and my brother Carl to ski the Pickets in mid-May, for a traverse from Hannegan Pass to Diablo on the North Cascades highway. We had all climbed in the Pickets before, so we were familiar with the terrain, but I knew it would be different on skis: Skiers and climbers see the mountains differently. They look for different routes; they appreciate different lines. Our intention was not to force a route where skis didn't belong or where they would be a handicap. I wanted to find a natural line, a skier's line—to experience that part of the Picket Range where skiing makes sense.

On the third morning of the trip, I got my chance. Leaving Whatcom Pass at dawn, we hurried across a steep frightening slope, racing the sun to minimize avalanche danger. Then we climbed easily up the Challenger Glacier. There were crevasses, so we roped up and skied in line. The glacier took a gradual turn and suddenly there was no more climbing to do. In front of us the slope dropped steeply to the Luna Cirque. Far below was the muffled sound of waterfalls. Spread out before us was the fluted, ice-draped 4,000-foot north wall of Mount Fury. We had arrived at the Pickets. We skied carefully into the magnificent, desolate hole of Luna Cirque, craning our necks to survey the ice cliffs and grim rock walls perched above us. At the bottom, I felt like an insect surrounded by poised flyswatters. Throughout the afternoon, we climbed the other side of the cirque to a ridgeline camp near Luna Peak.

During the fourth day, high on Mount Fury in the middle of the traverse, clouds and fog enveloped us. With no visibility, and obstacles on three sides, we pondered an escape route east to the Big Beaver Valley but feared that would involve a dangerous river crossing. Fortunately, the next day we awoke above the clouds, able to climb over the southeast summit of Mount Fury and rappel down the other side. Jens, Carl, and I finished the traverse by skiing above the clouds along Stetattle Ridge, one of the most beautiful days I've experienced in the mountains.

Carl Skoog crosses Stetattle Ridge during our Picket Range traverse in 1985.

Peaks, dominated by the Inspiration, McAllister, and Klawatti Glaciers. Brian Sullivan and Greg Jacobsen returned a year later and spent five days exploring that area on skis.

In the mid-1980s there was growing enthusiasm for long high-mountain ski trips in the western United States and Canada, inspired by the famous Haute Route from Chamonix to Zermatt in Europe. California skiers had the Sierra Crest route and the Redline Traverse. In the Rockies, Paul Ramer promoted his Colorado Grand Tour. In British Columbia, John Baldwin published *Exploring the Coast Mountains on Skis* in 1983, detailing routes such as the Spearhead Traverse, the Garibaldi Neve, and others in more remote areas (see Appendix for selected high-level routes).

In 1986 The Mountaineers published *Backcountry Skiing in Washington's Cascades*, a new guidebook by Rainer Burgdorfer. As the successor to 1968's *Northwest Ski Trails*, the book omitted lift skiing areas and featured an expanded list of backcountry tours, including destinations along the North Cascades highway. Backcountry skiing, it seemed, was taking off. There were more cars carrying skis along the highway than ever before. Jens Kieler and I planned a trip the following spring to explore the high country between Rainy Pass and the Cascade River, traveling over the summit of 9,087-foot Mount Logan. We called it the Thunder High Route since it traversed the headwaters of Thunder Creek for most of its length.

With Dan Nordstrom, we skied the route over five sunny days in May 1987. The trip was nearly all skiing, with just a mile or two of walking at either end and some forest to negotiate near Park Creek Pass. On the second day, Jens and I left our packs and climbed an unnamed 7,910-foot summit near Logan's Douglas Glacier. Its broad northwest slope, tapering for 3,000 feet from the valley floor to the summit horn, was a perfect ski run. A hundred skiers could have descended it without crossing a track, but today there were only two of us. After our descent, as I contemplated the ski tracks etched from the summit to our feet, it seemed they were already fading in the evening light. In my mind they would fade much more slowly. I suggested the name "Dream Peak" for this ethereal summit.

On the fourth day, we crossed the Boston Glacier and descended the Forbidden Glacier to Moraine Lake, then climbed to a camp below Eldorado Peak, a section that has since become known as the Forbidden Tour. After camping on the Inspiration Glacier, Dan, Jens, and I climbed and skied Eldorado Peak, then followed the divide to Hidden Lake Peak and our car at Sibley Creek.

A TRAVERSE OF THE AMERICAN ALPS

In *The Best Ski Touring in America*, Steve Barnett suggested that in the North Cascades "the pathfinding is almost complete for a ski route covering the entire glacial crest from the North Cascade Highway to south of Glacier Peak." It was an inspiring idea. By 1987, when the book was published, skiers had traversed the Cascade crest as far south as Dome Peak, but about 40 miles of the crest stretched from there to Glacier Peak. In 1989 my brother Carl and I made a plan to ski that section.

Rather than hike the trail along Downey Creek to Dome Peak, Carl and I took a shortcut to the high country by following the Sulphur Mountain trail to the ridge leading to Totem Pass. We would miss about five miles of the Cascade crest using this route, but we thought the shortcut to the high country would be worth it.

It wasn't. The country east of Sulphur Mountain was unpleasant to traverse on skis and not especially scenic. But it only cost us one bad day. The rest of the trip was beautiful, with highlights at Image Lake, over Chiwawa Mountain, and along the Dakobed Range to Glacier Peak.

Glacier Peak as seen from Image Lake in 1989 (Photo by Carl Skoog)

Following this successful trip, I was inspired to link the segments we had done between the North Cascades highway and Glacier Peak in a single two-week push, a route I called the American Alps Traverse. Family plans in 1990 precluded an attempt that spring, but in the fall I placed two caches, one near Boston Basin and the other near Lyman Lake, to support an attempt the following spring.

The year 1991 was bad for spring weather. While the eastern half of the United States was seeing record high temperatures, the Northwest was plagued by a series of wet weather systems. During the first full week of May, one to three feet of snow fell in the Cascades, and on the third weekend, the North Cascades highway was closed by a slide. Special avalanche warnings were issued by the Northwest Avalanche Center two weekends in a row that month.

Twice Carl and I made abortive attempts to ski another long route as a prelude to the American Alps Traverse. We did marathon car shuttles to place a car at either end of the route, then aborted the trip as the weather collapsed. We managed to squeeze in a short trip in early June, traversing Ragged Ridge from Mesahchie Pass to Fourth of July Pass. This route offered magnificent views of the summits surrounding Thunder Creek, the most glaciated drainage in North Cascades National Park. A storm dropped new snow below timberline the day after we ended our trip.

Obsessed with the idea of completing the American Alps Traverse, I had arranged to take most of June off from work. In mid-June, tempted by a promising weather forecast, Carl, Brian Sullivan, and I were finally able to launch our attempt. My obsession throughout the spring had been hard on my wife, Steph. The night before my departure, she woke at 2:00 a.m., weeping and wishing I wouldn't go. I didn't sleep after that. At 4:30 a.m. she was more stoic and we bid a long good-bye. I would owe her a great deal when I returned. I had burned through a lot of marital capital for this trip; I would need to earn it back.

Carl and I met Brian at the Marblemount Ranger Station, where District Ranger Bill Lester had agreed to let us borrow a Park Service radio. This would enable us to leave messages so Steph could check on our progress. Brian had planned to accompany us on just the first third of the journey, so we parked his car near the Cascade River, then continued toward Rainy Pass. We started near Rainy Pass instead of Diablo to explore terrain none of us had skied before.

The trip started well, with clear skies and continuous snow. We skied over a pass into Fisher Creek Basin, then climbed to our first campsite, at Silent Lakes. The next morning, clouds moved in from the south. We caught a forecast of rain the following day. Brian decided to return to the highway via Easy Pass and hitchhike back to

Scott Croll skis the Mount Redoubt high route in 1991. (Photo by John Dittli)

Marblemount. We took the Park Service radio and some extra food from Brian and bid him farewell.

Over the next three days, Carl and I skied deeper into the Cascades wilderness, but the weather continued to deteriorate. After we spent a day in our tiny tent on Mount Logan, the forecast predicted colder and wetter-than-normal weather for the next week and a half. Whiteout navigation and wet camping were not what we skied high routes for, so Carl and I pulled the plug. On the fifth day, we descended to the Fisher Creek valley, wrestled with the wet slide alder, and made our way over Easy Pass back to the highway.

"Total frustration," I wrote in my journal. "I'm shelving the trip for now. Who knows if we'll ever be as serious again about attempting this." In retrospect, 1991 was not the right year to pursue this dream. I concluded that the trip I had envisioned was not a good fit for my lifestyle, either at home or at work.

Years later, in 2000, I skied with Matt Firth and Bruce Goodson on an extended version of the Ptarmigan Traverse that continued from Dome Peak south to Lyman Lake. This trip completed all the segments of what I had called the American Alps Traverse, but I never again tried it as a continuous push. After describing my faded dream to Matt, however, he was inspired to give it a try. With Bob Nielsen of Stehekin, he skied from Diablo to Lyman Lake over nine days in 2002, a year with exceptionally good weather. They ended their trip at Holden Village (as the former mining town has been known since about 1957).

Between 2000 and 2007, I skied additional segments (during separate trips) to complete a route stretching all the way from Mount Baker to Mount Rainier, three times as long as my original goal. The full route from Diablo to Glacier Peak was finally completed in a single push by Jason Hummel and Kyle Miller in 2013. This pair eschewed caches and instead descended to roads at the Cascade River and Holden Village to resupply. Their sixteen-day trip ended at the White Chuck River, which had suffered extensive flooding over the previous decade. Most of the trail had been destroyed by washouts and fallen timber, making for an exhausting exit from the mountains.

True mastery of skiing the American alps was demonstrated a few years later. Over twenty-five days in April and May 2016, mountain guides Peter Dale and Aaron Mainer completed a ski traverse from Chilliwack Lake in British Columbia to Tall Timber Ranch, on the White River near Lake Wenatchee—a distance of well over 100 miles. The pair arranged food drops at two locations and made several noteworthy ski descents, including the complete northeast face of Mount Fury in the Picket Range. Later in the journey, they made a side trip to the Entiat Mountains to ski the north face of Mount Maude and the west face of Mount Fernow.

One year later, guides Trevor Kostanich and Forest McBrian completed an even longer continuous traverse from Snoqualmie Pass to the Canadian border. The journey spanned about 110 miles in straight-line distance and much more in actuality. The winter of 2016–17 was unusually cold and wet, and this continued through the early part of their trip, requiring continuous effort at "moisture management." Starting on May 1, they spent two weeks skiing along the Cascade crest from Snoqualmie to Stevens Pass, proceeding north toward Glacier Peak. Near Glacier Peak, they were joined by photographer Scott Rinckenberger and a friend who skied with them to Cascade Pass. I accompanied Kostanich's wife, Emily, to deliver the team's third resupply of food and fuel from the Cascade River up to timberline.

Kostanich and McBrian continued along the Isolation Traverse to State Highway 20, where friends drove to meet them for the first time since the pair had left Stevens Pass. They continued through the Picket Range nearly to the Canadian border before turning east to Ross Lake, from whence they chartered a boat back to civilization. The journey required thirty-four days and five resupplies. After their solar charger quit working, their phones went dead, so they navigated using paper maps and compass. A satellite phone enabled them to get weather forecasts and coordinate with friends. After their return, the adventure was front-page news in the *Seattle Times*. Human-powered skiing hadn't received this level of attention since the heady days of the 1930s.

Mount Olympus and its Blue Glacier (Spring Trust for Trails)

THE OLYMPIC MOUNTAINS

Olympic Mountains: A Climbing Guide describes the Olympics as "not a 'range' in the usual sense; rather, a compact cluster of steep peaks surrounded by a belt of densely timbered foothills." The book observes, "The drainage system is radial, with river valleys penetrating deeply into the mountain mass from all sides. Some valleys provide an extremely hostile

THE BAILEY RANGE

After exploring several high routes in the North Cascades, a group of my friends was inspired to try skiing the Bailey Range—the most famous high-level route in the Olympics, first explored by Billy Everett in the late 1800s. The route had been popularized by filmmaker Herb Crisler in the 1930s and 1940s. In 1989 we were unaware of any earlier attempts to ski the route.

After dropping off Joe Catellani, Jens Kieler, and Brian Sullivan at the Soleduck River trailhead, my brother Carl and I shuttled a car to the Hoh Visitor Center. There we filled out a backcountry permit with a skeptical ranger. "You going to do all that in five days?" he asked. "You know there's a lot of snow up there. I don't think anybody skis over there in the Bailey Range." We explained that we had done similar

Carl Skoog and Jens Kieler traverse the Bailey Range on skis in 1989.

trips in the Cascades, but the ranger replied, "Well, the Olympics are different. There are lots of white-outs this time of year." We thanked him for his counsel and headed back to the Soleduck.

After hiking the trail to the snow line, the five of us skied to the High Divide, where we found a beautiful campsite with a view across the Hoh Valley to Mount Olympus. The next day we followed the divide past Cat Peak to the Catwalk. While our friends continued traversing the west flank of Mount Carrie, Carl and I dropped our packs and skied to its summit. From its top we could see what appeared to be a much better ski route on its east flank, but since our packs were 2,000 feet below, we skied back down and spent the rest of the day grunting out the lower traverse toward Cream Lake Basin.

The rest of the trip went without problems, following the scenic glaciated divide to Bear Pass and continuing up the Humes Glacier to Blizzard Pass for our third night. We crossed Glacier Pass the next morning, dropped our packs, and skied up the Blue Glacier to climb the west summit of Mount Olympus. After camping that night at Elk Lake, we carried our skis down the Hoh Valley to the car on the fifth day.

East of the Bailey Range, a route of similar quality travels from Hurricane Ridge east to Obstruction Point and then south along a high divide to Lillian Basin. Park ranger Jack Hughes likely skied this section many times in the 1970s.

environment for travel, notorious for box canyons and frequent cliffy waterfalls." The guide continues, "Much of the Olympic Range is not ideal for over-snow travel. The snowline is variable and often quite high in elevation. Steep and heavily timbered slopes reach far up most peaks, and upper basins are mostly deep within the range."

Early skiing in the Olympics was focused at Deer Park and, later, Hurricane Ridge. The Flapjack Lakes cabin built by Bremerton and Shelton skiers provided a base for skiers in the southeast Olympics in the 1930s. Dwight Watson and his Seattle friends explored a few corners of the eastern Olympics in those days. Laurence A. Smith was said by his grandson to have carried skis to the Anderson Glacier from the Enchanted Valley around 1939. Because of the long valley hike, it's unlikely this destination was ever popular with skiers.

Attempts to climb Mount Olympus in winter in the late 1940s occasionally employed skis, but none of those ventures were successful. Use of skis by Ed LaChapelle and his colleagues on Mount Olympus during the International Geophysical Year in 1957–58 was documented by Ira Spring in his *Seattle Times* pictorials—but the scientists had been whisked to the Blue Glacier in Bill Fairchild's airplane.

In the summer of 1979, inspired by the mobility of Nordic downhill skiing, Steve Barnett and Dave Kahn approached Mount Olympus on foot via the Hoh River. They figured that July would be the optimal time for a ski trip on the mountain, with fewer hazards than in winter, better trail conditions than in spring, and a higher chance of good weather. "Our lightweight ski boots made excellent walking shoes," wrote Barnett. "The skis and poles weighed only five pounds, an insignificant additional load over what we would have carried for any hike in the Olympics. To other hikers we met on the trail, the very idea of hiking with skis in July seemed outlandish. Our only positive response came from climbers we met on their way down from Olympus; eyeing us enviously, they said, 'Wish we had had skis.' Thus encouraged, we walked on toward our goal."

Barnett and Kahn put their skis on at the edge of the Blue Glacier, roped up, and skied up the Snow Dome to the ridge between the middle and east summits. They made runs on the Blue Glacier and Hoh Glacier sides, following the best conditions. The next day they followed the Blue Glacier to Glacier Pass and did some exploring of the lower Hoh Glacier until they ran out of time. "Those new glaciers will have to wait until next year," wrote Barnett, "when we plan to return to this mythical mountain of the gods and some of the finest mountain skiing I know of anywhere."

There have been other long trips across the Olympics. In 2008 Eric Jackson and Mary Goodfellow continued south from Lillian Basin to Cameron Pass and traversed Mount Cameron to Gray Wolf Pass. Continuing east, they crossed the Needles to Royal Basin and hiked out to the Dungeness River road. A year later they returned to Royal Basin to carry on where the previous trip had ended, traveling southeast to Constance Pass. They reached Lake Constance by traveling over the pass between Inner Constance and Desperation Peak, then crossed a shoulder above Bull Elk Creek to reach the south fork of Tunnel Creek and its road.

Jackson and his friend Pat Whittaker embarked on a project to ski all the glaciers in Olympic National Park, which he described as "more or less an excuse to explore the Olympics." In summer they carried cutoff short skis and would ski at least a few turns on each new glacier. Their friend Larry Smith, whose grandfather introduced him to the Olympics in the 1950s, has also explored many corners of the range with skis, including the Humes Glacier east of Mount Olympus, the Queets Glacier south of Dodwell-Rixon Pass, the White Glacier on Mount Tom, Mount Christie near the Low Divide, the Carrie and Fairchild Glaciers in the Bailey Range, the Eel Glacier on Mount Anderson, the glaciers in Deception Basin, the north side of Mount Fricaba, and many others.

Tim Black wrestles slide alder during the Olympic Traverse East in 2016. (Photo by Jason Hummel)

Professional photographer Jason Hummel set himself a goal to ski all the named glaciers in the Washington Cascades and Olympics, which led to several strenuous trips. In 2018, with Jake Chartier and Carl Simpson, Hummel completed a circumnavigation of Mount Olympus high on its glaciers, laying ski tracks on the Blue, Hoh, Jeffers, University, Hubert, and Black Glaciers. Other glaciers with informal names were skied during their eight-day outing. Hummel also completed two long traverses through the Olympics traveling from north to south.

The first, which he dubbed the Olympic Traverse East, was done with Tim Black in May 2016. The pair traveled from Hurricane Ridge to Lake Cushman over nine days. The first three days took them to Grand Valley and Lillian Basin, fine ski country that had been traveled by previous parties. After skiing Mount Cameron, Hummel and Black continued over Lost Pass to Dose Meadow Camp.

On their fourth day, the pair skied and climbed over Sentinel Peak and Sentinel Sister and made a steep, brushy descent to Silt Creek. The Olympics' reputation for "an extremely hostile environment for travel" was realized during this descent. For several hours, Hummel and Black struggled through old-growth slide alder, grappling with stems as thick as a man's arms, sometimes balancing several feet above the ground, the skis on their packs becoming entangled with nearly every move.

After escaping the brush, the men climbed to Flypaper Pass, between the two summits of Mount Anderson, where they camped in fog. Waking the next morning above the clouds, Hummel and Black skied down into them and followed a circuitous route around the headwaters of the Duckabush and Skokomish Rivers to Flapjack Lakes. From there a trail led to the Staircase Ranger Station near Lake Cushman.

In June 2019, Hummel and Chartier joined Jeff Rich and Carl Simpson to ski another north-to-south traverse, which Hummel dubbed the Olympic Traverse West. This route started at the Soleduck River, and followed the Bailey Range traverse to Bear Pass, with ski descents of Mounts Fairchild and Carrie along the way. From Bear Pass they skied Mount Queets and its glacier, then passed Mounts Meany and Noyes to reach the Skyline Trail west of Mount Seattle. This took them to the Low Divide between the Quinault and Elwha Rivers.

On their fifth day, the foursome continued south to Martins Park and skied Mount Christie. Rough travel led to Mount Delabarre and its dwindling ice, the last in Hummel's quest to ski all of the Olympic glaciers. They skied an unlikely-looking narrow gully into Delabarre Creek, where they spent their fifth night. The sixth day involved several low-elevation problems, with heavy brush, a rappel with full packs, and a cold river crossing. They camped near the head of Rustler Creek and on their seventh day thrashed their way through the Olympic mountain jungle out to the Quinault River.

Opposite: *Kurt Beam, Dr. Otto Trott, Al Krupp, and Wolf Bauer transport Bill Degenhardt out of Commonwealth Basin following his avalanche accident on Mount Snoqualmie in 1954. (Spring Trust for Trails)*

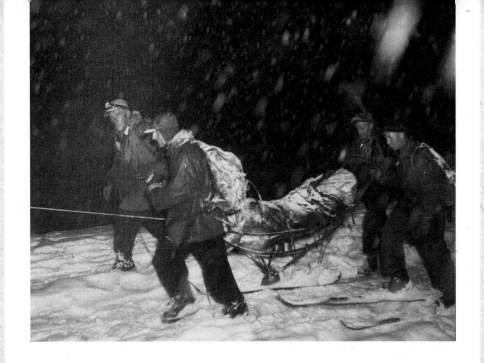

CHAPTER 13

TO THE RESCUE

Where snow falls on rugged mountains, there will be avalanches. In the Cascades, snowslides claimed victims as soon as men and women started working in the mountains in winter. In November 1894, as the mining town of Monte Cristo began its first winter of production, a slide swept over a cabin near the Pride of Mountains mine, trapping four men and killing miner Louis Erickson. Avalanches and crushing snowfalls were a recurring theme in accounts of winter at Monte Cristo.

The deadliest avalanche in Northwest history occurred in 1910 on the railroad through Stevens Pass, near the small town of Wellington. In late February, two trains were blocked by slides just west of the old Cascade Tunnel. The intense snowfall was described by mail clerk Alfred Hensel "[as if] somebody was plucking a chicken." For nearly a week, workers tried to clear the tracks as the storm dumped up to a foot of snow an hour and then, ominously, changed to rain. On March 1, as the

Men work to uncover a tanker truck buried in an avalanche on Stevens Pass in 1936. (The Mountaineers Archives)

rain grew into a thunderstorm, an enormous wet-slab avalanche released from the side of Windy Mountain and swept the trains into the Tye River canyon, killing ninety-six people.

The winter of 1936 spotlighted the danger that avalanches presented to the growing sport of skiing. On January 12, less than a month after the Mount Baker Development Company began operating its barge-like "ski escalator," the lift was struck by an avalanche from Panorama Dome, killing operator Arthur Branlund. A month later, on the eve of the Pacific Northwest ski jumping championships at Snoqualmie Pass, avalanches swept the highway, killing three drivers and burying many others. Driver Harold Devereaux, after being trapped for seven hours under nine feet of snow, was recovered alive in an air pocket next to his truck. Following this tragedy, the director of the Washington State Highway Department pushed for the construction of snowsheds to protect the highway at critical spots.

In March, after a storm dropped 18 inches of new snow on Mount Rainier, three skiers descended from Paradise to their car at Narada Falls, intending to drive to Longmire. Finding the road blocked, they decided to ski down. Just below the falls a slope above the road avalanched, burying all three men. Ranger Bill Butler summoned a rescue party that uncovered two skiers alive, but the third, Jack Northrop, could not be saved.

The need for a more organized approach to search and rescue had been underscored earlier that same winter. In January 1936, twenty-two-year-old Delmar Fadden went missing on Mount Rainier during a solo trip to ski, snowshoe, and climb the mountain. Following an unsuccessful ground search, from an airplane Ome Daiber spotted Fadden's body high on the Emmons Glacier on January 19. Daiber led the party that brought the body down the mountain. Following the search and recovery, which was national news for two weeks, Daiber became the focal point for an informal mountain rescue organization.

In 1948, the Seattle Mountain Rescue Council (MRC) was formed under the leadership of climbing and skiing pioneers Wolf Bauer, Ome Daiber, and Dr. Otto Trott. They brought broad expertise in summer and winter mountaineering to the council, which performed its first mission in October of that year. In 1952 and 1953 the MRC launched fifteen full-scale rescues for a variety of accidents—lightning strikes, crevasse falls, glissading accidents, falls on rock, rappelling accidents, rockfall, and four aircraft crashes that alone claimed forty victims.

Three high school boys were caught in an avalanche in February 1953 while skiing near Source Lake, upvalley from today's Alpental ski area. Edward Almquist escaped the slide and, after an unsuccessful search for his companions, skied down the valley for help. The local snow ranger organized a search party that uncovered Larry Schinke alive after an eight-and-a-half-hour burial. The third boy, Keith Jacobsen, was found dead the following day.

A year later, on Easter Sunday, Mountaineers president and MRC member Bill Degenhardt was ski touring with his wife, Stella, and a friend in Commonwealth Basin, one valley east of Source Lake. Degenhardt was caught in an avalanche on the slopes of Snoqualmie Mountain and swept over a cliff, fracturing his pelvis. Concluding that it would be too difficult to move him using a makeshift litter, Stella skied out for help. In response, MRC chairman Ome Daiber led an eleven-man team on an all-night mission to rescue him. After loading Degenhardt on a Stokeski stretcher, the usually grim rescuers laughed and joked with him as they hauled the litter along, relieved that his injuries were not too severe. When Degenhardt mumbled his thanks to his longtime friends, one replied, "That's all right, Bill. Next time you'll be pulling on these ropes."

In the years that followed, more mountain rescue units were organized throughout the Northwest. In 1957 the MRC released a movie by Bob and Ira Spring called *Mountains Don't Care* to raise public awareness of hazards and safe mountain travel. The national Mountain Rescue Association was formed in 1959, largely through the work of Seattle MRC members.

After ski touring became more popular in the 1970s, volunteer rescue groups specifically oriented toward backcountry skiing were formed. They include the Cascade Backcountry

Ski Patrol at Snoqualmie and Stevens Passes, the Ski Patrol Rescue Team (SPART) of King County, the Mount Rainier Nordic Ski Patrol, and Backcountry Avalanche Rescue K-9 (BARK) units operating out of the Stevens Pass, Snoqualmie Pass, and Crystal Mountain ski areas.

THE AVALANCHE HUNTERS

At the time of the 1910 Wellington disaster, avalanche science did not exist in the United States. But the lessons of Wellington were noticed by at least one forecaster. A few months after the tragedy, Edward Beals, head of the US Weather Bureau office in Portland, Oregon, wrote an article about avalanches in the Cascades and northern Rockies. As he monitored storms and the avalanches that resulted from them, he developed a feel for the conditions that caused snowslides.

The winter of 1915–16 was legendary in the western United States for cold temperatures and heavy snowfalls. It was the year of the "Big Snow," when Norwegian skiers staged a ski jumping exhibition on Queen Anne Hill in Seattle. The day after the exhibition, the *Seattle Times* published photos of the jumpers and reported that warming weather was causing Northwest rivers to reach flood stage. Next to the story was a warning from Beals of dangerous avalanches in the mountains over the next thirty-six hours. The Great Northern Railway (over Stevens Pass) canceled all trains, while the Chicago, Milwaukee, and St. Paul Railroad and the Northern Pacific (over Snoqualmie and Stampede Passes, respectively) doubled patrols in their danger areas. An article in the February 2009 issue of *The Avalanche Review* recognized this as the first published avalanche warning in US history.

Study of avalanches was much more advanced in Europe, and for many years the best English-language reference on the subject was the 1936 book *Snow Structure and Ski Fields* by Gerald Seligman, former president of the Ski Club of Great Britain. Clubs like The Mountaineers, the Mazamas, and the Ptarmigans had copies of this book and shared its lessons with their members, but few resources were available to the public to improve avalanche safety.

This began to change after World War II, as downhill skiing boomed. As ski areas were established throughout the western United States, the Forest Service realized that it administered a lot of avalanche paths that were being developed for ski areas and highways. Thus the Forest Service established avalanche research centers in the late 1940s and early 1950s at Berthoud Pass, Colorado; Alta, Utah; and Stevens Pass, Washington. The three centers were devoted to three different climate regimes—Rocky Mountain, Intermountain, and Pacific Coast—known to produce different avalanche conditions.

Ed LaChapelle at work in the 1950s (Spring Trust for Trails)

The Alta research center was led by a Tenth Mountain Division veteran of World War II, Monty Atwater, who took the job with the Forest Service after his discharge in 1945. Atwater used explosives to trigger avalanches during the winter of 1948–49. He abandoned electrical blasting, using long wires and a firing switch, and switched to time-delay fuses, which enabled him to "ski along a ridge tossing bombs like a newsboy delivering papers."

Ed LaChapelle joined Atwater at Alta in 1952–53. In his memoir *The Avalanche Hunters*, Atwater wished that LaChapelle had been there from the beginning. "To describe Ed LaChapelle," he wrote, "is to write the specifications for an avalanche researcher: graduate physicist, glaciologist with a year's study at the [Swiss] Avalanche Institute, skilled craftsman in the shop, expert ski mountaineer." LaChapelle would return to the Northwest a few years later to do glacier studies at the University of Washington and lead the International Geophysical Year project on Mount Olympus in 1957–58.

The avalanche research center at Stevens Pass in the Cascade Mountains was led by Frank Foto, who doubled as a Forest Service snow ranger, doing hands-on control work at the pass. As Seattle and Tacoma skiers studied Crystal Mountain for a potential new ski area in the 1950s, they recruited Foto, LaChapelle, and others to help survey the area. On a March weekend in 1958, a party of eight led by Walt Little skied up Silver Creek and spent

Elroy Burnett records measurements as Frank Foto tests the snow using a ram penetrometer at Stevens Pass in the 1950s. (Spring Trust for Trails)

a night at the miners' cabin in the valley. Also in the group were Foto's wife, Edie, and Dan Evans, a civil engineer then serving in the Washington State House of Representatives. The party toured the upper mountain, skiing Iceberg Ridge and Green Valley along the way. By midafternoon, they were working their way back to Silver Creek, about 1,000 feet above the valley bottom, when one of the skiers higher on the slope triggered an avalanche that caught most of the other party members.

Ironically, Foto and LaChapelle, the two most experienced avalanche men in the party, went the farthest in the avalanche. Foto was carried more than 500 feet, alternately buried and popped to the surface by the slide. He stopped when he was pinned against a tree, resulting in torn and bruised back muscles. LaChapelle took the longest ride. After being vigorously tumbled in the avalanche, he ended up on the surface near the tip of the slide with a pulled leg muscle. The party helped Foto reach the mining road along Silver Creek, then bundled him in one of their sleeping bags and made a sled using his skis. LaChapelle was able to ski out under his own power, and the other skiers pulled Foto four miles back to the Silver Springs Lodge.

Speaking to a newspaper reporter from his hospital bed in Enumclaw, Foto admitted, "It was just about a 'Foto-finish.' I never tell anybody I am an expert on avalanches. But every member of that party knew more about avalanches than the average skier. We probably got a little careless."

Six years later, Dan Evans was elected governor of the state of Washington. He served for twelve years, was president of The Evergreen State College, and served as one of Washington's US senators. During the North Cascades campaign in 1968, Evans pushed for establishment of the national park. Had fortune gone another way in the Silver Creek avalanche, Washington State history would have been very different.

A CLASSIC UNDERESTIMATION

Since the early 1900s, travelers in the Alps sometimes used avalanche cords, long strings tied around the waist of a skier or climber in hopes that, in an avalanche, the cord would remain visible on the snow surface. Over time, however, experience found the cords to be unreliable. As often as not, the cord would be completely buried in a slide.

Around 1968, Ed LaChapelle began experimenting with radios to locate a buried person. He built a transmitter that was about the size of a cigarette pack. Then he used a portable transistor radio to pick up the signal. While working to optimize the design, he talked with skier and electrical engineer John Lawton. Intrigued by the concept, Lawton redesigned the device to produce the first commercially successful avalanche beacon, called Skadi after the Norse goddess of winter and skiing. In the Sierra Club's 1972 book *Wilderness Skiing*, Lito Tejada-Flores and Allen Steck wrote, "It's been calculated that a Skadi-equipped searcher looking for a Skadi-equipped victim is the equivalent of nearly five hundred men with probing poles. But, since each unit costs over a hundred dollars, and you need at least two, the Skadi is not likely to become popular with touring skiers." Ski touring—and the cost of consumer electronics—have changed a lot since then. Today avalanche beacons are considered essential equipment for backcountry skiing.

Through his work in both Forest Service avalanche research and private consulting, Ed LaChapelle gained a reputation as one of the top experts on avalanche safety in North America. He was frequently called on for advice by government agencies and private businesses. In the mid-1960s, he directed the Forest Service avalanche study center at Alta during the winter and taught at the University of Washington in autumn and spring. In 1966 LaChapelle was hired by a consulting firm to do a feasibility study for a proposed residential ski area east of Stevens Pass called Yodelin. Plans called for four chairlifts, a lodge, and restaurants on the south side of US Highway 2. North of the highway, at the foot of Skyline Ridge, more than one hundred residential lots were proposed. LaChapelle warned against

USFS snow ranger Terry Norr loads a recoilless rifle at the Mount Baker ski area in the 1960s. Snow rangers were phased out in the 1970s and the task of ski area avalanche control was shifted to ski patrollers employed by the ski areas themselves. (Spring Trust for Trails)

construction in the residential area because of avalanche danger. Records indicated that avalanches large enough to hit the proposed development occurred every six or seven years.

Two years after delivering this report, LaChapelle was driving over Stevens Pass and noticed houses being built on the Yodelin residential site. The area had been sold to a developer, and LaChapelle was unsure whether his report had been conveyed to the new owner. Alarmed, he notified state authorities. The state Real Estate Division sent a letter to the developer requiring that the property owners be warned of the potential avalanche danger. In response, the developer threatened a lawsuit against the state claiming damages because of the letter. State officials determined that there were no laws in place giving the state authority to compel disclosure of the information. If the state acted, it was thought that state officials could be personally sued for losses. The state backed off.

During the spring of 1970, a small slide came through the back door of the cabin owned by the Barton Edgers family at Yodelin. The following winter, the cabin was hit by another small slide. Edgers ran a cable from a large rock behind the cabin to the main floor to keep it from being pushed off its foundation. An article in the 1975 edition of *The Snowy Torrents*, a compendium of US avalanche accidents, described this as "a classic underestimation of the destructive forces involved."

In January 1971, during a four-day storm that dropped more than four feet of snow, with winds gusting from 30 to 45 miles per hour, an avalanche released from the flank of Skyline Ridge, striking seven cabins. Five cabins were unoccupied, but inside the other two, sixteen people were caught, with four injured and four killed, including both parents of the Edgers family. Lawsuits followed. In 1973 Washington enacted a law requiring disclosure of any hazard on or around a land development.

In the early 1970s, the Washington State Department of Transportation (WSDOT) hired LaChapelle to complete a survey of avalanche activity along the North Cascades highway. His report included an atlas of avalanche paths with recommendations on how to set up control programs. The most dangerous section is just east of Washington Pass, where the road cuts under the east flank of the Early Winters Spires and traverses under eleven avalanche paths below Cutthroat Ridge. The hairpin turn below Early Winters Spires gives avalanches two opportunities to hit the road, on either side of the switchback. LaChapelle brought visiting Japanese colleagues to Washington Pass to observe the avalanche problems. "They looked around," he said, "and saw how the road comes up the west side and goes down the east side. Then they shook their heads and said, 'We would tunnel.'" Ultimately, the highway department used LaChapelle's report to argue against winter plowing of the

THE NORTHWEST AVALANCHE CENTER

Following the North Cascades highway survey, Ed LaChapelle was hired to map avalanche paths on all the other mountain passes in Washington. His team produced two more reports in 1974 and 1975, completing the project. As a result of this work, WSDOT became more interested in snowfall and avalanche forecasting. The agency found that it could save a lot of money deploying highway crews if it had more accurate snowfall forecasts.

Over the next three years, LaChapelle led a study of centralized avalanche forecasting for the highway department. Two of his graduate students at the University of Washington, Rich Marriott and Mark Moore, became key members of the study team. They were joined by Phil Taylor, who constructed instrumentation for remote weather stations at the major Cascade passes and ski areas. Sue

Early avalanche hunters associated with the Northwest Avalanche Center (NWAC). Top: Mark Moore and Sue Ferguson. Standing (L-R) Cindy Marriott, Richard Armstrong, Paul Baugher, Oscar (the avalanche wiener), Pam Speers, Betsy Armstrong. Kneeling: Rich Marriott, Ed LaChapelle. (Photo courtesy NWAC)

Ferguson helped the team develop a systematic procedure for avalanche hazard forecasting.

After the study was completed in the winter of 1978–79, representatives of WSDOT, the National Weather Service, the National Park Service, the US Forest Service, and the University of Washington created a permanent avalanche forecasting program under the Forest Service, the agency most involved in winter recreation in the Cascade and Olympic Mountains. The program was called the Northwest Avalanche Center (NWAC), and in 1979 Mark Moore and Rich Marriott became its first employees. Roland Emetaz, recreational assistant at the Forest Service regional office in Portland, became the avalanche center's supervisor and leading advocate.

For nearly forty years, NWAC consisted of just three staff members working out of the National Weather Service offices in Seattle. Funding came from WSDOT, the Forest Service, the National Park Service, and other organizations.

In the late 1990s, when funding problems threatened to shut down the center, a nonprofit group called the Friends of the Northwest Avalanche Center emerged to organize and coordinate fund-raising activities and increase public avalanche awareness. Increased fund-raising has enabled NWAC to expand education programs and hire field observers, most drawn from the growing guide community, to expand on-the-snow information for the public. Today NWAC has the largest network of remote weather stations of any avalanche program in North America, with more than ten million user hits per year.

North Cascades highway. Except for the snow drought of 1977, the highway has been closed in winter ever since.

IT DOESN'T COST THE MOUNTAIN ANYTHING

As one of the most active backcountry skiers in the Northwest in the years immediately following World War II, Chuck Hessey was sometimes asked to speak about winter travel and avalanches. Addressing a group of Yakima skiers and climbers in the 1960s, Hessey cautioned against being too goal oriented. "A safer approach to winter mountain travel," he said, "is to plan an outing, not a climb, and do the climbing if conditions guarantee a safe climb. Be casual. Sneak up on it. If your better judgment tells you to stay off that slope and you go anyway, you are betting your mighty sweet life—and win or lose, it doesn't cost the mountain anything."

At the fifth National Avalanche School, organized by the US Forest Service and National Ski Patrol in 1977, Knox Williams of Colorado painted a picture of the typical avalanche victim of the time: "The victim is male," he wrote, "twenty-seven years old, has had several years of skiing or mountaineering experience, and didn't know an avalanche from a snowball." Ed LaChapelle's study team had just completed their report on centralized avalanche forecasting, paving the way for the Northwest Avalanche Center to be established. Steve Barnett's book *Cross-Country Downhill* would appear in bookstores a year or so later. Interest in backcountry skiing in alpine terrain was growing, and so were avalanche accidents in the Cascade Mountains.

In April 1978, seven backcountry skiers were caught in an avalanche on the southeast slope of Panorama Point in Mount Rainier National Park. Four were partly buried and two were completely buried. Fortunately, all were uncovered alive. A few months earlier, three teenage climbers were descending the southwest slope of Panorama Point when Mike McNerthney triggered a small avalanche. He was buried for about forty minutes and died of suffocation. Panorama Point is one of several sites that have been repeat offenders for avalanches over the years. Source Lake basin, just two miles upvalley from the Alpental ski area near Snoqualmie Pass, has probably seen more avalanche accidents than any other location in the Cascade Mountains. Since Keith Jacobsen perished there in 1953, at least ten more accidents have been recorded around Source Lake, eight involving fatalities.

The mountains around Snoqualmie Pass are not especially tall by Cascades standards, but they are steep and heavily visited. Granite Mountain, five miles west of the pass along Interstate 90, rivals Source Lake basin for the number of accidents that have occurred there. The mountains stretching from Chair Peak to Kendall Peak have witnessed many tragic events, including the death of Monika Johnson, a strong and well-loved backcountry skier from Seattle, in 2011. Johnson perished when a cornice broke beneath her feet near the summit of Red Mountain.

For decades after the 1950s, the Snoqualmie Pass highway was protected—partially—by snowsheds on either side of the pass. Each snowshed protected uphill traffic only, so when an avalanche occurred, downhill traffic was blocked. In 1972 an avalanche over the east snowshed hit a car carrying three schoolteachers, breaking both the front and rear windshields and burying the car under six feet of snow. When rescuers probed the car through its broken windshield, the driver, Ralph McEwen, grabbed the probe and jerked it downward. "I wanted to make sure those people knew we were down there," he said. The rescuer was equally startled. "Someone's pulling my probe back down!" The rescue was a success.

While clubs such as The Mountaineers taught basic avalanche safety in ski touring and mountaineering courses, there was little instruction available for recreationists outside of a club setting. This began to change in the 1970s. Ray Smutek, a former Boeing engineer, started *Off Belay* magazine in 1972. Smutek had learned a little about avalanches through The Mountaineers and its book *Mountaineering: The Freedom of the Hills*, but his eyes were

Skiers swarm the southwest slope of Panorama Point. (Photo by Scott Rinckenberger)

really opened in 1977 when he attended the fifth US Forest Service National Avalanche School. He launched a crusade to increase public avalanche awareness in the late 1970s through an outfit he called the Mountain School.

In the early 1980s, Mark Moore teamed up with Paul Baugher, ski patrol director at Crystal Mountain, to start the Northwest Avalanche Institute, which taught both professional and nonprofessional students. By 1992 Jean Pavillard, then in Colorado, and Karl Klassen from Canada had collaborated on a national training program called the American Institute for Avalanche Research and Education. Today, AIARE provides more avalanche education than any other single avalanche education organization in the United States.

In the Northwest, avalanche education received a boost in 2007, when Michael Jackson, a commercial fisherman who enjoyed skiing in the off-season, organized the first Northwest Snow and Avalanche Seminar in Seattle. He collaborated with the Friends of the Northwest Avalanche Center to stage a daylong seminar at The Mountaineers clubhouse in Seattle with a dozen speakers drawn from NWAC staff, local ski patrols, WSDOT avalanche crews, equipment manufacturers, guides, instructors, and active skiers, snowboarders, and snowmobilers. The event was attended by more than 250 people. The avalanche seminar was the first time a large cross section of the backcountry ski community had gathered expressly to share safety knowledge and experience. It became an annual event and was renamed the Northwest Snow and Avalanche Workshop in keeping with similar regional events emerging across the United States. After 2014, NSAW was hosted by the nonprofit arm of NWAC.

Since 1967, the US Forest Service has published multiyear summaries of avalanche accidents throughout the United States in a report called *The Snowy Torrents*. Several editions have been printed, supplemented in recent years by data collected by the regional avalanche centers. Studying these records offers lessons on how to avoid accidents and respond more effectively when they occur. They also suggest trends, though they must be interpreted cautiously, since the record of avalanches is not complete.

For nearly fifty years following Keith Jacobsen's death near Source Lake in 1953, there were just four fatal avalanche accidents involving backcountry skiers recorded in the Cascades from Mount Hood northward. Then on December 29, 2002, seven skiers were caught in a slide in Cement Basin near the Crystal Mountain ski area. Dan Dovey perished in that avalanche. During the same period, more than seventy-five fatalities were recorded involving other recreationists, including hikers, climbers, snowshoers, lift skiers, ski patrollers, and "side-country" skiers—those who rode a ski lift and then went outside the boundaries of the ski area.

A ski patroller inspects the crown face of an avalanche in the Mount Baker side country in 2012. (Photo by Grant Gunderson)

The number of side-country accidents has grown dramatically since the 1990s, as competition for untracked snow prompts lift skiers to step outside boundaries and as better equipment makes deep snow accessible to more recreationists. At Mount Baker, construction of the Hemispheres chairlift in the early 1990s made Shuksan Arm easier to reach. The arm was the site of two fatal avalanches in 1999, a year when a record 95 feet of snow fell at the ski area.

In 2012 a side-country avalanche on Cowboy Mountain at Stevens Pass caught four skiers and killed three: Stevens Pass marketing manager Chris Rudolph, former president of the International Freeskiers Association Jim Jack, and ski patroller Johnny Brenan, a father of two. The accident was documented in a Pulitzer Prize–winning *New York Times* feature and prompted much soul-searching in the North American ski community.

Due to the dramatic growth of backcountry skiing and snowboarding since 2000, at least sixteen fatalities involving these groups were recorded in the Northwest from 2003 through the winter of 2020. This represented a tenfold increase in the annual fatality rate since Jacobsen's death near Source Lake in 1953. The first snowmobiling accident in the

Cascades documented in *The Snowy Torrents* occurred near Blewett Pass in 1998. Since then, most of the recorded snowmobile accidents have involved fatalities. It's unclear whether avalanches involving snowmobiles are really more deadly than those involving skiers and snowshoers, or whether the discrepancy is due to incomplete reporting. Remarkably, there have been no fatal avalanches recorded in the Olympic Mountains since 1900, due to limited winter access. Several nonfatal small avalanches have been reported in the Hurricane Ridge area.

RAINING DOWN THUNDER ON SKIS

Morning sun softens the snow as I climb on skis with John Stimberis and Aaron Opp above the Chinook Pass highway. In my backpack, in addition to lunch and personal gear, are thirty pounds of explosives. It's mid-May 2009, and I've joined John and Aaron to observe their work preparing State Highway 410 for its annual spring opening. Since its completion in the early 1930s, the road over Chinook Pass has been closed each winter. Each spring the highway is cleared by state maintenance crews using heavy equipment.

West of the pass, the road descends the southwest flank of Yakima Peak along a switchback route. While subject to avalanches, the danger zones on the west side are relatively short and easy to manage during the spring opening of the highway. East of the pass is a much bigger problem. Here the highway descends on a continuous grade for three miles while crossing some one hundred avalanche paths. Many paths start more than 1,000 feet above the road and end in the valley of the Rainier Fork American River 600 feet below.

During the first fifty years of the operation of State Highway 410, there were enough close calls during the spring opening effort that in the early 1980s WSDOT decided to apply avalanche control crews to better manage the problem. In 1983 Craig Wilbour and others from the WSDOT Snoqualmie Pass avalanche forecasting team began assisting highway maintenance crews on the Chinook Pass opening. Initially, Wilbour and his team would hike from the highway to the avalanche starting zones on foot. They started using skis a few years later. John Stimberis took over the program after Wilbour retired in 2011.

The Chinook Pass program is unique in the Northwest for its reliance on ski-assisted avalanche control work to support highway operations. Skis are used both to deliver explosive charges to avalanche starting zones and to trigger avalanches directly by ski cutting.

In spring snow conditions, ski cutting is not as dangerous as it sounds. High on a slope, a skier can skim across the top of a snowfield, releasing a few inches of sun-warmed snow that slides away beneath the skier's track. As the wet snow descends, it entrains more snow in an ever-increasing crescendo until, by the time it reaches the roadbed 1,000 feet below,

Rob Gibson climbs above heavy machinery on the Chinook Pass highway during spring snow-removal work. (Photo by John Stimberis)

it has swelled into a thundering torrent. Timing is everything, and it takes experience to judge when the surface has warmed enough to slide but not enough to endanger the skier.

John has experienced days when a snowball thrown onto the slope can start a sluff that grows large enough by the time it reaches the highway to bury a car, break trees, or destroy a small building. When conditions are right, a day of triggering can erase a week of work by the heavy equipment below. Whether John dreamed as a boy of being Thor and hurling down thunderbolts, that job is now his.

On the day when I join John and Aaron, conditions are not ideal for ski cutting, so we rely on explosive triggers. After arriving at a 6,200-foot knob above Deadwood Lakes, we bury the six bags of explosives we've carried across the top of the slope. John and Aaron connect the bags using detonation cord, which explodes at a rate of four to five miles a second, enabling all of the charges to be fired simultaneously.

When the blast goes off, I'm grateful for the earplugs Aaron gave me but concerned when my clothes and camera are showered by burned powder. John says he's had trouble getting through airport security because his backpack is typically coated with a layer of explosive dust. He's had to show airport screeners his WSDOT identification and blasting license to convince them he's not a threat.

Our shot produces modest results, since the slope below the knob has recently melted and consolidated. After doing some ski cutting along the ridge, we pause to watch Kevin Marston and Lee Redden, the other half of John's crew, fire a shot on a knob about a half mile west of us. Their shot triggers a wet-slab avalanche that sweeps powerfully over the highway and descends all the way to the valley bottom. Before the day is done, the heavy equipment operators will return along the highway to clear the piles of snow generated by the skiers on the ridge.

John recalled a day a few years earlier, when the elements of weather and snow combined to create a perfect moment. "The snowpack was like a late pregnancy," he wrote. "Nothing could stop the inevitable." The day dawned warmer than usual and the snowpack was becoming unstable ahead of schedule.

With Rob Gibson, John made two trips to the ridge to deliver explosive shots. By the time they reached the top the second time, clouds had moved in and thunderstorms could be heard to the southeast. "Quickly," he recalled, "we set up our final shot of the day, never pausing a moment." The explosion sent another large avalanche to the valley floor. "We raced to peel the skins off our skis, reload our packs, and squeeze in a quick sip of water. A ridge is no place to be when lightning is coming. The ski cutting was still prime, as good as it ever gets. The snow peeled away, gathering mass and speed quickly. When the slides hit the road, they sounded like enormous waves crashing into a seawall."

The conditions were impressive. "The sky was beginning to steal the show. Dark clouds created a bizarre light and color shift to the environment. Lightning began to flash across the clouds and one of the most surreal moments unfolded before us. Avalanches were crashing through trees and rocks onto the highway, amid the crack and boom of the lightning and thunder, and that odd and spooky light."

In a sentiment that would elicit a quiet nod from avalanche hunters since the days of Atwater and LaChapelle, he concluded, "We live for these moments."

Opposite: Gary Brill and Garth Ferber ski Shuksan Arm in 1988. Before the Mount Baker ski area installed its Hemispheres chairlift, this area received little ski traffic.

CHAPTER 14

THE BACKCOUNTRY BOOM

In their 1972 book *Wilderness Skiing*, Lito Tejada-Flores and Allen Steck described the Northwest as "the land of volcanoes and wet snow" and noted that "if you learn to handle all the heavy new snow that can be found in the Pacific Northwest, and then go to the Rockies for some true powder skiing, it will seem laughably easy." To their credit, the authors acknowledged that the stereotype of the Cascade Range as just a line of volcanoes rising above scrappy foothills was incomplete. "This is most clearly seen in *Northwest Ski Trails* by Ted Mueller," they wrote, "a fantastic guidebook to wilderness ski routes in the northwest. This book should serve as a model for future ski-touring guidebooks produced for other areas around the country."

Ironically, when *Northwest Ski Trails* was published in 1968, the book didn't sell. Lift skiing was booming, and trudging uphill with alpine skis, cable bindings, leather boots, and strap-on climbing skins didn't appeal to many skiers. Tejada-Flores and Steck described two styles in their book: Nordic cross-country, with lightweight boots and three-pin bindings, and alpine touring. Of the telemark turn, they noted its long history but admitted, "It's a matter of open debate among Nordic specialists whether or not it's still really useful for anything."

Steve Barnett, in his 1978 book *Cross-Country Downhill*, begged to differ about the telemark turn. The book helped spark a revival, not just of telemark skiing but of any sort of skiing away from groomed slopes. The Sierra Club took notice and released an updated book by Tejada-Flores called *Backcountry Skiing* in 1981. The most enduring contribution of the book may have been its title. "We were talking about the very same sport," Tejada-Flores wrote about Barnett's earlier book, "and it still doesn't matter whether you call it ski touring, wilderness skiing, cross-country skiing, ski mountaineering or, as I do here, backcountry skiing."

With the publication of Rainer Burgdorfer's *Backcountry Skiing in Washington's Cascades* in 1986 and Barnett's *The Best Ski Touring in America* in 1987, it seemed to the relatively small group of Northwest backcountry skiers that the sport was coming of age, maybe even getting too popular. But that was nothing compared to what was to come over the next two decades.

A BETTER MOUSETRAP

As telemark skiing grew in the 1970s and 1980s, it offered an alternative for younger skiers to explore untracked snow. "Free your heel and free your mind" was the mantra of the time. Alpine touring, with bindings that hinge at the toe for climbing and lock down the heel for descending, had a small but dedicated following among young skiers.

In the early 1970s, Paul Ramer was a research engineer at Rocky Flats, Colorado, who enjoyed skiing in his spare time. Around 1974, after being laid off from his engineering job, Ramer decided to try running his own business making ski-touring gear. He designed a frame binding with a pair of ball-and-socket hinges at the toe and a locking mechanism at the heel that would accommodate any boot with a sturdy welt. The ball-and-socket hinge provided both heel lift and a release mechanism, making the Ramer one of the first fully releasable touring bindings. The binding also featured a patented heel elevator, which reduced leg strain while climbing.

About a decade later, Fritz Barthel in Austria began experimenting with Ramer bindings, taking them apart and reimagining how the working parts could be configured. He revised

Stephanie Subak crosses a thin spot on Ramer bindings and mountaineering boots in 1986.

the ball-and-socket arrangement, mounting the ball components on spring-loaded pincers and embedding the sockets into the ski boot itself on either side of the toe. He designed a lightweight heel piece with steel pins that latched into reinforced slots carved into the boot heel. As a result, the ski boot itself connected the toe and heel pieces, eliminating the binding frame altogether. Barthel called his invention the Low Tech binding. In the late 1980s, Dynafit, a maker of alpine touring boots, licensed the binding design from Barthel to produce their Tourlite Tech binding, which initially worked only with Dynafit Tourlite boots. Lock Miller, owner of the Marmot Mountain Works shop in Bellevue, Washington, introduced tech bindings to North America in the fall of 1991.

Around the time Paul Ramer was tinkering with ski binding design, several innovators were experimenting with an entirely different approach to sliding on snow. In the mid-1960s, Sherman Poppen invented the Snurfer, a cross between a ski and a surfboard. A few years later, Dimitriji Milovich developed what he called the Winterstick, a swallowtail snowboard with a single strap running down the board for securing the feet. Writing in *Powder* magazine in 1976, Gene Hensley recalled his first experience riding the Winterstick. "I couldn't stop thinking about the concept of surfing in snow," he wrote. "I felt as if I were on a wave that would not break, that would not let go for its worth [sic]." In the mid-1970s, Jake Burton Carpenter of Vermont began building snowboards under the Burton brand, which would eventually become the largest snowboard manufacturer in the world.

Back in the Northwest, Bob Barci, Jeff Fulton, Eric Galleson, and Pat Quirke tried snowboarding in 1981 at the Mount Baker ski area after experimenting with a homemade board on sand dunes along the Oregon coast. There were just a handful of snowboarders in Washington at the time, and the only place to buy snowboards was at Barci's shop near Seattle, the BikeFactory. In the early years of the sport, snowboards were banned by many ski areas around the country. Mount Baker, under manager Duncan Howat, was one of the first to fully embrace snowboarding. In 1985 Barci, Fulton, and Galleson organized the first Mount Baker Halfpipe contest, a pivotal moment of national exposure for the sport. Competitor Tom Sims won the event with local rider Craig Kelly taking fourth. Within a few years, Kelly would become the world snowboarding champion, putting Mount Baker on the map as a cradle of the young sport.

It was not long before snowboarders took their passion to the higher mountains. In July 1990, Kelly Ball, Steve Matthews, Terri Rengstorff, Scott Spiker, and Matt Vining snowboarded from the summit of Mount Rainier via the Kautz Glacier route. At the Kautz ice chute, Rengstorff rappelled on a fixed rope, then Vining and Matthews descended on their snowboards. Ball fell while descending the chute and, after several failed attempts to self-arrest, stopped by grabbing an ice block. It was soon revealed that this was not the first snowboard descent of the mountain, however. Ned Randolph, a guide for Rainier Mountaineering Inc., reported seeing two anonymous 'boarders descending the standard route above Camp Muir four days earlier. A year later, John Erben and Kevin Slotterbeck made the first snowboard descent of Rainier's Emmons Glacier, the route chosen for the first ski descent of the mountain more than forty years earlier.

As ski areas gradually welcomed snowboarding, the sport grew in popularity, but it was limited in the backcountry since uphill travel involved either postholing on foot or switching to snowshoes. Further innovations in equipment would change this. Brett Kobernik made a visit in the early 1990s to Mark Wariakois of Voile, a Utah-based maker of backcountry ski equipment. Kobernik showed Wariakois a prototype snowboard that could be split in half like a pair of skis. The two men refined the idea and in 1995 released a do-it-yourself "split kit" that enabled snowboarders to saw their board in half to create a splitboard. When split, the two halves of the board could be used with skins to tour and climb. For the first time, snowboard riders had an easy way to access backcountry powder snow.

A splitboarder applies skins in preparation for the next climb. (Photo by Jason Hummel)

While splitboarding grew as a branch of backcountry riding in the 1990s, ski equipment was evolving as well. In the mid-1990s, manufacturers began marketing "super side-cut" skis to alpine skiers. These skis, with a narrower waist and wider tip and tail than previous models, were found to make carving turns easier for intermediate skiers. They also offered advanced skiers a level of performance formerly attainable only by elite racers.

Then, inspired by the performance of snowboards in deep snow, manufacturers began making skis wider. In the 1980s and early 1990s, most skis used by backcountry skiers measured less than 70 millimeters wide at the waist. By 2005 "fat" skis had proliferated so much they were being grouped into classes from "low fat" (up to an 80-millimeter waist) to "super fat" (a more than 100-millimeter waist). A pair of super fat skis placed side by side was nearly as wide as a snowboard.

Manufacturers also modified the flex profile of skis to perform better in unpacked snow. Since the 1930s, skis have been built with camber, a gradual bend in the ski between the turned-up tip and the tail—similar to the bend of an archer's bow—which helps distribute the skier's weight over the snow. When laid unweighted on a table, a cambered ski arches up in the middle and presses on the table only near the tip and tail. In the early 2000s, designers began making skis with reverse camber, or "rocker," with the forebody and tail bending slightly upward, away from the snow. A fully rockered ski, when placed on a table, touches the table only at the center of the ski. Most rockered skis are built using a blend of camber and rocker. When combined with a wide footprint, a rockered ski becomes much easier to ski on in soft snow. If the design is taken to extremes, such a ski becomes unstable on firm snow, so most models are built as a compromise.

TECHNOLOGY AND SAFETY

On a blustery autumn day in North Cascades National Park in 1994, a cellular phone call made history. The call, from a group of climbers high on the east ridge of Forbidden Peak, was placed to the backcountry desk at the Marblemount Ranger Station. The climbers were stuck in a whiteout, unsure of which gully to descend, and they called the rangers for advice—the first time a distress call had ever been made from a cell phone within the park.

Ranger Kelly Bush, who took the call, recalled that her first impulse was to rule out a prank. She matched the names of the calling party against the climbing register and concluded that the call was genuine. "We gave them some rudimentary information," she recalled, "but we felt like we were out on a limb, liability-wise, not knowing their exact location." The climbers told Bush that they would try climbing down and call back in thirty minutes. They never made the call. Concerned for their safety, Bush organized a rescue party. A few hours later, the climbing party was found safe but unapologetic, claiming they never actually called for a rescue. "We were dumbfounded," said Bush.

Such technology began to change the nature of outdoor recreation in Northwest mountains. When I started backcountry skiing in the 1970s, navigation was done entirely using paper maps, compass, and altimeter. GPS devices began to appear in the 1990s, but they didn't really catch on until the 2000s, after the US government lifted military restrictions on their accuracy. When we attempted a two-week ski traverse through the North Cascades in 1991 (see chapter 12), my brother Carl and I didn't yet own a GPS device. In case of an emergency, we made a special arrangement to borrow a Park Service radio from Ranger Bill Lester, Bush's predecessor. Later, I began carrying a ham radio that enabled me to make autopatch phone calls to my family through a hobbyist repeater service. Even today, cell phone coverage in Northwest mountains can be hit-or-miss.

Today, GPS-equipped smartphones enable navigation with almost pinpoint accuracy. Satellite devices make it possible to call out from the wilderness virtually anywhere in the world. These tools have changed the psychology of wilderness recreation in complex ways and have facilitated some of the remarkable adventures completed by Northwest ski mountaineers since 2010.

This evolution of ski design erased the advantage that snowboarding once held in soft snow. By about 2010, snowboarding had peaked, much as telemark skiing had about a decade earlier. In 2005 the patent on Dynafit's Tourlite Tech binding expired. Other manufacturers started making what have come to be known simply as tech bindings, resulting in more innovation and a broad range of products. Having absorbed innovations from other snow sports since the 1970s, alpine touring has emerged as the most popular style of backcountry skiing today.

BUILDING COMMUNITY

One of the most significant changes in backcountry skiing since the 1980s has been the development of a community that is largely independent of traditional ski clubs. An early sign of this took place in 1979, a year after the publication of Barnett's *Cross-Country Downhill*. Telemark skier Suze Woolf invited a group of friends for a Mother's Day ski-brunch at Stevens Pass after the ski area had closed for the season. The telemark party became a spring tradition that continued for years. Woolf's invitation read, "You are cordially invited to the first annual free-wheeling free-heelers party and champagne breakfast. Formal attire, though not required, is strongly suggested. Best-dressed skier takes home remaining liquor."

Tuxedos, party dresses (several worn by the men), and elaborate costumes were the theme of the telemark party. Woolf arrived in a sequined Gore-Tex ball gown, slit up the side so she could do a proper telemark turn. Co-organizer Earl Hamilton showed up in knickers, a white shirt, a British driving cap, and a duct-tape bow tie. Over the years, Ken Ritland arrived as the maestro Telemann (complete with violin), as a used Karhu salesman (after the tele-ski brand), and as the Reverend Ken, a televangelist in a plaid suit with a copy of *Hustler* magazine in one pocket and Rainer Burgdorfer's ski bible in the other. A skier wearing a top hat with shrubs growing out of it got puzzled looks until he explained he had come as a head plant. The telemark party at Stevens Pass was an annual event through 1995. Frequent attendee Kathy Phibbs brought the costume tradition to Mount St. Helens, when she wore a red chiffon dress to the summit of the mountain in 1987, inaugurating the Mount St. Helens Mother's Day tradition that continues to this day (see chapter 11).

Another forum for community building took shape through popular ski magazines and local tabloids. Seattle brothers Dave and Jake Moe founded *Powder* in 1972. After selling the magazine in 1981, Jake founded a new company that got into broadcasting, event production, and the publication of *Sports Northwest*. For a decade, the tabloid provided one of the only channels outside of a club environment for Northwest skiers to share experiences

Turns All Year founder Charles Eldridge skiing in summer on Mount Rainier (Photo by Steve Barnett)

beyond their small circle of friends. *Sports Northwest* went out of business around 1991, followed a few years later by John Garibaldi's *free snow*, a tabloid specifically for backcountry skiers. After *free snow* petered out in 1996, its place was filled by *Off-Piste*, published by Dave Waag from 1999 through 2015. These local publications provided a Northwest complement to *Couloir* magazine, launched in California in the fall of 1988, and *Backcountry* magazine, which started in Colorado in November 1994.

The 1980s, the dawn of the personal computer era, brought new ways for people to connect, as Microsoft and machines from IBM and Apple began to appear in many households. Connectivity was initially limited to email and text-only chat forums using dial-up networking. The Usenet, a worldwide discussion forum, began in 1980 and was expanded in 1987. Users, primarily university students or technology workers at the time, could read and post messages in newsgroups. Many an hour that should have been devoted to work was instead spent on these forums by tech-savvy skiers. For the first time, skiers around the country could discuss, debate, and share stories almost instantaneously.

With the emergence of the World Wide Web in 1991, and the development of "point and click" web browsers a few years later, commercial sites like Outside Online and

Seattle-based MountainZone.com began to offer magazine-quality stories about outdoor sports that could be released and updated on a much shorter publishing cycle than print media. Web-based discussion forums for skiers began to form around 1998, including TelemarkTips.com, founded by California skier Mitch Weber, and WildSnow.com, from Lou Dawson of Colorado.

By far the most important catalyst for the Northwest backcountry ski community in the early 2000s was the website Turns All Year (TAY), launched by Seattle's Charles Eldridge in 2002. Several of the early contributors to TAY were connected with The Mountaineers and other local clubs, but the website built a community of its own. CascadeClimbers.com, a site devoted to climbing and, to a lesser extent, skiing, developed around the same time. Enthusiasm for real backcountry skiing (without lifts or helicopters) was growing, and Turns All Year offered a way for Northwest skiers to communicate and share experiences beyond their usual group of friends. The immediate effect of online communication on the backcountry community was like pouring gas on a smoldering fire.

Another venue for the growing community of backcountry enthusiasts in the Northwest emerged out of the "alpine races" (later called randonnée or "skimo" races) started by Swiss skiers in the 1920s. These events—involving technical terrain, multiple summits, and at least 10,000 feet of combined elevation gain and loss a day—grew in popularity during the 1980s in Italy, Switzerland, France, and Spain, in the mountains of Catalonia. Competitors were required to carry crampons, a headlamp, and some food, water, and emergency gear. European races were typically made up of two- or three-person teams, especially in races over glaciated terrain.

A race billed as the first of its kind in the United States took place at Jackson Hole, Wyoming, in March 2001. The Life-Link/Dynafit Randonnee Rally featured a Le Mans–style start in which competitors ran to their skis, clicked into their bindings, and surged up the hill on climbing skins. Upon reaching the top of the climb, each racer would strip off the skins—preferably without removing their skis—stuff them in a shirt pocket, lock their bindings, and race downhill to the start of the next climb. The racing-class event included more than 5,000 feet of climbing while the recreational class covered more than 3,000 feet. Life-Link vice president John Scott had seen ski mountaineering races while traveling for business in Europe. "I thought it would help grow alpine touring in the States," he said, "and bring the backcountry community together."

The following year, Life-Link expanded its randonnée rally into a series, with the second race of the season at Alpental, Washington. I entered this race out of curiosity after a completing a scouting trip along The Mountaineers' Patrol Race route (described in the

Racers sprint to their skis during the start of the first Life-Link/Dynafit Randonnee Rally at Alpental in 2002. (Photo by Chad Coleman)

prologue) a few days before the event. Racers could use whatever ski gear they wanted but had to carry a shovel, avalanche probe, and rescue beacon. Andrew McLean, who grew up in Seattle skiing at Alpental, had traveled with friends from his home in Utah for the race. Sixty-eight entrants lined up outside the day lodge after positioning their skis side by side about 50 feet up the slope. After a short countdown, John Scott blew a boat horn and we sprinted up the slope toward our skis in a Le Mans–style start.

McLean and I got off to a good start, and we were soon near the front of the pack with Slovakian mountain guide Miki Knizka. Andreas Schmidt was close behind but having trouble with skin traction on borrowed skis. Knizka was pulling away by the time we reached Piss Pass, but he ran into trouble during a short descent where most of the racers kept their climbing skins on. He broke a ski binding around this time and had to drop out of the race. After retracing the route to the lodge and completing a second lap to Source Lake and Pineapple Pass, McLean and I and Schmidt finished one-two-three in the race. Petra Pirc of Utah won the women's event, with Brigid Sterling and Corinne Jeuch finishing second and third.

The event was well received. Writing in the October issue of *Off-Piste* magazine, photographer Chad Coleman observed, "Backcountry touring in North America has long been a sport of small groups, or even a solitary pursuit with many people keeping their favorite lines and powder stashes secret. This is no longer true as a new tradition emerged last winter with the

Life-Link Randonnee Rally Race series." Life-Link product manager Tim Kelley was pleased. "The backcountry ski community rarely gets together for any event," he said. "It is a close-knit group and a hugely spread-out and secretive group all at the same time."

Randonnée rallies, later known as "skimo" (ski mountaineering) races, continued to grow, and Life-Link races were held the following season at Whistler, British Columbia; Crested Butte, Colorado; Alpental and Stevens Pass, Washington; and Jackson Hole, Wyoming. Seattle's Outdoor Research became a cosponsor in 2006 and took over the race in 2007, renaming the event VertFest, "a celebration of backcountry VertiCulture." Backcountry skier Monika Johnson won the women's division race at most of the VertFest events in Washington between 2007 and 2010. After she died in a cornice accident on Red Mountain in 2011—a shock to the Northwest mountaineering and skiing community—the Alpental race was renamed the Monika Johnson Memorial Race in her memory.

Born in 1970, Johnson had been introduced to ski mountaineering as a student with The Mountaineers. She became an instructor and for years introduced beginners to the sport she loved. After a friend died in an avalanche accident in 2002, Johnson carried a tiny stuffed tiger on her ski trips to keep her friend "Kitty" in her thoughts. Johnson suffered a serious head injury in a bicycling accident in 2007, but drawing on her skills as a physical therapist, she fought her way back to health and strength, returning to the mountains to make several first women's descents in the Cascades.

THE GROWTH OF SKI GUIDING

Since Walt Little launched the first ski mountaineering course for The Mountaineers in 1941, outdoor clubs have played a key role in introducing skiers to the Northwest backcountry. After World War II, lift skiing lured skiers away from touring and mountaineering, and it wasn't until 1962 that The Mountaineers revived their course. Other clubs such as the Washington Alpine Club and the Mazamas have long-running ski mountaineering programs as well. The biggest change in recent years has been the emergence of teaching and guiding programs offered by commercial outfitters.

In 1979 a small group of climbing guides in a bar in Moose, Wyoming, sketched out the charter for a proposed organization of American mountain guides with two purposes: to promote the highest possible standards for professional mountain guides in the United States and to become a member of the Union Internationale des Associations de Guides de Montagnes (UIAGM). The new organization, later called the American Mountain Guides Association (AMGA), didn't make much progress on those goals for several years, but by the late 1980s it began developing an accreditation program and guide exams.

During the 1980s, there were several established guiding companies in the Northwest, but they were mostly involved in summer climbing on the Cascade volcanoes, particularly Mounts Baker, Rainier, and Hood. Longtime Northwest climber and guide Alan Kearney recalled that there was very little ski guiding in the early part of the decade. Some skiers hired him in 1981 to guide them on the north side of Mount Baker, but the group didn't try to reach the summit. A few years later, Tim Boyer started a ski guiding company out of Bellingham but, as Kearney recalled, "he just could not get the clients." The company folded before long.

When Eric Sanford started Liberty Bell Alpine Tours in the Methow Valley, winter guiding was focused mainly on helicopter skiing. But several of the local guides, especially Eric Burr, felt it was important to offer more-affordable programs, so the company put together what Sanford called the Super Tour. A single helicopter ride would whisk skiers up Goat Peak, where they could ski back down the mountain to the valley under their own power. In the late 1980s, after Randy and Kathy Sackett took over the Methow Valley heli-skiing

Martin Volken, Andy Dappen, and Mike Hattrup check the map on the Snoqualmie Haute Route in 1999. (Photo by Carl Skoog)

permit, they continued the Goat Peak outing and added a similar trip to Silver Star Mountain and other nearby slopes. Skiers were dropped off on the mountain to ski on their own for the day, then picked up by helicopter in the afternoon. The establishment of a yurt near Windy Pass in 1997 gave the biggest boost to the company's backcountry skiing program.

In the early 1990s, Swiss guides Bela Vadasz and Jean Pavillard, working in California and Colorado, respectively, led the effort to develop a ski guiding program for the AMGA. Ski guiding was the weakest link in US mountain guiding at the time. After several years of effort, the program was brought up to international standards, and the AMGA was admitted to UIAGM in 1997. Acceptance by UIAGM meant that guides certified by AMGA were qualified to work anywhere in the world.

Northwest guide Martin Volken, who had grown up in Switzerland near the Matterhorn, really focused on ski guiding. Attracted by the idea of wilderness, he moved to North Bend, Washington, in the foothills of the Cascades, in 1994. He opened a ski shop in Seattle and pursued Swiss guide certification, which he achieved in 1999. He led several pioneering trips in the North Cascades and Alpine Lakes Wilderness, and in the early 2000s he coauthored two guidebooks to the Cascades and an instructional book on backcountry skiing.

As improved equipment and online media has boosted the popularity of backcountry skiing, the number of active ski guides has grown considerably. At least a dozen companies now offer ski guiding, and several independent guides have been certified, although it's hard to make a living at it. Most independent guides have other sources of income, and making guiding a sustainable profession remains a big topic in the American guiding community.

SKI HUTS

In the early 1900s, cabins and shelters of various kinds were scattered throughout the Cascade and Olympic Mountains. Some were left over from mining and prospecting; others were built by the US Forest Service as guard stations. Old-time skiers found shelter and warmth at Mount Baker's Kulshan Cabin, the Storbo hotel in Mount Rainier's Glacier Basin, the snow survey cabin at Lyman Lake, Spanish Camp in the Pasayten country, the Hannegan Pass cabin below Ruth Mountain, and the Flapjack Lakes cabin in the Olympic Mountains. There were probably other cabins that have been lost to memory. Some cabins succumbed to neglect or were crushed by winter snows. Others were removed as sections of the Cascades and Olympics were protected as parks or wilderness areas. Today, the few huts that exist are most often associated with commercial operations just outside of protected areas. For example, the Windy Pass yurt established by Randy and Kathy Sackett in 1997 is located near the Pacific Crest Trail just outside the Pasayten Wilderness.

Mountaineers skiers (William J. Maxwell, Paul Shorrock, Norval Grigg, two unknown skiers, and Rudy Amsler) at the old Storbo hotel in Glacier Basin on the northeast side of Mount Rainier, 1930 (Rudolf Amsler collection, The Mountaineers Archives)

In 1978 Bill and Peg Stark established what they called the Scottish Lakes High Camp, a collection of small cabins near the edge of the Alpine Lakes Wilderness east of Stevens Pass. The camp remains in operation under newer ownership. On the west side of Stevens Pass, an outfit called Cascade Powder Guides operates a yurt on the north flank of Windy Mountain that is accessed in winter by snowcat. The Rendezvous Huts system above the Methow Valley offers hut-to-hut skiing on groomed Nordic trails. Near Mount Rainier, a similar system operated by the Mount Tahoma Trails Association includes three huts and a yurt near Ashford.

In Olympic National Park around 1970, local skiers installed a small A-frame structure at the Waterhole campground, about halfway between Hurricane Ridge and Obstruction Point. The hut could be assembled in fall, before the snow fell, and removed in summer. Skiing ranger Jack Hughes supported the hut enthusiastically, but his superiors did not.

When the park superintendent learned of the hut, he ordered it removed, but the snow had come already, so the hut was allowed to stand for emergency use only. Skiers posted a register in the hut to sign in case of "emergency" use. By the end of the winter season, the roster was so long, and contained so many influential names, that the park administration allowed the hut to stay.

For decades, an uneasy truce existed between local skiers, who overwhelmingly favored the shelter, and Park Service managers, who continued to urge its removal. The hut was so

Bill Stark surveys Mount Cashmere for a potential ski area in the early 1970s. A few years later, with his wife Peg, he established the Scottish Lakes High Camp a few miles to the north, just outside the Alpine Lakes Wilderness. (Spring Trust for Trails)

popular that for many years the park held lotteries for spaces and required reservations for weekend use. In 2010 the Hurricane Ridge Winter Sports Club proposed a ski hut system between Hurricane Ridge and Deer Park, an idea first put forth in the 1930s. The system would incorporate the Waterhole ski hut and add removable winter shelters below Hurricane Hill and at the end of the Obstruction Point road. The Deer Park Ranger Station would be adapted for winter overnight use.

In 2012 the Waterhole ski hut was abruptly demolished by the Park Service. Local skiers were stunned, since there had been no prior public announcement or explanation of the decision. In 2008 an exclusion had been granted that allowed park management to remove the structure without further public notification or comment.

In the Washington Cascades, several fire lookouts have been used for overnight shelter by skiers. Administered by the Forest Service, some of these lookouts have been adopted by local hiking clubs, which do their best to maintain them. However, with backcountry skiing booming in an era of social media, this arrangement has not always ended well. Built by the Forest Service in 1935, the Winchester Mountain lookout was restored by the Mount Baker Club in 1982 and added to the National Register of Historic Places.

As backcountry skiing took off in the 2000s, the lookout came under heavy use by skiers and snowboarders, who propped open the storm shutters in winter and sometimes left the storm door unsecured, leading to broken hinges, windows, and shutters. Skiers kicking their boots to remove snow ruined the door threshold. The remote location made it impractical for volunteers to check on the lookout during winter, and though the club and Forest Service pleaded with users for years, they were unable to stem the damage. The Winchester Mountain lookout was closed to winter use in the fall of 2017.

Mount Hood has several older huts, including the Cloud Cap Inn, constructed in 1889 on the northeast flank of the mountain. Maintained by the Hood River Crag Rats, the inn is generally not open for overnight use. The Tilly Jane A-Frame, a half mile southeast of Cloud Cap Inn, is heavily used by backcountry skiers today, available by reservation only and managed by the Oregon Nordic Club.

Opposite: *Rene Crawshaw climbs Black Peak for the first ski descent in 1997.* (Photo by Carl Skoog)

CHAPTER 15

BEYOND BOUNDARIES

Mount Rainier so dominates its surroundings that its 11,138-foot satellite, Little Tahoma, seems a minor peak by comparison. Yet "Little T" is taller than every other summit in Washington except Mount Adams, and it is steeper than most. On three sides, the summit looms thousands of feet above crumbling cliffs and teetering crags. The Whitman Glacier extends high on the peak's southeast flank, offering the only easy climbing route.

During the first ski ascent of Little Tahoma in April 1933, Paul Gilbreath and Wendell Trosper climbed within eight feet of the summit on skis. Skis with metal edges were beginning to appear in the Northwest by this time, and Gilbreath and

Sylvain Saudan talks with Rene Farwig following his ski descent of Mount Hood's Newton Clark Headwall in 1971. (Western Ski Promotions collection)

Trosper likely had the best equipment available. Both men would compete in the first Silver Skis race the following year, and Gilbreath would win the race twice, in 1940 and 1948. Trosper guided on Mount Rainier for many years, becoming the first person to climb the mountain by ten different routes. In *The Challenge of Rainier*, mountaineer Dee Molenaar described their 1933 ski climb as "a delicate feat considering the high angle of the upper several hundred feet of the peak." Along with the 1931 ski ascent and descent of Mount Hood by Hjalmar Hvam's party, it was one of the earliest instances in the Northwest of skis being used on seriously steep terrain. Many years later, skiing slopes once thought suitable only for climbers would become a significant branch of the sport.

Born in Switzerland in 1936, mountain guide Sylvain Saudan had been working as a ski instructor for several years when he realized he'd spent an entire winter on skis without falling. Needing new challenges, he set his sights on skiing classic climbing routes. He trained by skiing moderate slopes in difficult conditions, including slopes of dirt and loose stones in the middle of summer. One year he skied Japan's Mount Fuji in September entirely without snow. In the late 1960s, Saudan made a series of steep descents in the Alps and decided to make his living through films and public appearances. He began looking for challenges in other parts of the world. Rene Farwig, director of the Mount Hood Meadows ski school, encouraged Saudan to come to Oregon to ski Mount Hood.

Saudan flew to Portland during the winter of 1971. Two weeks of bad weather followed his arrival. Running out of time, he hired a helicopter to fly to the summit of Mount Hood during a brief clearing on the afternoon of March 1. Not having climbed the mountain before, he initially started down the wrong chute, one that ended above a cliff. Fortunately, he realized his mistake and sidestepped back up and traversed to the proper gully. He then descended the Newton Clark Headwall to the gentle slopes of Clark Canyon and the Mount Hood Meadows ski area. Speaking to reporters, he said, "The run was much shorter than the ones I did in Europe, but it was just as dangerous. If I had fallen on Mount Hood, it would have been the same as if I had fallen on the Eiger. I would not have lived to tell about it." Three years later, Brian Raasch, a ski racer from Hood River, repeated the descent.

Perhaps inspired by Saudan's ski on Mount Hood, ski instructor and mountain guide Bill Briggs completed the first ski descent of the Grand Teton in Wyoming in June of the same year. Briggs was a member of the party that first skied Mount Rainier's Ingraham Glacier a decade earlier. Also in June 1971, Fritz Stammberger of Aspen skied the north face of North Maroon Bell in Colorado. These descents, reported in the premiere issue *Off Belay* magazine in 1972, seeded the idea of steep ski mountaineering in the American climbing community. The idea germinated slowly.

In a good snow year, one of the most obvious snow chutes in the Cascade Range is the north gully of McClellan Butte, a 5,162-foot "Little Matterhorn" rising above Interstate 90 near Snoqualmie Pass. College roommates Karl Erickson and Greg Wong were part of a younger generation of Northwest ski mountaineers attracted to climbing routes detailed in Fred Beckey's new

Karl Erickson contemplates the north face of Mount Shuksan before hiking in for the 1979 ski descent. (Photo by Greg Wong)

Cascade Alpine Guide. Every time Erickson and Wong drove from the pass toward Seattle, the chute "just begged us to ski it." The pair finally climbed and skied the gully in 1978. After descending the snow chute, Wong recalled, they had to stumble through thick underbrush to return to their car. There was no trail. "All of a sudden we heard a nonorganic 'clang,'" he said, "and realized we were standing on top of the old railroad avalanche sheds." They had returned to civilization, almost.

A year after their McClellan Butte venture, Erickson and Wong set their sights on a bigger objective, the north face of Mount Shuksan, the picture-postcard summit towering above the Mount Baker ski area. They approached the mountain in late June, hiking in leather climbing boots and carrying alpine ski boots in their overnight packs. Focused on skiing the north face, they didn't climb the summit pyramid during their 1979 venture. On the descent, they belayed each other on skis for several rope lengths. They chose a line west of the normal climbing route that forced them to rappel over a rock band at one point.

A month or two before their Shuksan trip, Erickson and Wong had attempted to ski Mount Stuart, the crown peak of the central Cascades. They hiked over Longs Pass as soon as the Teanaway road was drivable, but found the south flank of the peak had already melted out. In 1980 they climbed the peak in early May and skied Ulrichs Couloir from the true summit nearly all the way to the Ingalls Creek valley. Stuart had been skied from the false summit a year earlier by the father-and-son team of Eric and Kurt Feigl. Their 1979 descent was made via the Cascadian Couloir.

STEEP SKIING COMES TO MOUNT RAINIER

Prior to May 1980, only two routes on Mount Rainier had ever been skied: the Emmons and Ingraham Glaciers. A party led by Dan Davis skied the Fuhrer Finger route for the first time on May 3 and 4. Davis began his descent at the 14,410-foot summit, while Tom Janisch and Jeff Haley began skiing a short distance below. After spending another night at their 10,000-foot high camp, the party continued down to the Nisqually River bridge at 3,900 feet, for a total skiing descent of 10,500 feet, surely one of the longest ski runs in the conterminous United States.

On May 3, while the Davis party was skiing from the summit of Rainier, Chris Landry of Aspen, Colorado, and Doug Robinson of Bishop, California, hiked toward the mountain from the White River road. After three days of bad weather, they climbed to the summit and skied the Emmons Glacier, with Robinson making the first complete descent from the top on three-pin Nordic gear. After resupplying with food from a party that had become discouraged by the weather, the pair moved camp to Curtis Ridge, where they were stormbound

Chris Landry skis Mount Rainier's Liberty Ridge in 1980. (Photo by Doug Robinson)

for several more days. When the weather improved, Landry and Robinson waited a day for avalanche hazard to diminish, then moved camp to the toe of Liberty Ridge.

At 1:30 a.m. on May 12, they began climbing the ridge with Landry carrying skis, reaching the summit of Liberty Cap around 10:00 a.m. After a short rest, they began their descent, with Landry on skis and Robinson on foot. The initial slope below Liberty Cap was the crux of the descent, described by Landry as "hard as nails and about a 50-degree slope." He later recalled, "That was the one place I was kind of spooked." Landry dropped down this pitch "with no control to speak of" and found more manageable conditions on the ridge below. Robinson down-climbed the route on foot, taking photographs while Landry skied. The descent was considered a landmark at the time, but Landry retired from steep skiing a year later after a scary fall on the west rib of Denali in Alaska.

Dale Farnham was an all-around mountaineer known for bold climbs in both summer and winter on Mount Index, Baring Mountain, Rainier's Willis Wall, and other Cascade summits. He added two ski routes on Mount Rainier during his lifetime. He skied the Kautz Glacier and its chute in 1985 and repeated the route four times, all solo, deeming it the best ski route on the mountain. In 1988 he climbed the Gibraltar Ledges to the summit, intending to ski back down the route. When he came to the juncture of the ledge and the Nisqually-Gibraltar Chute, Farnham found the chute so inviting that he started down it instead. After he'd made a few turns, the chute narrowed to the length of his skis and steepened considerably. He was struck by rocks many times during the short time he spent in the narrowest part. He later called it "probably the most stupid thing I've ever done." Farnham made sixteen ski descents of Rainier by various routes and attempted the Mowich Face in 1995, turning back due to "a raging sinus infection." He died of a heart attack in 2017 at age sixty-four.

OTHER EARLY FORAYS

In the South Cascades, Mount Hood became the center of attention for a new generation of ski mountaineers. Mike Kirby joined three friends for a ski circumnavigation of the peak combined with a climb of the mountain in May 1979. The group circled from Timberline to a bivouac on Cathedral Ridge, then climbed the Sandy Glacier Headwall the next morning. Kirby carried his skis up, hoping that the slope would be skiable. While his friends continued to the summit, Kirby napped for an hour near the Queens Chair and awoke to find the snow softened enough for skiing. With his ice axe taped to a ski pole as a self-arrest tool, he skied the headwall without incident. The party eventually regrouped and completed their circuit of the mountain the following day.

In the late 1970s and early 1980s, Steve Lyford explored more routes on Mount Hood than any other skier. His descents included the standard south-side route many times, the Leuthold Couloir, Sandy Glacier Headwall, Sunshine route, Cooper Spur, north face (three times, via the climber's-left gully), and Wy'east route. During one of his ventures on the north face, Lyford climbed the right-hand gully and prepared anchors to rappel the two rock steps if necessary, but was hit in the leg by a falling rock. Concerned about leg cramps, he decided to ski the left-hand gully instead. The climber's-right gully was snowboarded (with a rappel over the lower step) by Stephen Koch of Jackson, Wyoming, in May 1992.

As for Mount Adams, it had been skied by its South Spur as early as 1932, but many years elapsed before descents on other flanks of the mountain were recorded. In June 1988, Jeff Berrens skied the northwest face of the north ridge after a solo ascent of the ridge. W. D. Frank skied the Adams Glacier in 1990 and, a year later, the Avalanche Glacier with Gary Nesvig. Matt Perkins skied the Pinnacle Glacier headwall around 1995.

In the North Cascades, skiers exploring remote high routes in the 1980s generally avoided steep descents, since they were using equipment better suited for cross-country travel than steep skiing. But a few set their sights on more challenging routes on individual peaks. Jens Kieler and friends skied from the knife-edge summit of Eldorado Peak in April 1981, and Kieler skied the northwest flank of Del Campo Peak in the Monte Cristo group a couple years later. Mount Spickard, a beautiful summit accessed from the Canadian border, was likely skied from the north by Canadians around this time. Though Whitehorse Mountain had been skied via the standard Lone Tree Pass route in the 1940s, descents of the steep and avalanche-prone Snow Gulch were rarely, if ever, done. In March 1985, Gary Brill and Jens Kieler climbed the mountain on skis via the standard route, and Kieler descended the Snow Gulch in cold powder snow. Electing not to follow

The summit pyramid of Mount Shuksan

him, Brill took a photo of Kieler beginning his descent that was printed on the cover of Rainer Burgdorfer's backcountry ski guidebook in 1986.

Around 1987, Steve Vanpatten and Jim Witte made a ski ascent of Mount Shuksan with several friends. Finding the summit pyramid coated with rime ice and dusted with fresh snow—conditions that looked ideal for skiing—the pair decided to carry their skis to the top while their friends climbed on foot. With a belay from their friends, both skiers sidestepped the first 20 to 30 feet down from the top, then untied and skied the rest.

One of the finest descents made deep in the North Cascades during this period was the north couloir of Tenpeak Mountain, completed by Andreas Schmidt around 1993 during a traverse of Glacier Peak from the White Chuck River. Schmidt climbed the volcano via Kennedy Peak and Frostbite Ridge, then descended the Cool, Suiattle, and Honeycomb Glaciers to the base of Tenpeak. After climbing and skiing the north couloir, he returned to Kennedy Hot Springs via the Honeycomb and White Chuck Glaciers.

During their early adventures together, Karl Erickson and Greg Wong made an attempt to ski the Coleman Headwall on Mount Baker in March 1981. They cut short their attempt due to deep snow after climbing halfway up the face. The headwall was eventually skied by visiting guides Bela and Mimi Vadasz in May 1990.

EXTREMITIS

The 1970s and 1980s were a golden age of steep skiing in the Alps, when hundreds of alpine climbing routes, many steeper than 50 degrees, were descended on skis for the first time. "Extreme skiing" became the handle for this branch of the sport, a term popularized in American media by a 1981 profile of Chris Landry in *Sports Illustrated* magazine. Though Landry later explained that he had been quoted out of context, the profile became famous for its stark definition of extreme skiing: "If you fall you die."

In the United States, this period was the golden age of a different branch of skiing: free-style, an acrobatic form of the sport that basically grew out of skiers showing off under-neath the chairlift. Freestyle consisted of three disciplines: mogul skiing, ballet, and aerials. Competitive events were formalized in the 1970s, and freestyle became a demonstration sport at the 1988 Winter Olympics in Calgary.

Freestyle skier and aspiring moviemaker Gregg Stump struck the idea of combining these two branches of skiing on film. In 1988 he produced *The Blizzard of Aahhhs*, which followed three freestyle skiers, Mike Hattrup, Glen Plake, and Scot Schmidt, skiing in the French Alps around Chamonix, the hotbed of European extreme skiing. Stump lamented that American skiing, burdened by lawsuits and crushing insurance rates, didn't promote

Dean Collins and Rene Crawshaw drop off a cornice just outside the Mount Baker ski area in the 1990s. (Photo by Carl Skoog)

the type of ski heroes he cared about. "Believable ski heroes," Stump said, "are the ones who ski the extreme." Filmed in rockumentary style, the movie was a huge success. The film included scenes of the three skiers dropping off cliffs and tackling couloirs in a fast, dynamic style, an image that became synonymous in American media with extreme skiing. Glen Plake later acknowledged, "We were just freestylers hotdoggin' around. We had zero alpine skills."

The film inspired skiers to push high-level skiing outside the boundaries of traditional ski areas. This led to an event in 1991 billed as the World Extreme Skiing Championships at Valdez, Alaska. Competitors were supported by helicopters to reach the start of the runs. The first event was won by Doug Coombs, who had honed his skiing at Bridger Bowl in Montana. Competitive extreme skiing was judged on style, flow, and the difficulty of the line chosen by each skier. It was neither freestyle skiing nor steep ski mountaineering, but a blend of the two that later came to be known as freeriding.

In the Northwest this branch of skiing was centered around the ski areas at Mount Baker and Stevens Pass. Baker, with world-record snowfalls and steep terrain surrounding the lift-serviced area, became the home of world champion snowboarder Craig Kelly and acrobatic skiers including Dean Collins and Rene Crawshaw. Stevens, with Cowboy Mountain that gets only slightly less snowfall than Mount Baker, built a freeride community around skiers such as Robbie Capell and snowboarders including Matt Goodwill.

By the mid-1990s, "extreme" had become the hottest new superlative for advertisers. Previous favorites included "super," "ultra," and "mega," but "extreme" was now king. While media-driven "extreme skiing" dominated the news, casual skiers could be forgiven for being confused about what, exactly, the term meant.

Meanwhile, steep ski mountaineering—the descent of difficult routes climbed by the skier—continued to develop in the Northwest. Doug Coombs lived in Hood River, Oregon, for a time and he made the first ski descent of the Lava Glacier Headwall on the north face of Mount Adams. In 1995, with Glen Plake, Coombs skied the north face of the northwest ridge on Adams, which since then has become the most popular steep descent on the mountain. He also skied the climber's-left gully on the north face of Mount Hood in 1997, unaware of the previous descent by Steve Lyford. After Martin Volken settled in North Bend and opened his ski shop, he began systematically exploring ski descents on the small but rugged summits surrounding Snoqualmie Pass. In 2002 he published *Backcountry Skiing Snoqualmie Pass*, the first guidebook to Washington skiing that included seriously steep descents.

One of the most publicized steep descents was the 1997 ski of the Edmunds Headwall on the Mowich Face of Mount Rainier. Organized by Doug Ingersoll, the effort included Armond DuBuque, Andrew McLean, and my brother Carl Skoog. The descent was probably not much harder than Chris Landry's ski of Liberty Ridge in 1980, but its significance lay in the way it was reported and the level of attention it received in the ski community.

Ingersoll wrote a long article about the adventure for *Backcountry* magazine and made several public presentations, using photographs taken by Carl. The article described some of the decision-making involved in steep skiing, emphasizing how important good conditions are for such a venture. At their camp below the face, Ingersoll wondered, "Would it be warm enough to soften the snow at 14,000 feet? How would it feel to watch a friend lose an edge and plunge to his death? Was it really worth playing around with this mountain in this way?" Fortunately, the day of the

Armond DuBuque skis the Edmunds Headwall on Mount Rainier's Mowich Face in 1997. (Photo by Carl Skoog)

climb brought sunshine and high freezing levels, and the team waited near the summit until the afternoon sun warmed and softened the face. The descent was made without incident. (See Appendix for selected ski descents.)

THE BOLD RUSH

The new millennium brought a surge of ski exploration that would continue unabated for twenty years (see Appendix). In July 2000, Rene Crawshaw and my brother Carl skied the north ridge of Mount Baker, a route that Crawshaw had attempted seven times before. The north ridge was as much a mountaineering problem as a skiing challenge, with a nearly vertical brow of glacier ice perched atop the ridge, requiring steep ice climbing during

Rene Crawshaw climbs the north ridge of Mount Baker during a ski attempt in 1997. (Photo by Carl Skoog)

the ascent and a rappel during the descent. Crawshaw had been foiled at various times by lightning, hard-frozen ice, unconsolidated snow, and ill-preparedness when a partner underestimated the difficulty and neglected to bring two ice climbing tools. During their successful attempt, Rene and Carl climbed a pitch on the west side of the prow that could be descended on skis with a single rappel from ice screws.

The North Cascades became a focus of ski exploration in the 2000s, as skiers took advantage of better equipment to seek out remote ski descents. An extreme example of this trend was the descent of the northwest face of the southwest summit of Dome Peak in 2001 by twin brothers Jason and Josh Hummel with Ben Manfredi. In late August they carried skis, poles, and boots through forest, brush, and talus more than 15 miles before setting foot on the snow of the Dome Glacier. They crossed the glacier in tennis shoes, switched to boots to climb and ski the northwest face of the southwest summit (finding poor late-season conditions), then shouldered their ski gear and walked back out. In total, they hiked more than 30 miles for a ski run of less than a mile.

Manfredi was one of the first Northwest skiers to combine enthusiasm for steep skiing with internet savvy. In 2001 he created a website called CascadeClassics.org to document and share his skiing and kayaking adventures. Teaming with his brother Troy, the Hummel twins, their friend Sky Sjue, and a few others, Manfredi fully embraced steep skiing. The opening page of his website began, "Can you feel it? The mysterious horizons, the nauseating steeps, the adrenaline hazed lines. Nature's temptations doing battle with common sense. The mind-numbing commitment as you question each turn, each step, each breath. Will this be the last?" His ski descents included Stormy Monday Couloir, Lava Glacier Headwall, and North Lyman Glacier on Mount Adams; Mount Baker's Roosevelt Glacier; the north face of Mount Maude in the North Cascades; Fisher Chimneys and Price Glacier on Mount Shuksan; and the upper northeast face of Mount Fury in the Picket Range.

Manfredi was as enthusiastic about kayaking as he was about steep skiing, and he made many difficult whitewater descents throughout the Northwest. In November 2003 he drowned while kayaking the Grand Canyon of the Elwha River in the Olympic Mountains. He was just twenty-four years old.

Several other parties achieved firsts in the North Cascades in the early 2000s. In 2002 Andrew McLean and two Utah friends came to Washington hoping to ski a route on Mount Rainier. Finding poor conditions there, McLean's group joined Martin Volken to ski the north face of Mount Buckner. Their trip brought attention to the potential of the Cascade Pass area, with its high glaciated summits, for steep skiing. A couple weeks later, my brother Carl partnered with Alan Kearney to ski the Ptarmigan Traverse, making descents of the southwest gully of Spider Mountain and the north face of Sentinel Peak. Carl also joined

Sky Sjue during one of his ski adventures on Mount Rainier in the early 2000s (Photo courtesy Sky Sjue)

Andreas Schmidt and me to ski Pelton Peak and the S Glacier on Hurry Up Peak that summer. Volken and Peter Avolio skied the north face (left side) of Spider Mountain in 2003, a peak named for the "spidery" appearance of its snow gullies.

One of the most sought-after Cascades descents of the early 2000s was the central Mowich Face of Mount Rainier. Andrew McLean drove from Utah with his friend Mark Holbrook to meet Armond DuBuque for an attempt on the route in July 1999. During the two-day approach from Mowich Lake, DuBuque commented that the Mowich Face looked like it was covered with blue ice. When they started up the face on the third day, they found it just as icy as it had appeared from a distance. DuBuque turned back, while McLean and Holbrook continued to Liberty Cap and the summit. The face hadn't softened any when the two skiers returned from the summit, so they decided to descend the Edmunds Headwall, which McLean had skied in 1997. After a few good turns, they once again found themselves in the middle of a vast icefield. They sidestepped down on skis for more than 1,000 vertical feet, swinging the picks of their ice axes into the slope for security. Conditions gradually improved and, as McLean later wrote, they reached the lower glacier "slightly shell shocked."

Manfredi attempted the central Mowich Face with the Hummel brothers in July 2001. They, too, found the upper face icy, and they turned back before the crucial rightward snow ramp near 12,500 feet. They managed to switch to skis and descend from a point a short distance below the ramp. Four years later, the Hummels returned with Sky Sjue and three others to make another attempt on the route. Four turned back during the climb, but Sjue and Hannah Carrigan continued to the top. Carrigan, who was not carrying skis, continued to the summit to descend by a different route. Sjue found himself alone on Liberty Cap around noon and eager to return to his friends. He made his way on skis back toward the crux section of the face, only to find himself off route and perched above a cliff. Fortunately, he was able to traverse northward to the critical steep ramp. He stopped where the ramp rolled off to reveal the face below. "I was gripped when it quit rolling," Sjue recalled. "It was getting steeper and just staying icy. Once I realized I was off the roll and on the sustained face, it was totally icy." After he descended 1,000 feet of tentative skiing, the snow gradually softened and Sjue was able to relax. "Decompression took a while," he wrote.

A year later, in June 2006, Sjue skied the Kautz Glacier Headwall alone based on a tip from Carrigan, who had climbed it by herself a few days before. In 2007 he skied Sunset Ridge, again solo, following a reconnaissance trip two weeks earlier and a climb over Rainier's summit via the Kautz Glacier. The crux of the descent was an exposed slope above the Edmunds Headwall, where thinly covered ice required switching to crampons for safety.

The west flank of Sunset Ridge offered enjoyable, sun-warmed skiing, and Sjue continued down the South Mowich and Puyallup Glaciers to Tahoma Creek. Carrigan met him at the West Side Road twenty hours after he'd left Paradise.

Sky Sjue pioneered some of the most compelling lines in the Cascades and Olympics in the early 2000s, including the Degenhardt Glacier in the Picket Range, the north face (right side) of Spider Mountain, the northwest buttress of Bonanza Peak, and the northeast chute of Mount Deception in the Olympics. In 2010, he launched a web-based bulletin board called SkiSickness.com. The site offered an alternative to Turns All Year and attracted many skiers interested in steep descents.

Originally from New England, Dan Helmstadter learned to ski in Vermont and Massachusetts. He moved west in the early 2000s, gaining experience on bigger peaks in the Tetons and Rockies. In May 2009, Helmstadter skied the east face of Greybeard Peak near Rainy Pass on the North Cascades highway with Eric Wehrly. The Greybeard adventure was remarkable in that the east face had never been climbed before the two men made its first ascent and then skied it. The following spring, Helmstadter focused his attention on the peaks of the Stuart Range, completing new descents on Dragontail, Sherpa, and Argonaut Peaks. All these adventures were launched solo, but on Dragontail, Helmstadter encountered John Plotz and Will Terrano and joined them to pioneer the north face variation of the Triple Couloirs route. In mid-May, Helmstadter made a continuous descent of the Stuart Glacier Couloir on Mount Stuart, including the narrow section that is often unskiable ice. Partnering with Wehrly, Helmstadter made a continuous ski descent of Rainier's Sunset Ridge that summer and a descent (also including Pete Hirst) of the mountain's Ptarmigan Ridge route a year later.

Helmstadter skied four major new routes on Mount Shuksan in 2011 and 2012, all solo. The most striking of these was the Curtis Glacier Headwall (called the southwest face in Fred Beckey's *Cascade Alpine Guide*), a soaring pillar of rock rising 2,000 feet above the lower Curtis Glacier with a clean, nearly fall-line chute that provides a skiable route. Halfway down, the line slants to skier's right, where a hasty traverse and descent are required to pass beneath the seracs of the Upper Curtis Glacier. Helmstadter had skied the lower portion a month earlier, so he was familiar with the route and could negotiate it quickly.

Helmstadter and Wehrly teamed up for several other remarkable descents. The northwest face of Black Peak, climbed and skied by the pair in May 2012, is an alpine rock climb that becomes sufficiently plastered by winter snow to provide a skiable descent from the summit ridge. In 2013 the pair climbed and skied the north face of Big Four Mountain in the Monte Cristo region in soft-snow conditions. Photos from the climb show the men

Dan Helmstadter skis the northwest face of Black Peak in 2012. (Photo by Eric Wehrly)

postholing up tree-studded chutes and skinning exposed snow ramps high on the mountain. Stable snow enabled them to ski the entire 4,000-foot face with just one short rappel that Wehrly thought could have been avoided. With other partners, Wehrly completed other steep descents in the 2010s, including three routes on the east face of Mount Constance in the Olympics and the north couloir of Goode Mountain in the North Cascades in 2015.

Although the discipline of steep skiing has been pursued most avidly by men, a number of women have also participated in this branch of the sport. One of the earliest in the

Monika Johnson climbs the northeast couloir of Colchuck Peak prior to a ski descent in 2008. (Photo by Ryan Lurie)

Northwest was Hope Barnes, a gifted athlete who was captain of the US Olympic women's rowing team in 1984. With her partner Sprague Ackley, Barnes skied adventurous routes in the Cascades and Olympics in the late 1980s, including Mount Stuart's Ulrichs Couloir, the east face of Robinson Mountain, the north couloir of Oval Peak, Frostbite Ridge on Glacier Peak, and a two-day round-trip to Mount Olympus. In January 1991 she and friend Kathy Phibbs perished in a climbing accident on Dragontail Peak.

Mount Shuksan has attracted women on skis for many years, and several steep routes have been completed. Heather Wolfe skied the north face of Shuksan from the north shoulder with her husband, Mark Simon, in May 1999, completing the first known descent by a woman. Monika Johnson skied the central couloir of Shuksan's Curtis Glacier around 2010, and Molly Baker skied the peak's Hanging Glacier during the winter of 2011, taking the skier's-left variation below the ice cliff.

On Mount Rainier, Lel Tone skied the Fuhrer Thumb, a route west of the Fuhrer Finger, in May 1999 with Aaron Martin and Tom Wayes, making the first known descent of that route. As probably the first woman to do so, Monika Johnson skied the Edmunds Headwall on the Mowich Face. Laura Ogden skied the central Mowich Face in June 2014. On Mount Baker, mountain guide Liz Daley made the first female snowboarding descent of the Coleman Headwall, in May 2011.

Erin Smart, who started working as a mountain guide in 2010, made new ski descents on Alta Mountain, Lemah Thumb, and the Four Brothers in the Alpine Lakes region a couple years later. In 2013 she skied the Isolation Traverse with Forest McBrian and Kurt Hicks, pioneering a variation of the route that descended a steep 3,000-foot chute from Backbone Ridge to the lower McAllister Glacier. Monika Johnson made the first women's descents of the southwest face of Chikamin Peak, the northeast couloir of Colchuck Peak, the Cool

THE GUIDES

Before 2000, ski mountaineering in the Northwest was almost entirely the domain of enthusiastic amateurs. Since then, the growth of professional guiding has introduced a cadre of well-trained alpine and ski guides to the community. Several guides have made their mark on the steep skiing landscape. In 2008 Aaron Mainer and Oliver Deshler skied Mount Rainier's Nisqually Icefall route, making at least one rappel (over an ice cliff) during the descent. The two worked as ski patrolmen at Crystal Mountain, and Mainer later became an internationally certified guide. Mainer, Forest McBrian, and Dan Otter skied the Hanging Glacier route on Mount Shuksan in 2010. Their adventure began with a descent of the summit pyramid, then they skied the westerly of two routes below the glacier's massive ice cliff.

Andy Bond, a guide on Mount Rainier, skied the Sunset Amphitheater Couloir with Jesse Dudley in 2010. This route drops into the Sunset Amphitheater from the shoulder west of Rainier's Liberty Cap and requires a rappel on skis over a 30-foot cliff. A year later, Bond joined with Tyler Jones and Seth Waterfall to ski the Nisqually Ice Cliff route. Two weeks after that, Bond returned by himself to Point Success to attempt the South Tahoma Headwall. From a saddle a short distance northwest of the top, he skied the upper 300 feet of the headwall, then made two rappels. The rest of the descent to the South Tahoma Glacier was a fairly straightforward 40-degree slope. The upper flanks of Mount Rainier were well covered with snow in 2011, so Bond continued his streak of new ski routes with a descent of the South Edmunds Headwall in July.

Aaron Mainer and Oliver Deshler skied an eastern variation on Rainier's Liberty Ridge in May 2012 that intersected the *Thermogenesis* climbing route a few hundred feet above its base. With the White River road not yet open to summer traffic, they pedaled bicycles up the road to the White River campground, then continued to a camp on the Carbon Glacier. They climbed Liberty Ridge to Liberty Cap and began their descent with two rappels to bypass unskiable ice. The heart of the route, down the east flank of Liberty Ridge, went smoothly, and they rappelled over the bergschrund at the bottom by burying a couple of rocks for an anchor. The name *Cryogenesis* was suggested for this new route. Mainer returned with mountain guide Peter Dale to ski *Thermogenesis* in 2017.

Glacier Headwall on Glacier Peak, the north couloir of Tenpeak Mountain, and the Ice Cliff Glacier on Mount Stuart.

SLIPPERY SLOPES

In 1981 my older brother Gordy skied the north face of Mount Shuksan with Jens Kieler. They followed the original climbing route (east of the 1979 line used by Erickson and Wong) and completed the descent without a rappel. Gordy concluded that, for him, risking life and limb for a ski descent was not what skiing was about. An experienced mountaineer, Gordy had been a freestyle skiing champion in the 1970s, and I regarded him as a role model. For the next decade and beyond, as I explored high-level ski routes in the Cascades and Olympics, I remained uninterested in skiing must-not-fall terrain. So it was with some surprise that I learned of my younger brother Carl's descent of Mount Rainier's Edmunds Headwall in 1997. He and I had done many trips together, none of which involved dangerously steep skiing. But his pursuit of photography as a career in the 1990s had led him to adventures of a different sort with a new group of friends.

Steep skiing was still on the fringe of the sport: accidents were noted but generally not discussed in depth by the skiing community. David Persson, a Swedish citizen living in Vancouver, British Columbia, fell to his death in May 1999 while attempting to ski Mount Rainier's Liberty Ridge. After the fall, Persson's climbing partners called for help on a cellular phone, saying they last saw him "cartwheeling out of control" toward the Carbon Glacier below Thumb Rock. His body was recovered by helicopter the next day.

Shortly after Persson's death, I began researching the history of human-powered skiing in the Northwest, largely to satisfy my own curiosity. I was unable to interest a publisher in the project for many years, due to the small market at the time. Yet I persisted, and as steep skiing grew in popularity, I felt a desire to better understand this branch of the sport by dabbling in it myself. So I reached out to Carl and suggested we do a few steep ski descents together. The first of these trips was to the Cascade Pass area in July 2002, where Carl and I, with Andreas Schmidt, skied a couple new routes on Pelton and Hurry Up Peaks. The next Memorial Day, we skied Ulrichs Couloir on Mount Stuart, and a few weeks later I suggested a more demanding descent in the North Cascades: the north ridge of Forbidden Peak—one of my favorite summits in the range.

The northwest flank of the north ridge is an elegant ice face that sweeps from the Forbidden Glacier to the crest of the ridge about 500 feet below the summit of the mountain. The upper north ridge is a fun rock climb, and we decided that if we were going to ski the ridge, we should of course climb to the summit. We completed the climb in our ski boots

Carl Skoog skis the northwest face of the north ridge of Forbidden Peak in 2003.

and returned to our skis at the top of the snow face around 2:00 p.m. Unsure of the snow conditions, we tied in to our climbing rope, and I made the first tentative turns with a top belay from Carl. I cut back and forth across the slope, trying to get the softening snow to slide. Only an inch or two of the surface snow slid, gently clearing a path at first but growing to a torrent by the time it reached the bottom of the face. We descended the face without incident, skiing one at a time while the other took pictures.

"Steep skiing under these conditions is seductively easy," I wrote in my journal. "It's important to remember the seductive side and not be fooled by the easy side." Carl and I did a couple steep descents the next year, and on Memorial Day in 2005 we joined Jason and Josh Hummel and my friend John Mauro to ski the north face of Sinister Peak in the Glacier Peak Wilderness. This descent was especially meaningful for Carl because he had made the first ascent of the route twenty-five years earlier with our brother Gordy. It was the last time I would ski with my younger brother.

On the morning of October 20 of that year, I was awakened by a phone call from the US Embassy in Buenos Aires, Argentina. The consular officer informed me that Carl had died in a fall on 22,014-foot Cerro Mercedario, one of the highest peaks in the Andes. He and his friend Rene Crawshaw were descending the peak's southwest face, a route never before skied in its entirety. The snow surface was rough, with big waves of wind-eroded snow that made it tricky to sideslip the skis or carve a controlled turn. As they were sideslipping, Rene heard Carl say, "Whoa!" and watched him lose his balance. In Carl's left hand was an ice axe strapped to his ski pole and in his right was a ski pole with a self-arrest pick. They were not enough. Once Carl's fall began, he could not stop it. Rene watched for several agonizing minutes as Carl tumbled 4,500 vertical feet to the flats at the bottom of the face. With infinite care, Rene skied down, reaching Carl's body three hours later.

During the early 2000s, there was a rash of accidents in rugged mountains around the world involving well-known skiers. Several of these—Hans Saari in the Alps (2001), Aaron Martin and Reid Sanders in Alaska (2002), Doug Coombs and Chad VanderHam in France (2006), Arne Backstrom in Peru (2010), Fredrik Ericsson in Pakistan (2010)—occurred during steep ski descents. Others involved avalanches. Some took place during extreme skiing competitions.

The December 2012 issue of *Powder* magazine, which for years had been one of the biggest boosters of steep skiing, freeriding, and "big mountain skiing" (a blend of the other two), commissioned an article that asked "Why are so many of the best skiers dying?" Author Matt Hansen wrote, "People started to wonder when skiing had evolved from being

The aftermath of Carl's fall on Cerro Mercedario in 2005. One of his ski poles and a ski became lodged in the snow high on the southwest face. Carl continued tumbling for thousands of feet. (Photo by Rene Crawshaw)

a fun activity, where the day's thrills, spills, and excitement would be recounted later over beers, to a sport where any little mistake would cost you the ultimate price."

In a follow-up story a couple years later, Hansen noted, "Since the early 2000s, skiing has lost more iconic athletes than any other action sport aside from BASE jumping. But while BASE [building, antenna, span, earth] jumping might be considered a 'fringe' sport with fewer than 5,000 participants, skiing is a global activity with a glorious history that affects 65 million people each winter. And when you start comparing the safety of your sport to BASE jumping, you might have a problem."

After my brother Carl's death in 2005, I lost interest in steep ski descents. The following spring, I scattered some of Carl's ashes on a favorite peak in the North Cascades. As I scanned a horizon filled with memories, I conceived a task to bring closure to the adventures Carl and I had shared: I would ski the remaining segments of the Cascade crest between Mount Baker and Mount Rainier, connecting the trips we had done together into an unbroken chain. It took five different trips, each covering terrain I hadn't skied before; I did one segment solo, the others with friends. In 2007, I completed that journey, linking my memories of Carl with experiences I'd found in the tracks of early ski pioneers.

In the Pacific Northwest, since about 2015, the number of descents pioneered each season has tapered off somewhat. Given the intensity of activity that came before, this may be inevitable—there are only so many compelling ski routes remaining to be discovered. Focus seems to have shifted to repeating some of the "classic" routes. But, sadly, accidents have not ended. In 2012 Keith Hardy, a sports medicine doctor from Kirkland, Washington, died in a fall while attempting to ski the Coleman Headwall on Mount Baker. Hardy had climbed to the summit of the mountain and was approaching the top of the route when he slipped on frozen snow and could not arrest his fall. While skiing Mount Rainier's Liberty Ridge in June 2020, Matthew Bunker suffered a fatal fall near Thumb Rock in roughly the same area where David Persson had fallen in 1999. Born in the Midwest, Bunker was an army veteran who had done some mountain guiding, leading trips up Mount Baker and Glacier Peak. The tragedy occurred during the worldwide coronavirus pandemic, as climbing and skiing in the Northwest were beginning to resurge after several months of lockdown.

FLOW

When I skied the Ptarmigan Traverse with Gary Brill and friends in 1982, we scrambled a few peaks and dropped our packs to make a few ski runs, but in general we kept moving steadily to avoid being caught by bad weather. Three years later, I returned with friends in July to spend a week backpacking the route. This time we explored the region more thoroughly, climbing nearly all the named summits between Cache Col and Gunsight Peak.

By the late 1980s, I had done enough ski touring to realize there is something special about high-mountain skiing. There's an intimacy with the snowy landscape—its contours, its continuity, its relationship to sun and wind. There's a heightened sense of movement. To reach a high col, strip off the climbing skins, then push away on a fast gliding traverse evokes a feeling much like flying. Arnold Lunn described this perception in the 1940s: "On the smooth unchanging gradients of a gentle glacier you lose the sense of personal movement. You feel as if you were stationary and as if it were your surroundings that are moving."

In the early 1990s, I encountered Mihaly Csikszentmihalyi's book *Flow: The Psychology of Optimal Experience*. The author, a professor of psychology, observed that people are happiest when they are in a state of *flow*—of complete absorption that occurs when one's skills are well matched to a challenging task. Skiers experience flow in several ways. There is the sense of immersive movement found while gliding on skis. And there is the sense of engagement described by Csikszentmihalyi. Before I had words to describe what I was looking for, I had begun seeking this experience on skis.

Carl Skoog climbs the Dana Glacier during the one-day crossing of the Ptarmigan Traverse in 1988.

On a cloudy evening in June 1988, my brother Carl and I drove separate cars to the Suiattle River at the edge of the Glacier Peak Wilderness. Parking my car near the Downey Creek trailhead, we drove Carl's car to the Cascade Pass trailhead, about 30 miles away. Well before dawn, we began hiking toward Cascade Pass by headlamp, carrying our skis. We continued to Cache Col, gateway to the Ptarmigan Traverse. In the morning chill, the snow was firmly frozen, so we continued walking on crampons. When the sun finally found us near the Spider-Formidable Col, we switched to skis and began gliding.

The Ptarmigan Traverse is named for the Ptarmigan Climbing Club, a Depression-era group of former Boy Scouts whose members were the first to complete the traverse fifty years earlier. Carl and I envied their adventure, and we shared the sense of discovery they must have experienced. As we pushed off from Spider-Formidable Col, the texture of the snow beneath our feet was a blur. In the middle distance, islands of rock and heather passed effortlessly. Far away, the valley of Flat Creek and the Le Conte Glacier wheeled gracefully before us.

During the long daylight hours, we moved continuously—not rushing, but relishing the cycle of ascent and descent, feeling our skins grip the snow as we climbed to a new viewpoint, then gliding with skins off as far as gravity and skating could take us. We crossed the Cascade crest a half dozen times, wandering from west to east and back again as we wended our way across glaciers, between summits, and above deep valleys while the sun slowly rolled across the sky.

We reached our final high point near Spire Point in midafternoon. We were both tired and felt like napping, but a forty-five-minute rest with boots drying in the sun was all we figured we could afford. Numbed with fatigue, we struggled down the so-called trail in the Bachelor Creek drainage. I slipped off a log on the Downey Creek trail and fell butt-first into a stream. We arrived at the Suiattle River road tired but thoroughly satisfied after twenty-one hours on the go.

In later years, I made other attempts at what I'd begun to call "flow days." There was an effort to encircle Mount Rainier in a day with my brother Gordy in 1999. It was thwarted by a poor route choice on a day when I wasn't feeling quite right. A few years later, six of us skied the Forbidden Tour as a day trip, with Bruce Goodson and Andreas Schmidt joining me to tag the summit of Eldorado Peak. I had long been interested in skiing the Isolation Traverse as a flow day, but I never made it happen.

In July 2011, Gregg Cronn and Ryan Lurie completed a flow day *plus*—skiing and climbing Mounts Baker and Shuksan in a twenty-six-hour push. They started from the Heliotrope Ridge trailhead at 3:00 p.m., climbing Baker via the Coleman Glacier in about five and a half hours. After descending the Park Glacier, they paused near Coleman Pinnacle around 11:00 p.m. to warm a late dinner, rest an hour or two, and let the snow refreeze. Around 3:00 a.m. Cronn and Lurie skied over Artist Point and made their way to the Fisher Chimneys on Mount Shuksan. Climbing the chimneys at sunrise, they reached the summit of Shuksan in early afternoon.

Lurie later wrote, "It never ceases to amaze me how much ground one can cover on skis, and how absorbing such travel can be. In a way, time stands still. Or simply doesn't matter. The further we traveled, the more absorbed I became in my immediate surroundings, while my sense of what was immediate continued to grow."

The pair met a group of climbers below the summit of Mount Shuksan who were hiking out the Sulphide Glacier route. Reaching their car around 5:00 p.m., the climbers offered them a ride back to Bellingham, and another friend returned Ryan to his truck. As the trip was completed five months after their friend Monika Johnson had perished on Red Mountain near Snoqualmie Pass, Cronn and Lurie suggested the name "Monika's Traverse" for this adventure.

The path toward flow doesn't have to be linear. Skiing from the infamous Point A to the mythical Point B may be just the beginning. This was demonstrated by Kristoffer Erickson of Montana and Jamie Laidlaw of Idaho during a trip to the Cascades in 2009. On July 11 the two men climbed the northwest side of Mount Adams, intending to ski back down their ascent route. Finding themselves with hours to burn before the north-facing snow softened, they decided to ski the southwest chutes, a descent of around 5,000 vertical feet on the opposite side of the mountain. After rehydrating at the bottom of the chutes, they started back up toward the summit, reaching the top around 6:00 p.m. By this time conditions on the northwest flank were just what they'd hoped for, and they made an enjoyable descent of the Adams Glacier, requiring a short down-climb to pass an icy section. They returned to their camp thirteen hours after leaving it, having made descents of both sides of Mount Adams in a single day.

Over the following three days, Erickson and Laidlaw drove to Mount Rainier and hiked from the Mowich Lake road to a bivouac around 8,000 feet on the North Mowich Glacier. They awoke on the morning of July 15 at 4:00 a.m. and climbed the Edmunds Headwall to the summit. "With brisk winds blowing across the summit," Erickson wrote, "we quickly made the call to give the second twofer a go with a descent of the Emmons to start things off. Conditions began to soften at nearly 13,500 feet and by the Corridor the skiing was the best of the day."

They skied the Emmons Glacier to the flats around 9,600 feet near Camp Schurman, on the opposite side of the mountain from their camp. Around 2:30 p.m., they started back up, returning to the top of Liberty Cap around 6:30 p.m. It was still blowing hard, and Erickson recalled, "Due to our lightweight efforts, we needed to keep moving in order to stay warm." They carried their skis through a field of *nieves penitentes* to the top of the Edmunds Headwall. There was one small chute still skiable on the south side of the face, so they carefully skied onto the headwall itself and descended it, working around four bergschrunds near the bottom. Erickson and Laidlaw's round-trip over the mountain and back required thirteen hours.

As randonnée racing began attracting more young skiers, and lighter equipment made it possible to climb and ski with less fatigue, one-day trips for speed became more commonplace. Fastest known time (FKT) is a yardstick applied to many sports, and web-based sharing has made it easier to log and compare experiences.

Seattle arborist Allen Taylor became interested in skimo racing in the 2010s, and he won the VertFest men's race in 2017. Two years later, his team won The Mountaineers' Patrol Race. Taylor became interested in fast ski tours accessible from the Cascade River Road. The Ptarmigan Traverse, Forbidden Tour, and Isolation Traverse all share this starting point. Taylor partnered with his later Patrol Race teammate Todd Kilcup in May 2018 to

Todd Kilcup traverses the Boston Glacier during an FKT (fastest known time) ski of the Forbidden Tour in 2018. (Photo by Allen Taylor)

ski the Forbidden Tour, including the summit of Eldorado Peak, in 8 hours, 22 minutes. A week later, he joined Sam Lien to ski the Isolation Traverse south-to-north in 14 hours, 30 minutes. With Brian Melvin, Taylor completed the Ptarmigan Traverse in about 18 hours, 30 minutes in 2017—thought to be an FKT until it was learned that outdoor equipment designer Eben Sargent had skied the Ptarmigan solo from the Cascade Pass trailhead to the Downey Creek trailhead in 2011 in 11 hours, 41 minutes.

The nature of FKTs is that these times will inevitably be improved, but as some of the earliest examples of this pursuit in the North Cascades, they provide an interesting record. Speed outings and "flow days" are different animals. A flow day needn't be hurried, but it should cover a lot of varied terrain. The goal is to enjoy continuous movement, to experience the broad sweep of the landscape in an unbroken thread of conscious action, to savor flight without wings. An FKT attempt can embrace all of these experiences, but the primary goal is to move fast.

Sam Lien and Allen Taylor achieved both flow and an FKT in May 2019 during the first one-day circumnavigation of Mount Rainier on skis. Leaving Paradise at 3:45 a.m., they circled the mountain counterclockwise, finding the trickiest routefinding on the Emmons Glacier early in the day. They used skimo racing gear but carried extra equipment to spend a night out if necessary. During our attempt on the one-day circuit of Rainier in 1999, my brother Gordy and I were thwarted by scary crevasses around 9,000 feet on the Nisqually Glacier. The route chosen by Lien and Taylor avoided that area, crossing the Nisqually late in the day on their way back to Paradise. They completed the loop in 13 hours, 54 minutes.

Sam Lien traverses the Emmons Glacier below Little Tahoma during a one-day ski circumnavigation of Mount Rainier in 2019. (Photo by Allen Taylor)

Speed climbs of Mount Rainier are a long-running tradition, initially done by guides on their day off. The quickest way to the summit and back begins at Paradise, and various routes have been used to race to the top over the years. A well-known early speed ascent of the mountain was made in 1959 by twin brothers Jim and Lou Whittaker, with Oregon rancher and sportsman John Day. Their roundtrip time was 7 hours, 20 minutes. The time was shaved by forty minutes a couple weeks later by guides Dick McGowan and Gil Blinn. As the years passed, climbers gradually shaved the roundtrip time until 2016 when long-distance runner Uli Steidl reduced the time to 4 hours, 24 minutes, 30 seconds. These times were all recorded by climbers traveling on foot.

Skimo racers Eric Carter and Nick Elson broke the climbers' speed record on Rainier for the first time in May 2013. Their round-trip was completed via the Disappointment Cleaver route in 4 hours, 19 minutes, 12 seconds. Modern ski gear, it seems, is now so light and efficient that the overall speed record on Mount Rainier is unlikely to ever be reclaimed by a climber traveling on foot. Improvements to the ski record are sure to continue. In May 2019, skiers Jason Dorais and Tom Goth established a new roundtrip record to the summit and back of 3 hours, 24 minutes, 46 seconds.

Most backcountry skiers aren't out to seek records. They seek experiences—the silence of winter, the magic of skis running on snow, the bond of a shared adventure, the tonic of a day well spent. Each skier has unique boundaries, and adventure comes in many forms. The beauty of skiing is that there are so many paths to enjoyment.

EPILOGUE:

THE BIG THAW— SKIING INTO THE FUTURE

During the International Geophysical Year in the late 1950s, while Ed LaChapelle and his team studied the Blue Glacier on Mount Olympus, a young scientist named Charles David Keeling established a carbon dioxide monitoring station on Mauna Loa in Hawaii. In 1960 Keeling published results suggesting that atmospheric carbon dioxide might be rising from year to year. Further studies found that the increase was correlated with a rise in global temperatures.

Since then, evidence from around the world has confirmed that the world is warming and that human activity is the main driver. Warming was already under way when Keeling began his measurements. In the ensuing years, not only has the concentration of carbon dioxide kept growing, but the pace has accelerated nearly every year.

In 1978, around the time I started backcountry skiing, the US Congress passed a National Climate Act to enable the United States and other nations "to understand and respond to natural and man-induced climate processes and their implications." The act had little effect. In my lifetime, climate change in the Northwest has caused

Greg Louie near the location of the former Paradise Ice Caves in 2005. A warning sign from the final years of the ice caves lies at his feet. (Photo by Kam Leang)

annual snowpack to decline, glaciers to shrink, stream flow to change, and stresses to increase on wildlife, forests, and fisheries. Future warming is expected to raise average snow levels in winter and change weather patterns that enable skiing at lower elevations like Snoqualmie Pass.

Since the 1930s, skiing at Snoqualmie has benefited from cold air that pools in central Washington in winter, shielding the slopes somewhat from the effect of warm storms from the Pacific Ocean. Guy Lawrence, manager of the Summit at Snoqualmie ski area, has observed, "We joke about building a shrine to the easterly air flow. It is such a nice benefit for us."

Climate change is expected to end that benefit. In a 2012 story in the *Seattle Times*, Cliff Mass, a professor of atmospheric science at the University of Washington, summarized the results of recent climate modeling: "By 2050, there won't be any more skiing at Snoqualmie; it's over."

Higher ski resorts in the Cascades and Olympics may have skiable conditions over the next few decades, but we can expect shorter ski seasons and more frequent poor snow years. Backcountry skiers may be able to venture beyond the ski areas to find snow, but established routes are likely to become more difficult as trees reclaim old avalanche clearings and glaciers become thinner and more broken.

Skiing—especially backcountry skiing—is an activity pursued for the most part by individuals and small groups. Individual skiers can reduce their climate impact by ride sharing, reducing the number of trips, and using cleaner forms of transportation. While important, those actions by themselves will do little to solve the climate problem, even if widely adopted. Instead, we need to pursue political solutions, joining with others in movements big enough to make a difference. What's needed is a worldwide effort to replace an energy system based on fossil fuels with one based on sun and wind.

Skiers eager to address the climate problem can take several concrete steps. First is to get better educated on the issues and to support groups like Protect Our Winters, the American Alpine Club, and the Outdoor Alliance (see Resources at the back of this book) that are working to coordinate action in the outdoor community. Skiers need to recognize the impact we each have through our actions and how that impact, for good or ill, is multiplied within our community.

Bill McKibben, a founder of the grassroots climate campaign 350.org, has stressed the need to organize: "It's very important to make your own life responsible. . . . But by far the most important thing an individual can do is be less of an individual. Join together with others in movements big enough to matter." That means speaking out, organizing, writing letters, fund-raising, and voting.

Naturalist John Muir wrote in 1901, "Climb the mountains and get their good tidings. . . . The winds will blow their own freshness into you and the storms their energy, while cares will drop off like autumn leaves." We skiers must harness the optimism and energy that the mountains inspire within us and bring them to the public square. We need to support policies and elect representatives who will work toward systemic change. The future of skiing will be written in the statehouses as much as in the snows.

ACKNOWLEDGMENTS

I thank the following select individuals who personally provided information for this book (as well as hundreds of others who provided help during this twenty-year project):

Sprague Ackley, John Baldwin, Steve Barnett, Wolf Bauer, Paul Baugher, Fred Beckey, Jeff Berrens, Gary Bisgaard, Andy Bond, Matt C. Broze, Eric Burr, C. E. "Buster" Campbell, Greg Cronn, Matie Daiber, Peter Dale, Stella Degenhardt, Oliver Deshler, John Dittli, Armond DuBuque, Harland Eastwood Jr., Dorothy Egg, Karl Erickson, Kristoffer Erickson, Dale Farnham, Joe Firey, Matt Firth, W. D. Frank, Peter Giese, Kirby Gilbert, Mel Gourlie, Dan Helmstadter, Marion Hessey, Steve Hindman, Jack Hughes, Jason Hummel, Eric Jackson, Tom Janisch, Josh Kaplan, Alan Kearney, Jens Kieler, Mike Kirby, Jan Kordel, Trevor Kostanich, Ed LaChapelle, Erick Larson, Walt Little, Kathleen Long, John Lundin, Ryan Lurie, Steve Lyford, Tom Lyon, Cal Magnusson, Aaron Mainer, Harry Majors, Ben Manfredi, Harvey Manning, Chester Marler, Forest McBrian, Andrew McLean, John and Irene Meulemans, Mark Moore, Larry Penberthy, Ross Peritore, Matt Perkins, Glen Plake, Don Portman, Irv Pratt, Hank Reasoner, Tyler Reid, Doug Robinson, Lon Robinson, Gary Rose, Randy Sackett, Eric Sanford, Eben Sargent, Andreas Schmidt, Pete Schoening, Mark Simon, Sky Sjue, Larry Smith, Steve Spickard, Ira Spring, John Stimberis, Karl Stingl, Allen Taylor, Will Thompson, Lel Tone, Steve Vanpatten, Martin Volken, Duke Watson, Eric Wehrly, Chuck Welsh, Pat Whittaker, Ingrid Wicken, Craig Wilbour, Jim Witte, Greg Wong, Wilfred Woods, John Woodward, Suze Woolf.

COURSE OF RACE

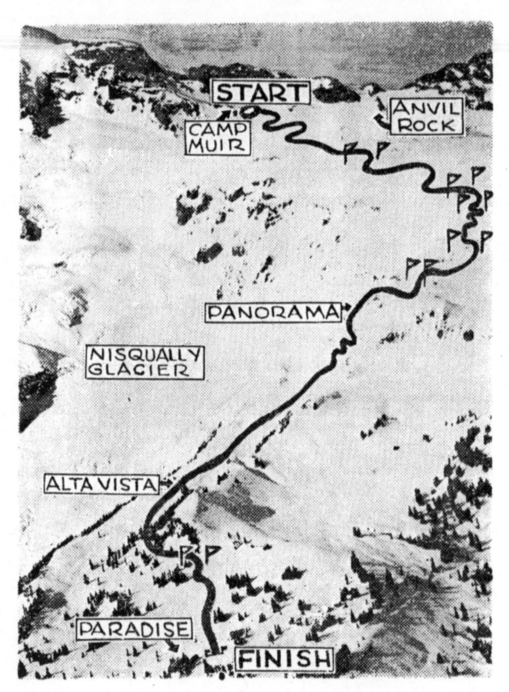

SKI MOUNTAINEERING HIGHLIGHTS

MOUNTAINEERS' PATROL RACE WINNERS, 1930–41		
YEAR	**TEAM**	**TIME**
1930	Andrew Anderson, Fred Ball, Hans Otto Giese	7:30:50
1931	No race was held	—
1932	Fred Ball, Hans Otto Giese, Norval Grigg	unknown
1933	Don Blair, Herbert Strandberg, Art Wilson	unknown
1934	No race was held	—
1935	Bill Degenhardt, Scott Edson, Art Wilson	5:35:22
1936 (last club race)	Wolf Bauer, Chet Higman, Bill Miller	4:37:23
1936 (first open race)	Howard Dalsbo, Roy Nerland, Ole Tverdal (Seattle Ski Club)	4:50:39
1937	Bill Degenhardt, Scott Edson, Sigurd Hall (Mountaineers)	5:13:00
1938	Scott Edson, Sigurd Hall, Art Wilson (Mountaineers)	4:57:45
1939	Sigurd Hall, Bert Mortensen, Roy Nerland (Seattle Ski Club)	4:39:20
1940	Carlton Greenfield, Grant Lovegren, Art Wilson (Washington Alpine Club)	5:13:00
1941	Carlton Greenfield, Grant Lovegren, Art Wilson (Washington Alpine Club)	5:27:55

Course diagram for the first Silver Ski Championships in 1934 (Courtesy John Woodward)

MOUNTAINEERS' PATROL RACE WINNERS SINCE 2014

YEAR	DIVISION	TEAM MEMBERS	TEAM NAME	TIME
2014	—	Cody Lourie, Luke Shy, Jed Yeiser	R&Ski	7:09:00
2015	—	No race was held	—	—
2016	—	Seth Davis, Brandon Kern, Lowell Skoog	Wet & Scrappy	4:52:07
2017	Open	Seth Davis, Aaron Ostrovsky, Lowell Skoog	Wet & Scrappy	4:19:23
2017	Women's	Holly Davis, Heather Kern, Anne Marie Stonich	Mountain Mamas	6:09:29
2018	Open	Seth Davis, Brandon Kern, Lowell Skoog	Wet & Scrappy	5:05:29
2018	Women's	Leia Hansen, Liza Hodgins, Sophia Whittaker	Dirty Bird SkiMo Club	6:53:50
2019	Open	Todd Kilcup, Ethan Linck, Allen Taylor	Fastest Known Team	4:35:46
2019	Women's	Leia Hansen, Liza Hodgins, Sophia Whittaker	Valley Girls	6:58:41
2020	Open	Elsa Klein, Linden Klein, Evan Williams	Team Klipspringer	6:43:55
2020	Women's	Ali Forelli, Elena Horton, Liz Webber-Bruya	No Debris in the Skin Track	9:03:04
2021	Open	Seth Davis, Aaron Ostrovsky, Dave Braun	Old Age and Treachery	4:44:48
2021	Women's	Esther Opersteny, Holly Davis, Anne Marie Stonich	Snoqualmie Skimo Sisters	6:33:26

SILVER SKIS WINNERS 1934–48

YEAR	MEN'S RACE	WOMEN'S RACE
1934	Don Fraser	Marguerite Strizek
1935	Hannes Schroll	Ellis-Ayr Smith
1936	Hjalmar Hvam	Peggy Harlin
1937	Weather cancellation	
1938	Don Fraser	Gretchen Kunigk
1939	Peter Radacher	Dorothy Hoyt

1940	Paul Gilbreath	Nancy Reynolds
1941	Bill Taylor	Shirley McDonald
1942	Matt Broze	Shirley McDonald
1943–45	Cancelled due to World War II	
1946	Weather cancellation	
1947	Willard South	No women's race
1948	Paul Gilbreath	No women's race

SELECTED HIGH-LEVEL ROUTES

DATE	REGION	ROUTE	PARTY
1932	Mount Baker	Mount Baker Lodge to Mount Baker, partial orbit	Darroch Crookes, Don Henry, Ben Thompson
1934	Mount Rainier	Paradise to White River traverse	Orville Borgersen, Ben Spellar, Otto Strizek
1934	Mount Hood	Ski orbit	Ralph Calkin, James Mount
1938	Olympics	Deer Park to Hurricane Ridge	Max Borst and party
1939	Mount Baker	Kulshan Cabin to Mount Baker Lodge (summit traverse)	Andy Hennig, Erick Larson, Dwight Watson
1981	North Cascades	Ptarmigan Traverse (Cascade Pass to Bachelor Creek)	Dan Stage, Brian Sullivan
1982	North Cascades	Eureka Creek Loop (Pasayten Wilderness)	John Almquist, Steve Barnett, Greg Knott, Doug Veenhof
1982	North Cascades	Dakobed Range traverse (Glacier Peak to Clark Mountain)	Gary Brill, Joe Catellani, Brian Sullivan
Early 1980s	North Cascades	Sawtooth Range traverse (Hoodoo Peak to Washington Pass)	Tom Baker and party
1983	North Cascades	Isolation Traverse (Snowfield Peak to Eldorado Peak)	Gary Brill, Mark Hutson, Lowell Skoog, Brian Sullivan
1984	North Cascades	Inspiration–Klawatti Glacier route	Greg Jacobsen, Brian Sullivan
1985	North Cascades	Picket Range traverse (Hannegan Pass to Diablo)	Jens Kieler, Carl Skoog, Lowell Skoog
ca. 1985	North Cascades	US-Canada border traverse (Iron Gate to Ross Lake, continuing to Hannegan Pass)	Brent Harris, Steve Hindman, Alan Millar
1986	Mount Rainier	High-level orbit (clockwise from Paradise)	N. L. Kirkland, Terry Pritchards, Dana Rush, Dr. Roy Walters

1987	North Cascades	Thunder High Route (Rainy Pass to Mount Logan, Boston Glacier, Eldorado Peak)	Jens Kieler, Dan Nordstrom, Lowell Skoog
1989	North Cascades	Buckindy Range traverse (Green Mountain to Snowking Mountain)	Carl Skoog, Lowell Skoog, Brian Sullivan
1989	North Cascades	Mystery Ridge traverse (Watson Lakes to Whatcom Pass)	Scott Croll, John Dittli
1989	Olympics	Bailey Range traverse (Soleduck River, High Divide to Mount Olympus)	Joe Catellani, Jens Kieler, Carl Skoog, Lowell Skoog, Brian Sullivan
1989	North Cascades	Suiattle high route (Sulphur Mountain to Image Lake, High Pass, Glacier Peak)	Carl Skoog, Lowell Skoog
1991	North Cascades	Ragged Ridge traverse (Mesahchie Pass to Fourth of July Pass)	Carl Skoog, Lowell Skoog
1991	North Cascades	Mount Redoubt high route (Depot Creek to Whatcom Pass)	Scott Croll, John Dittli, Mark Long
1999	Alpine Lakes	Snoqualmie Haute Route (Big Snow Mountain to Mount Hinman, Chikamin Peak, Snoqualmie Pass)	Peter Avolio, Andy Dappen, Mike Hattrup, Carl Skoog, Martin Volken
1999	North Cascades	Forbidden Tour (circuit of Forbidden Peak and Inspiration Glacier region)	Don Denton, Murray Gailbreth, Mike Hattrup, Greg Lange, Dave Metallo, Martin Volken
2000	North Cascades	Extended Ptarmigan Traverse (Cascade Pass to Holden Village)	Matt Firth, Bruce Goodson, Lowell Skoog
2002	North Cascades	"American Alps" traverse (Snowfield Peak to Holden Village)	Matt Firth, Bob Nielsen
2002	Alpine Lakes	Alpine Lakes traverse (Snoqualmie Pass to Mount Daniel)	Joe Catellani, Matt Firth, Bruce Goodson, Lowell Skoog
2006	Alpine Lakes	Chiwaukum Mountains traverse (Whitepine Creek to Chatter Creek)	Ben Mitchell, John Race
2007	Washington Cascades	"Skiing the Cascade Crest," twenty-five-year linkup from Mount Baker to Mount Rainier completed (eighteen segments)	Lowell Skoog with various partners
2008	Alpine Lakes	Central Cascades traverse (Icicle Creek to Hyak)	Peter Avolio, Trevor Kostanich
2008, 2009	Olympics	Hurricane Ridge to Royal Basin to Mount Constance (in two segments)	Mary Goodfellow, Eric Jackson

2011	North Cascades	North-central Cascades traverse (Holden to Mount Fernow, Dumbell Mountain, High Pass, Dakobed Range, North Fork Sauk River)	Peter Avolio, Rob Bolton, Trevor Kostanich, Adam Vognild
2013	North Cascades	"American Alps" traverse (Snowfield Peak to Glacier Peak)	Jason Hummel, Kyle Miller
2016	North Cascades	US-Canada border to Lake Wenatchee	Peter Dale, Aaron Mainer
2016	Olympics	Olympic Traverse East (Hurricane Ridge to Lake Cushman)	Tim Black, Jason Hummel
2017	Alpine Lakes, North Cascades	Snoqualmie Pass to US-Canada border	Trevor Kostanich, Forest McBrian
2019	Olympics	Olympic Traverse West (Sol Duc Hot Springs to Quinault River)	Jake Chartier, Jason Hummel, Jeff Rich, Carl Simpson

SELECTED SKI DESCENTS 1971–99

DATE	REGION	ROUTE	PARTY
1971	South Cascades	Mount Hood, Newton Clark Headwall	Sylvain Saudan
1978	Alpine Lakes	McClellan Butte, north gully	Karl Erickson, Greg Wong
1979	Alpine Lakes	Mount Stuart, Cascadian Couloir	Eric Feigl, Kurt Feigl
1979	South Cascades	Mount Hood, Sandy Glacier Headwall	Mike Kirby
1979	Mount Baker	Mount Shuksan, north face	Karl Erickson, Greg Wong
ca. 1980	South Cascades	Mount Hood, north face (left)	Steve Lyford
1980	Alpine Lakes	Mount Stuart, Ulrichs Couloir	Karl Erickson, Greg Wong
1980	Mount Rainier	Fuhrer Finger	Dan Davis, Jeff Haley, Tom Janisch
1980	Mount Rainier	Liberty Ridge	Chris Landry
1985	Mount Rainier	Kautz Glacier	Dale Farnham
ca. 1987	Mount Baker	Mount Shuksan, summit pyramid	Steve Vanpatten, Jim Witte
1988	South Cascades	Mount Adams, northwest face of north ridge	Jeff Berrens
1990	South Cascades	Mount Adams, Adams Glacier	W. D. Frank
1990	Mount Baker	Mount Baker, Coleman Headwall	Bela and Mimi Vadasz
1992	South Cascades	Mount Hood, north face (right)	Stephen Koch

ca. 1992	Mount Rainier	Wilson Glacier Headwall	Jim Collinson
ca. 1993	North Cascades	Tenpeak Mountain, north couloir	Andreas Schmidt
1995	South Cascades	Mount Adams, north face of northwest ridge	Doug Coombs, Glen Plake
1990s	South Cascades	Mount Adams, Lava Glacier Headwall	Doug Coombs
1997	Alpine Lakes	Kaleetan Peak, S-E-NE spiral	Steve Martin
1997	Alpine Lakes	Snoqualmie Mountain, Slot Couloir	Jan Kordel, Steve Martin
ca. 1997	Alpine Lakes	Mount Stuart, Sherpa Glacier and Couloir	Jeff Mazinko, Shane Wilder
ca. 1997	Mount Baker	Mount Shuksan, White Salmon Headwall	Rene Crawshaw
1997	North Cascades	Black Peak, south route	Rene Crawshaw, Andy Dappen, Carl Skoog
1997	Mount Rainier	Tahoma Glacier	Rob Gibson, Darrel Howe, Aaron Horwitz
1997	Mount Rainier	Mowich Face, Edmunds Headwall	Armond DuBuque, Doug Ingersoll, Andrew McLean, Carl Skoog
1998	Mount Baker	Park Glacier Headwall	David Orsatti
1998	Mount Rainier	Success Glacier Couloir	Luke Edgar, Chad Kellogg
1999	Mount Baker	Mount Shuksan, northwest couloir	Rene Crawshaw (George St. James snowboarded from below Hanging Glacier entry in 1993)
1999	North Cascades	Mount Buckner, southwest route	Garth Ferber, Lowell Skoog

SELECTED SKI DESCENTS 2000–2017

DATE	REGION	ROUTE	PARTY
2000	Mount Baker	North ridge	Rene Crawshaw, Carl Skoog
2002	North Cascades	Mount Buckner, north face	Fred Marmsater, Andrew McLean, Petra Pirc, Martin Volken
2002	South Cascades	Mount Adams, Stormy Monday Couloir	Jason Hummel, Josh Hummel, Ben Manfredi
2002	North Cascades	Sentinel Peak, north face	Alan Kearney, Carl Skoog
2002	North Cascades	Mount Maude, north face	Ben Manfredi

2003	Mount Baker	Mount Shuksan, Price Glacier (upper)	Ben Manfredi, Sky Sjue
2003	Alpine Lakes	Mount Stuart, Stuart Glacier Couloir (down-climb narrows)	Mark Simon (complete ski by Dan Helmstadter in 2010)
2003	South Cascades	Mount Adams, North Lyman Glacier	Corey Bloom, Jason Hummel, Ben Manfredi, Sky Sjue
2003	North Cascades	Spider Mountain, north face (left)	Peter Avolio, Martin Volken
2003	North Cascades	Forbidden Peak, north ridge	Carl Skoog, Lowell Skoog
2004	South Cascades	Mount Adams, South Lyman Glacier	Amar Andalkar, Sam Avaiusini, Cyril Benda, Corey Bloom, Jason Hummel, Sky Sjue
2004	North Cascades	Mount Degenhardt, Degenhardt Glacier	Ross Peritore, Sky Sjue
2005	North Cascades	Jack Mountain, northeast glacier	Ross Peritore, Sky Sjue
2005	North Cascades	Goode Mountain, east face	Ross Peritore, Sky Sjue
2005	North Cascades	Sinister Peak, north face	Jason Hummel, Josh Hummel, John Mauro, Carl Skoog, Lowell Skoog
2005	North Cascades	Bonanza Peak, northwest buttress	Paul Belitz, David Coleman, Phil Fortier, Sky Sjue
2005	Mount Rainier	Central Mowich Face	Sky Sjue
2006	North Cascades	Spider Mountain, north face (right)	Ben Kaufman, Sky Sjue
2006	Alpine Lakes	Dragontail Peak, Triple Couloirs	Ross Peritore
2006	Alpine Lakes	Mount Stuart, Ice Cliff Glacier	Casey Ruff, Sky Sjue
2006	North Cascades	Mount Formidable, northwest face	Ross Peritore, Sky Sjue
2006	North Cascades	Snowfield Peak, true summit	Josh Kaplan
2006	South Cascades	Mount Adams, Lava Ridge	Phil Fortier, Jason Hummel, Josh Hummel, Sky Sjue
2006	Mount Rainier	Kautz Glacier Headwall	Sky Sjue
2007	Olympics	Mount Deception, northeast chute	Phil Fortier, Sky Sjue

2007	North Cascades	Mount Fernow, north face	Phil Fortier (from base of summit gully; later done by Jason Hummel and Kyle Miller)
2008	Mount Baker	Mount Shuksan, Curtis Glacier	Pete Durr, John Wells
2008	North Cascades	Bandit Peak, "Black Hole" couloir	Phil Fortier, Ryan Lurie
2008	Mount Baker	Mount Shuksan, southwest face couloir	Ryan Carter, Jason Hummel, Paul Kimbrough, Davide de Masi
2008	North Cascades	North Early Winters Spire, north couloir	Michael Shaffer
2008	Alpine Lakes	Colchuck Peak, northeast couloir (complete ski descent)	Monika Johnson, Ryan Lurie, Sky Sjue, Eric Wehrly
2008	Olympics	Sundial Peak, east-southeast face	David Coleman, Phil Fortier
2008	North Cascades	Phantom Peak, southeast face	Todd Karner, Eben Sargent
2009	North Cascades	Greybeard Peak, east face	Dan Helmstadter, Eric Wehrly
2010	Mount Baker	Mount Shuksan, north face (northwest variation)	Alex Gibbs, Casey Ruff, Sky Sjue, Andy Traslin, Eric Wehrly
2010	Mount Baker	Mount Shuksan, Hanging Glacier	Aaron Mainer, Forest McBrian, Dan Otter
2010	South Cascades	Mount Adams, Klickitat Glacier Headwall	Jason Hummel, Josh Hummel, Adam Roberts
2010	Mount Rainier	Sunset Amphitheater Couloir	Andy Bond, Jesse Dudley
2011	Mount Baker	Mount Shuksan, northwest connection	Dan Helmstadter
2011	Mount Rainier	Ptarmigan Ridge route (with rappel, crampon traverse at 11,200 ft.)	Dan Helmstadter, Pete Hirst, Eric Wehrly
2011	Mount Rainier	South Tahoma Headwall	Andy Bond
2012	Mount Baker	Mount Shuksan, Curtis Glacier Headwall	Dan Helmstadter
2012	Olympics	Mount Constance, east face	Eric Wehrly
2012	North Cascades	Glacier Peak, Scimitar Glacier	Eben Sargent
2012	Mount Rainier	Liberty Ridge east (*Cryogenesis*)	Oliver Deshler, Aaron Mainer

2012	North Cascades	Black Peak, northwest face	Dan Helmstadter, Eric Wehrly
2012	Mount Baker	Lincoln Peak, X Couloir	Aaron Scott
2013	Olympics	Mount Angeles, southwest peak (*Pipeline*, *Hourglass*)	Jack Ganster, Tyler Reid, Solveig Waterfall
2013	North Cascades	Copper Peak, northwest couloir	Eduardo Blanchard, Seth Holton, Eben Sargent
2013	North Cascades	Three Fingers, east face couloir	Dan Helmstadter
2013	North Cascades	Big Four Mountain, north face	Dan Helmstadter, Eric Wehrly
2014	Mount Baker	Mount Shuksan, Price Glacier (complete)	Seth Holton, Nick Ley, Ben Price, Kevin (last name unknown)
2014	Olympics	Mount Johnson, northwest couloir	Tyler Reid
2015	North Cascades	Goode Mountain, north couloir	Eric Noll, Eric Wehrly
2016	Alpine Lakes	Mount Stuart, west ridge couloir	Matt Bowen, Aaron Scott
2016	North Cascades	Mount Fury, northeast face (complete)	Peter Dale, Aaron Mainer
2017	North Cascades	Hoodoo Peak, north face	Michael Shaffer
2017	Mount Rainier	*Thermogenesis*	Peter Dale, Aaron Mainer

Note: The exploits listed in this table represent fewer than a third of the ski descents completed in the Northwest between 2000 and 2020. Details of more than two hundred routes pioneered during this period can be found at http://alpenglow.org/ski-history.

GLOSSARY

For terms related to early skiing techniques, see the sidebar in chapter 3, Skis Triumphant.

alpine touring Skiing with bindings that hinge freely for climbing and hold the heels on the skis for the descent

cross-country skiing Self-propelled skiing, typically over gentle, rolling terrain

downhill skiing Skiing with lifts, where the skier doesn't have to climb the hill

four-way skier Competitor in downhill, slalom, cross-country, and ski jumping events

free-heel skiing Skiing with free-heel bindings using either telemark or parallel turns

freeriding A blend of freestyle skiing and steep ski mountaineering

freestyle skiing Acrobatic skiing (which emerged in the 1970s) with three disciplines: mogul skiing, ballet, and aerial acrobatics

randonnée Generally, touring in mountainous terrain using alpine touring equipment

schuss To run a slope as straight as possible on skis

ski ascent A climb completed on skis. Ski ascents (without corresponding descents) have seldom been recorded since World War II.

ski-climb A climb in which a significant portion of the route is done on foot. Historically, ski-climbs preceded ski ascents. Ski mountaineers would climb as high as possible on skis, then abandon them and continue to the summit on foot.

ski descent A descent completed entirely on skis

ski mountaineering Ski touring in terrain that may require mountaineering skills, such as the use of an ice axe, crampons, or a rope for safety

ski traverse A trek from Point A to Point B substantially made on skis. A ski traverse over a summit follows different routes on the ascent and descent. A loop or orbit ends near its starting point, but does not retrace its route.

slalom A down-mountain race with many turns, over a course marked with flags that racers must ski around

SELECTED REFERENCES

Allen, Dale. Interviewed by Harry Majors, August 16, 1974. Special Collections, accession 2311, tape 180, University of Washington Libraries, Seattle.

American Mountain Guides Association. "40 Years of American Guiding." *AMGA Guide Bulletin* (Spring 2019): 7.

Ancient Skiers Association. *Ancient Skiers 1904–1984*. Seattle: Ancient Skiers Association, 1984.

Armbruster, Kurt E. *Orphan Road: The Railroad Comes to Seattle, 1853–1911*. Pullman, WA: Washington State University Press, 1999.

Armstrong, Betsy, and Knox Williams. *The Avalanche Book*. Golden, CO: Fulcrum, 1986.

Atwater, Montgomery M. *The Avalanche Hunters*. Philadelphia: Macrae Smith Co., 1968.

Ball, Fred. "The Patrol Race." Unpublished manuscript, The Mountaineers Archives, Seattle, n.d. Typescript.

Barnett, Steve. *Cross-Country Downhill*. Seattle: Pacific Search Press, 1978.

Bauer, Wolf. "Telemarks, Sitzmarks, and Other Early Impressions." *Mountaineer Annual* (1963): 9.

Beckey, Fred. *Cascade Alpine Guide*. 3 vols, 1st, 2nd, 3rd eds. Seattle: Mountaineers Books, 1973–2008.

———. *Range of Glaciers*. Portland, OR: Oregon Historical Society Press, 2003.

Bradley, Charles. *Aleutian Echoes*. Fairbanks: University of Alaska Press, 1994.

Brower, David R., ed. *Remount Blue: The Combat Story of the 3rd Battalion, 86th Mountain Infantry*. Berkeley, CA: Self-published, 1948.

Burgdorfer, Rainer. *Backcountry Skiing in Washington's Cascades*. Seattle: Mountaineers Books, 1986.

Burton, Hal. *The Ski Troops*. New York: Simon and Schuster, 1971.

Bush, Evan. "Snoqualmie Pass to Canada in 24 Days—On Skis." *Seattle Times*, June 16, 2017, A1.

Cle Elum Miner-Echo. Stories about Cle Elum ski tournaments 1921–33, accessed on microfilm. Central Washington University, Ellensburg.

Corff, Nicholas Campbell. *The Making of a Rescuer: The Inspiring Life of Otto T. Trott, M.D.* Bloomington, IN: Trafford Publishing, 2008.

Crews, Paul. *Early Hiking in the Olympics, 1922–1942.* Seattle: Peanut Butter Publishing, 1996.

Daiber, George C. "Skiing in the Olympics." *Mountaineer Annual* (1933): 15.

Dederer, Mike. "Silver Skis: Derring-Do on Mount Rainier." *Skiing Heritage,* September 2004, 25.

Degenhardt, Stella. "Boards Without Hordes." *Mountaineer Annual* (1963): 37.

Devin, Doug. *Mazama: The Past 125 Years.* Winthrop, WA: Shafer Historical Museum, 2008.

Donahoe, Mike. "Uphill and Downdale: Patrol Race on Tomorrow." *Seattle Post-Intelligencer,* February 18, 1939.

Dostie, Craig. "Paul Ramer: Crazy Like a Fox." *Couloir,* Spring 2000, 12.

Eastwood, Catherine. "Lookout Bride." *The Saturday Evening Post,* December 18, 1937, 7.

Erben, John. "Hardcore—Mt. Baker Snowboarders Take on the World." *Sports Northwest,* November 1987, 16.

Eyraud, Pete. "Adventuring on Skis." *Washington Sportsman,* March 1936, 9.

Gourlie, Melvin R. Memoirs. Unpublished manuscript, held by Lowell Skoog, Seattle, 1989. Photocopy.

Hall, Sigurd. "Mount Rainier on Skis." *Mountaineer Annual* (1939): 30.

Hansen, Matt. "The End Game." *Powder,* December 2015.

Hanson, Howard A. "Pioneer Ski Tournament at Mount Rainier." *Seattle Times Magazine,* April 7, 1946, 9.

Heller, Ramon. *Mount Baker Ski Area: A Pictorial History.* Bellingham: Mount Baker Recreation Co., 1980.

Helleson, Linda. "The History of Skiing in Mt. Rainier National Park." Unpublished manuscript (used by interpretive staff), Mount Rainier National Park, Longmire, WA, ca. 1972.

Hellyer, David Tirrell. *At the Forest's Edge: Memoir of a Physician-Naturalist.* Seattle: Pacific Search Press, 1985.

Hessey, Charles D., Jr. "Scratching the Surface of the North Cascades." *American Ski Annual* (1947): 84.

Holt, Gordy. "Avalanche Danger at Yodelin Known." *Seattle Post-Intelligencer,* January 28, 1971, 7.

Ingersoll, Doug. "Wicked Wich of the West." *Backcountry,* January 1998, 22.

Jacobi, Wayne. "Skiing Down Mt. Rainier." *Seattle Post-Intelligencer,* June 8, 1980.

Jank, Milana. "Back to Nature on Wings of Wood." *Physical Culture,* February 1932, 22.

Jay, John. *Ski Down the Years.* New York: Award House, 1966.

Johnson, William Oscar. "It's Got Its Ups and Downs." *Sports Illustrated,* March 30, 1981, 54.

Kirby, Donald M. *Mission Ridge: The First 20 Years.* Wenatchee, WA: World Publishing Co., 1986.

Kirk, Ruth. *Sunrise to Paradise*. Seattle: University of Washington Press, 1999.

Krist, Gary. *The White Cascade: The Great Northern Railway Disaster and America's Deadliest Avalanche*. New York: Henry Holt and Co., 2007.

Kubin, Patrick. "Longview Ski Club Celebrates 75 Years." *The Daily News*, March 11, 2010.

Lang, Otto. *A Bird of Passage*. Helena, MT: Falcon Press, 1994.

Langdon, James. "TRACK!" Unpublished manuscript (Snoqualmie Pass ski patrol work starting in 1947), courtesy of Gretchen Besser and New England Ski Museum, Franconia, NH, ca. 1982. Typescript.

Leich, Jeff. *Tales of the 10th: The Mountain Troops and American Skiing*. Franconia, NH: New England Ski Museum, 2003.

Manfredi, Ben. "Cascade Classics" (largely a collection of trip reports). Accessed November 25, 2003. http://CascadeClassics.org.

Mapes, Lynda V. "With Warming, Winter Isn't What It Used to Be." *Seattle Times*, December 21, 2012, A1.

Marler, Chester. *East of the Divide: Travels through the Eastern Slope of the North Cascades: 1870–1999*. Leavenworth, WA: North Fork Books, 2004.

Maxwell, William J. "Skiing Eight Months a Year." *Mountaineer Annual* (1930): 53.

McConnell, Grant. "Wilderness World." *Mountaineer Annual* (1958): 7.

Mills, Peggy. "Seventy Years of Mazama Skiing: 1897–1967." Mazamas Archives, Portland, OR, 1966.

Molenaar, Dee. *The Challenge of Rainier*. 4th ed. Seattle: Mountaineers Books, 2011.

——. *Mountains Don't Care, But We Do*. Seattle: Mountain Rescue Association, 2009.

Mosauer, Dr. Walter. "Here's Your Real Summer Sport—Skiing." *Seattle Times Magazine*, July 9, 1933, 2.

Mueller, Ted. *Northwest Ski Trails*. Seattle: Mountaineers Books, 1968.

Nalder, Eric. "Having a Blast on Mount St. Helens—There's Less Mountain Now, But More Fun." *Seattle Times*, June 5, 1987.

Northwest Skier. "The Dilemma at Mt. Pilchuck." January 5, 1979, 2.

——. "Swiss Conquers Unclimbed Mt. Hood Route on Skis." April 1971, 11.

Off Belay. "Ski Descents of Difficult Routes." January 1972, 42.

Olympic Mountain Rescue. *Olympic Mountains: A Climbing Guide*. 4th ed. Seattle: Mountaineers Books, 2006.

The Oregonian. "New Climb Record Set." April 27, 1931.

Parker, Robert W. *What'd You Do in the War, Dad?* Santa Fe, NM: Rio Grande Publishing, 2005.

Perryman, Charles. "EXTRA! Selznick Cameraman Climbs Mt. Rainier in Dead of Winter." Selznick newsreel, 1922. Mountaineers Film Collection, PH 1047, Special Collections, University of Washington Libraries, Seattle. https://content.lib.washington.edu/filmarchweb/mountaineers.html

Port Angeles Evening News. "Explorers See Great Skiing Possibilities." April 25, 1938, 6.

Prater, Yvonne. *Snoqualmie Pass: From Indian Trail to Interstate.* Seattle: Mountaineers Books, 1981.

Roberts, Milnor. "A Wonderland of Glaciers and Snow." *National Geographic* (1909): 530.

Roe, JoAnn. *North Cascades Highway: Washington's Popular and Scenic Pass.* Seattle: Mountaineers Books, 1997.

———. *The North Cascadians.* Seattle: Madrona Publishers, 1980.

Seattle Post-Intelligencer. "Mayor Opens Seattle Ski Plant at Pass." January 22, 1934.

———. "Post-Intelligencer to Stage Thrilling Downhill Ski Race." February 2, 1934.

———. "7 Dare Death to Eat Lunch atop Rainier." April 11, 1928.

———. Stories about the 1916 "Big Snow" in Seattle (February 1–7) and the February 4, 1917, Scenic Hot Springs ski tournament, accessed on microfilm. University of Washington Libraries, Seattle.

Seattle Times. Stories about the 1916 "Big Snow" in Seattle (February 1–7) and the February 4, 1917, Scenic Hot Springs ski tournament, accessed on microfilm. University of Washington Libraries, Seattle.

———. "3 Killed; Rescuers Dig Out 50 Buried Alive in Snow." February 23, 1936, 1.

Shattuck, Denny. "Ski Club Preparing White Pass Resort for Winter." *Yakima Herald*, October 11, 1953.

Shorrock, Paul. "Patrol Races Highlight the '30s." *Mountaineer Annual* (1956): 60.

Simmons, Drew. "Wilderness Technology." *free snow,* Winter 1995, 8.

Simplecast.com. "Give Up Your Climate Guilt." Accessed November 12, 2020. https://a-matter-of-degrees.simplecast.com/episodes/give-up-your-climate-guilt.

Skoog, Lowell. "High Skiing: A Decade of Exploration in the Cascades and Olympics." *Mountaineer Annual* (1991): 32.

Sperlin, R. B. "To Mount Baker's Summit on Skis." *Mountaineer Annual* (1930): 50.

Stanford, Jim. "Peak Punishment." *Couloir,* Spring 2002, 16.

Stevens Pass Ski Area. *Stevens Pass: 75 Years of Pure PNW.* Skykomish, WA: Stevens Pass Ski Area, 2012.

Tacoma News Tribune. Stories about Mount Rainier summer ski tournaments 1917–23, accessed on microfilm. University of Washington Libraries, Seattle.

Taylor, Derek. "Alpine Extreme." *Adventure Journal*, no. 3 (Winter 2017): 26.

Thompson, Ben. "Ski-Scraping Mt. Baker." *American Ski Annual* (1935): 68.

Trotter, William R. *A Frozen Hell: The Russo-Finnish War of 1939–40*. Chapel Hill, NC: Algonquin Books of Chapel Hill, 1991.

Van Pelt, Julie. *Crystal Mountain, Built by Skiers*. Virginia Beach, VA: Donning Co., 2012.

Walsh, Mrs. Stuart P. "Women Can Ski as Expertly as Men." *Seattle Times*, March 12, 1930, 19.

Watson, Dwight. Interviewed by Harry Majors, August 30, 1973. Special Collections, accession 2170, tape 132, University of Washington Libraries, Seattle.

——. Mountain scrapbook, n.d. Special Collections, accession 2170-004, University of Washington Libraries, Seattle.

Watters, Ron. "Jack Meissner and His Remarkable Ski Journey." *Cross-Country Skier*, December 2007.

Weart, Spencer R. *The Discovery of Global Warming*. Cambridge, MA: Harvard University Press, 2003.

Wenatchee World. "Stevens Pass to Be Winter Playground," April 26, 1935, 10.

Western Skier. "Just Seven Miles of Real Work." March 24, 1938 (skiing Stevens Pass from Berne).

Whitesell, Edward A., ed. *Defending Wild Washington: A Citizen's Action Guide*. Seattle: Mountaineers Books, 2004.

Whiting, Keith. "The Azurite Story." *Okanogan County Historical Society Heritage* 13, no. 1 (Winter 1974–75).

Woodhouse, Philip R. *Monte Cristo*. Seattle: Mountaineers Books, 1996.

Zalesky, Philip. "Mountaineer Conservation: Contribution to Destiny." *Mountaineer Annual* (1966): 53.

RESOURCES

The Alpenglow Gallery
Website founded in 1999 by Lowell Skoog; includes the Alpenglow Ski Mountaineering History Project. http://alpenglow.org.

The American Alpine Club
Committed to taking action on climate change to preserve healthy mountain environments, communities, and economies. www.americanalpineclub.org.

Bob and Ira Spring Films
Mountaineers Film Collection, PH Coll 1048, Special Collections, University of Washington Libraries, Seattle. https://content.lib.washington.edu/filmarchweb/mountaineers.html

CascadeClimbers.com
Online forum founded in 2000 for Northwest climbers and backcountry skiers, featuring trip reports and topical discussions.

Charles and Marion Hessey Films
Mountaineers Film Collection, PH Coll 1050, Special Collections, University of Washington Libraries, Seattle. https://content.lib.washington.edu/filmarchweb/mountaineers.htm.

Dwight Watson Films
Mountaineers Film Collection, PH Col 1049, Special Collections, University of Washington Libraries, Seattle. https://content.lib.washington.edu/filmarchweb/mountaineers.html

MountainZone.com
Launched in the late 1990s to provide "the first digital meeting space for the outdoor community," it continues to offer news, trip reports, editorials, and stories.

Outdoor Alliance

Nonprofit coalition of national advocacy organizations united to conserve public lands and ensure those lands are managed in a way that embraces the human-powered experience. www.outdoor alliance.org

***Outside* magazine**

Active- and adventure-lifestyle magazine founded in 1977; website launched in the late 1990s. www.outsideonline.com

Protect Our Winters

Nonprofit organization created in 2007 by professional snowboarder Jeremy Jones to encourage systemic solutions to curb climate change. www.protectourwinters.org

SkiSickness.com

Website and forum founded by Sky Sjue for trip reports and discussions of adventurous back-country skiing and climbing

TelemarkTips.com

Website founded by Mitch Weber in 1998 for discussing backcountry skiing; the site crashed in 2013 and was superseded by a new site called TelemarkTalk.com

350

International movement working to end the age of fossil fuels and build a world of community-led renewable energy for all. www.350.org

Turns All Year

Website and forum founded in 2002 by Charles Eldridge of Seattle for trip reports and discussions of both lift-served and backcountry skiing, with emphasis on the latter; from the beginning, it has had a strong Northwest orientation. www.turns-all-year.com

WildSnow.com

Website founded in 1998 by Lou Dawson of Colorado for reviews, reports, stories, and tips about backcountry skiing

IN GRATITUDE

Thank you to the many donors whose generosity supports transforming lives through books like *Written in the Snows*. To learn more about how you can support powerful stories and publications about the lessons and pleasures of the great outdoors published by Mountaineers Books, please visit mountaineersbooks.org/donate.

Each of our giving levels has been named in honor of a Pacific Northwest glacier.

Pinnacle - $5,000
For Sam, Addis, and Gus Goldman who are lucky enough to call the North Cascades home

Rainbow - $1,000
Craig McKibben and Sarah Merner

Lowell Skoog
With love to:
Tom Skoog
Nancy Mattheiss
R. Philip Skoog
Anita Skoog
Gordy Skoog

In memory of:
Dick and Ingrid Skoog
Stephanie Subak
Larry Skoog
Carl Skoog

Meany Lodge in Honor of Lowell Skoog
(Art Freeman, Brian Finrow, Pat Boyle, Alicia Fahey, Dan Nord, Patti Polinsky and Dave Claar, Matt Simerson, Gregory Smith, Nigel and Sarah Steere, and Chuck Welter)

Paradise - $500
Fred and Anandhi Bumstead
Mike Riley
Chris and Kathy Robertson
Curt and Katherine Simonson
Emily Simonson
John E. Spring Family
Anita Wilkins

Inspiration - $250
Shail Casey
Carla Firey
Don and Natala Goodman
Martinique and Eliot Grigg

Francois Godcharles in memory of
    Jim Rothwell
Roger Johnson
Linda Lewis in memory of Doug Walker
Anne Smart and Frank McCord
John Ohlson
Patrick Vilbrandt
Norm Vigus
LaVerne Woods and Eric Zobel
Gavin and Sara Woody
Brian and Amy Young

Cool - $100
John Baldwin
Aaron Banse
Cynthia Bellomy
Megan Bond in memory of Fred Beckey,
    who earned his turns
Maureen Brinck-Lund
Amber Carrigan and Seth Dygert
Helen and Arnie Cherullo
Kristina Tursi with love for baby Lucca
Karen Daubert and Jared Smith
Bob and Larina Davis
Vivian Doorn
Kurt Harris Fengler
The Robert and Peggy Ferber Family
Dave Galvin - Sahalie Ski Club

Bruce Goodson
James Groh
Renee Harn
Peter Hendrickson and Nancy Temkin
Margaret Hunt in memory of
    Ed LaChapelle
Jan Kordel
Eric B. Larson
Eric and Marilyn Lindahl in memory of
    family friend Rudy Amsler
Randy and Vicki Lord
John Lundin
Chester Marler and Ann Fink
Roger Mellem
Aaron Miller
Anita Skoog Neil and Bill Neil
Patrick and Janice Noonan
Franklin Rumi Oppenheim
Dean Petrich
Suzan Reiley in memory of Dan Davis
Eric Noll
Christopher Roberts
Mike Rolfs
Alice Salcido in honor of Grace Garwin
Robin Stump
Brianne Vanderlinden in honor of
    Kelly Nolan
Tony Weida

INDEX

Note: Page numbers in **boldface** denote photographs; "ci" denotes color insert

ABOUT THE
AUTHOR

The grandson of Swedish immigrants, **Lowell Skoog** was introduced to skiing by watching his father jump at the Kongsberger Ski Club hill near Washington's Snoqualmie Pass. He became a ski instructor in high school and took up climbing in college. He began backcountry skiing after graduating from the University of Washington in 1978. Since then, Skoog has explored the Cascade and Olympic Mountains, becoming the first person to ski, in stages, over 350 miles of the Cascade Crest from Mount Baker to Mount Rainier. Along the way, he gained a deep appreciation for the region's outdoor history, serving as chairman of the Mountaineers History and Library Committee, publishing the online Northwest Mountaineering Journal, and helping launch the Washington State Ski and Snowboard Museum in 2015. Skoog founded the Alpenglow Gallery (alpenglow.org) in 1999. Following a career in electrical and software engineering, he lives in Seattle with his wife, Nancy Mattheiss.

recreation · lifestyle · conservation

MOUNTAINEERS BOOKS is a leading publisher of mountaineering literature and guides—including our flagship title, *Mountaineering: The Freedom of the Hills*—as well as adventure narratives, natural history, and general outdoor recreation. Through our two imprints, Skipstone and Braided River, we also publish titles on sustainability and conservation. We are committed to supporting the environmental and educational goals of our organization by providing expert information on human-powered adventure, sustainable practices at home and on the trail, and preservation of wilderness.

The Mountaineers, founded in 1906, is a 501(c)(3) nonprofit outdoor recreation and conservation organization whose mission is to enrich lives and communities by helping people "explore, conserve, learn about, and enjoy the lands and waters of the Pacific Northwest and beyond." One of the largest such organizations in the United States, it sponsors classes and year-round outdoor activities throughout the Pacific Northwest, including climbing, hiking, backcountry skiing, snowshoeing, camping, kayaking, sailing, and more. The Mountaineers also supports its mission through its publishing division, Mountaineers Books, and promotes environmental education and citizen engagement. For more information, visit The Mountaineers Program Center, 7700 Sand Point Way NE, Seattle, WA 98115-3996; phone 206-521-6001; www.mountaineers.org; or email info@mountaineers.org.

Our publications are made possible through the generosity of donors and through sales of 700 titles on outdoor recreation, sustainable lifestyle, and conservation. To donate, purchase books, or learn more, visit us online:

MOUNTAINEERS BOOKS
1001 SW Klickitat Way, Suite 201 • Seattle, WA 98134
800-553-4453 • mbooks@mountaineersbooks.org • www.mountaineersbooks.org

An Independent nonprofit publisher since 1960